MW01595759

TEXTXET

Studies in Comparative Literature 66

Series Editors
C.C. Barfoot and Theo D'haen

Literature and Terrorism
Comparative Perspectives

Edited by
Michael C. Frank and Eva Gruber

Amsterdam - New York, NY
2012

Cover design: Inge Baeten

The paper on which this book is printed meets the requirements of
'ISO 9706: 1994, Information and documentation - Paper for
documents - Requirements for permanence'.

ISBN: 978-90-420-3498-3
E-Book ISBN: 978-94-012-0773-7
© Editions Rodopi B.V., Amsterdam - New York, NY 2012
Printed in The Netherlands

Printed by Printforce, the Netherlands

CONTENTS

LITERATURE AND TERRORISM:
INTRODUCTION

MICHAEL C. FRANK AND EVA GRUBER

I

Like other academic disciplines that contribute to the current research on terrorism, the field of literary studies is still strongly marked by the impact of "9/11", an event that was immediately identified as constituting not only a historical and political, but also a cultural watershed. Before the fires at Ground Zero were extinguished, debates concerning the future of such diverse forms as action movies, satirical TV shows, and the novel appeared in the press.

More often than not, changes were demanded rather than foretold. Thus, on September 16, 2001, distinguished American writer and journalist Roger Rosenblatt triumphantly declared the "end of irony". By "irony", Rosenblatt understood a particular attitude to life according to which nothing "was to be believed in or taken seriously" because "Nothing was real". While the author's opposition to "irony" clearly went back further than 9/11, he apparently felt that the general grief and dismay following the tragedy were the right context for exposing the cynicism of "ironists".[1] In the face of recent events, Rosenblatt exclaimed, even the most stubborn of ironists had to acknowledge the undeniable reality of the disaster – even though the reality of the event had never been called into question. Rosenblatt's essay was a reaction against the perceived moral relativism of postmodernism with its constructivist epistemology. Because irony is one of the generally accepted characteristics of postmodern art, literature,

---

[1] Roger Rosenblatt, "The Age of Irony Comes to an End", *Time Magazine*, 24 September 2001: http://www.time.com/time/magazine/article/0,9171,1000893,00.html (accessed 16 November 2011).

and thinking, the debate on the end of irony – which proliferated in print and on the Internet – also pertained to the future of fiction: had the events of 9/11 heralded the demise of postmodern modes of story-telling and would they lead to the (re)emergence of "non-ironic" narr-atives?

Other prognostications and demands for the development of fiction had different concerns. In an essay written for *The Guardian* in early October 2001, influential literary critic James Wood called for a renewal of the American novel. The terrorist attacks, he hoped, would cause "casualties" among those types of fiction that he disliked on aesthetic grounds. Against the backdrop of the mass casualties of Sep-tember 11, however, Wood's critique acquired an additional ethical dimension, implying a moral obligation for change. Programmatically entitled "Tell Me How Does It Feel", the article was aimed at three distinct targets: the "trivia and mediocrity" of New York writers Jay McInerney and Bret Easton Ellis; Don DeLillo's "idea of the novelist as a kind of Frankfurt School entertainer" and the more general ten-dency among contemporary authors to use fiction for "displays of knowledge"; as well as the "hysterical realism" of Salman Rushdie, Thomas Pynchon, and others who pursue "vitality at all costs". Under-lying this multiple polemic was Wood's discontent with the tradition of the sweeping "social novel"[2] and its panoramic, all-encompassing pretensions. After 9/11, he asserted, writers should put the individual character back at the center of their plots, focusing on his or her per-sonal experience and emotion. Apart from a new sincerity, then, crit-ics expected – or rather stipulated – a stronger emphasis on feelings.

After the first wave of New York-set novels about the attacks and their emotional aftermath had appeared (from the English translation of Frédéric Beigbeder's 2003 novel *Windows on the World* in March 2005 to Don DeLillo's much-anticipated *Falling Man* in May 2007), the debate on the future of fiction was no longer limited to the arts sections of daily newspapers, blogs, or periodicals; it was also carried on at scholarly conferences and in edited volumes. In the process, the speculative anticipation of the "novel to come" was superseded by a critical assessment of the novels that had actually been published since the September 11 attacks. Yet the principal focus of the discussion

---

[2]   James Wood, "Tell Me How Does It Feel?", *The Guardian*, 6 October 2001: http://www.guardian.co.uk/books/2001/oct/06/fiction (accessed 30 August 2010).

remained the same. *9/11 as a Cultural Caesura* is the symptomatic title of a recent German collection of essays,[3] which starts from the premise that the attacks have had a lasting impact on what is (somewhat vaguely) described as "modalities of thought".[4] Accordingly, the task laid out in the Introduction is not to critically reflect the general postulation of discontinuity, but to demonstrate in what ways the assumed "caesura" may be said to manifest itself in representations of 9/11.[5] What is thereby ignored is the strong possibility that the very expectation of discontinuity may itself be an example of the said changes in critical thought: is it not a presupposition that we bring to the texts – under the possibly premature assumption that the current escalation of global terrorism and counterterrorism goes hand in hand with a cultural and intellectual paradigm shift?

The editors of the first English-language book on the subject come to a different conclusion. According to Ann Keniston and Jeanne Follansbee Quinn, the question of continuity or discontinuity is directly addressed by the literary representations of 9/11 themselves; as Keniston and Quinn emphasize, however, the event's status as a "caesura" is still a matter of debate. In the Introduction to *Literature after 9/11*, they explain that the essays collected in their volume "refuse to interpret 9/11 *either* as a rupture with the past *or* as continuous with (and even anticipated by) earlier historical events", because the literature analyzed does not allow such an unequivocal interpretation; rather, the literary negotiation of the question is itself marked by a shift: "while the initial experience of 9/11 seemed unprecedented and cataclysmic, the experience of incommensurability generated a culture-wide need for explanatory narratives, not simply as a means for countering the

---

[3] *9/11 als kulturelle Zäsur: Repräsentationen des 11. September 2001 in kulturellen Diskursen, Literatur und visuellen Medien*, eds Sandra Poppe, Thorsten Schüller, and Sascha Seiler, Bielefeld: Transcript, 2009.

[4] The blurb describes the attacks of September 11 as constituting "not only a political and social caesura", but also a "trauma of thought (*Trauma des Denkens*)". Both here and in the editors' Foreword, it is further stated that the events have changed "modalities of thinking (*Denkmodalitäten*)" (*ibid.*, 7).

[5] See Sandra Poppe, "Einleitung", in *9/11 als kulturelle Zäsur*, 9-17.

trauma, but as a means for refusing incommensurability, prompting attempts to place 9/11 into an historical framework."[6]

It is essential in this context to distinguish two vantage points or frames of reference from which the "cataclysmic" nature of the event is experienced, observed, or postulated. Keniston and Quinn's statement moves within a trauma-theoretical framework. There can be no question that for surviving victims and immediate witnesses an event such as the September 11 bombings has the power to fracture life into a "before" and an "after". In his 2009 monograph *Out of the Blue*, Kristiaan Versluys is interested precisely in this emotional impact of the September 11 attacks. He reads 9/11 novels as an attempt to deal with the dilemma that the traumatic experience cannot be represented while, at the same time, representation is unavoidable (since even the insistence on the event's unrepresentability provides some kind of representation). There is also an ethical obligation to bear witness and – most importantly for Versluys – a therapeutic necessity to frame the trauma in narrative form. Accordingly, Versluys contends that narrativizations of 9/11 do not only offer a means of remembering the violence and its victims, but that they may also enable survivors and witnesses to engage with – and work through – the trauma in an imaginative mode: "in a gesture that is familiar to therapists and writers alike, the novels affirm and counteract the impact of trauma."[7]

But who exactly are the patients in need of such a therapeutic effort? "In a time of globalized witnessing and shared vicarious experience", Versluys asserts, "an event like 9/11 is a rupture for everybody. As a consequence, there is a globalized need to comprehend, to explain, and to restore."[8] Even though the author is careful not to use the concept of "trauma" too lightly (by indiscriminately applying it to everybody who followed the event on television), this statement is still remarkably sweeping. It unhesitatingly moves from New Yorkers and Americans to an international and even global audience, implying that the whole of humanity shared the same experience of 9/11 – namely

[6]   Ann Keniston and Jeanne Follansbee Quinn, "Introduction: Representing 9/11: Literature and Resistance", in *Literature after 9/11*, eds Ann Keniston and Jeanne Follansbee Quinn, New York and London: Routledge, 2008, 3.
[7]   Kristiaan Versluys, *Out of the Blue: September 11 and the Novel*, New York: Columbia University Press, 2009, 13.
[8]   *Ibid.*, 4.

one of "rupture". Instead of generalizing the experience in such a way, we should perhaps distinguish more clearly between the level of individual life stories and that of world history, complementing the trauma-theoretical framework with a look at global politics. In doing so, we may acknowledge the traumatic rupture caused by 9/11 while at the same time leaving open the question as to whether the event has by itself initiated a whole new historical era – even outside the communities (the city of New York, the American nation) most immediately affected by it.

From the perspective of a history of international terrorism, there are strong reasons for considering the September 11, 2001 attacks not only as the starting point of a new war (which they soon became), but also as the culmination of a longer series of anti-US attacks, which were themselves rooted in earlier political conflicts. In the words of David Holloway, "9/11 was long in the making, and the pre-9/11 and post-9/11 worlds were broadly continuous not discontinuous".[9] This, however, is not how the event was officially perceived. Public discourse on 9/11 – both in American mainstream media and in statements by government officials – strongly stressed the singularity and, hence, unpredictability of the bombings. Instead of calling back to memory the February 1993 attempt at bringing down the twin towers of the World Trade Center, the September 2001 bombings were immediately placed under the category of "unprecedented". Disregarding two calls for jihad against US citizens signed by Osama bin Laden (in August 1996 and February 1998 respectively), as well as the ensuing campaign against US embassies and military installations (with large-scale attacks in Kenya, Tanzania, and Yemen in 1998 and 2000), the discontinuity topos relies – at least to a certain extent – on historical forgetting. And this forgetting, we should add, has serious political implications. For, as Holloway notes, "the idea that 9/11 was a moment when 'everything changed' … played directly to partisan political agendas in Washington"; after all, "historical rupture on 9/11 was precisely the case [the administration] argued in defence of the 'Bush doctrine' of pre-emptive war, unilateral policy-making and 'regime change' in 'rogue states'".[10] If 9/11 does indeed institute a new histor-

---

[9] David Holloway, *9/11 and the War on Terror*, Edinburgh: Edinburgh University Press, 2008, 2.
[10] *Ibid.*, 4.

ical period, then it not only legitimizes, but also necessitates equally unprecedented counterterrorist measures. Before literary scholars proclaim new epochs, they should therefore carefully consider the political weight of this declaration.

Keniston and Quinn refrain from such strong claims, limiting themselves instead to a discussion of literary reflections of the question. As they note, "the history of literary representations of 9/11 can be characterized by the *transition* from narratives of rupture to narratives of continuity".[11] This observation refers to the whole body of texts dedicated to the September 11 attacks, including the essays, personal reminiscences, and often anonymous poems that were published only days after the event. In the specific case of the novelistic genre, things seem to be slightly different, however. One of the earliest New York-set 9/11-novels, Jonathan Foer's *Extremely Loud and Incredibly Close* (April 2005), juxtaposes the nine-year old narrator's grief work over his father's death in the World Trade Center with his grandparents' traumatic experience of the firebombing of Dresden in 1945; and the novel also features a brief reference to Hiroshima.[12] The analogy here consists less in the respective events themselves than in the narratives of personal loss that Foer associates with them. For Kristiaan Versluys, Foer's novel thus "universalizes grief", "tak[ing] the side of the victims, irrespective of their national origin or allegiance".[13] This early example suggests that novels immediately combined "narratives of rupture" with "narratives of continuity", emphasizing breaks in the life of the protagonist and society at large, while simultaneously establishing a wider historical framework – referring to earlier events that affected large urban populations, though noticeably avoiding the history of terrorism (and, more specifically, the political entanglements involved in the rise of anti-Western Islamist terrorism).

While several studies have shown that 9/11 fiction is concerned with the event's place in global history, the question remains whether this fiction in turn constitutes a break within the novelistic tradition. Surprisingly, despite their emphasis on the question of continuity or

---

[11]   Keniston and Quinn, "Introduction", 3.
[12]   Jonathan Safran Foer, *Extremely Loud and Incredibly Close*, Lanham, MD: Hamilton, 2005.
[13]   Versluys, *Out of the Blue*, 82.

discontinuity, all studies mentioned so far choose a purely synchronic focus. This, we think, is indicative of a more general tendency within the research on terrorism in contemporary literature. Before we can say anything definite about the specificities of current engagements with terrorism and its aftermath – and thus about cultural breaks or general shifts – we need to consider post-9/11 literature in a comparative, diachronic perspective. By this we do not only mean a discussion of the general questions raised in forecasts about the future of fiction (such as those cited at the outset of this Introduction), but also, more specifically, a comparison of contemporary novels about terrorism on or since September 11 with thematically related works of earlier decades and periods.

It is worth remembering that the literary history of terrorism (to say nothing of the literary history of "terror" *tout court*) goes back at least 140 years. Originating with authors such as Fyodor Dostoevsky, Robert Louis Stevenson, and Henry James, the narrativization of terror began in the last three decades of the nineteenth century, when the social revolutionary, the political assassin, and the dynamiter entered the stage of political and literary history. After a first vogue of "anarchist" and "dynamite novels" at the turn of the twentieth century, there followed a period of relative silence on terrorism during and after the two world wars. As Robert Appelbaum and Alexis Paknadel have recently reconstructed, however, terrorism has since become "a prominent subject for English language novels", "increasing year by year, with notable booms in the late seventies and then again in the mid-nineties".[14] From their extensive article it can be deduced that we are currently witnessing an unprecedented peak in terrorism-related fiction, but that this trend already set in at the close of the twentieth century – that is, *before* September 11, 2001. The theme had just experienced a vogue in American literature (from the pens of authors like Don DeLillo, Ann Patchett, or Philip Roth) when the events of 2001 radically challenged previous – sometimes sympathetic – literary engagements with terrorism and its protagonists.

Appelbaum and Paknadel combine their encompassing quantitative with a loosely structuralist approach. They suggest a typology of fiction dealing with terrorism on the basis of the following criteria: the

---

[14]   Robert Appelbaum and Alexis Paknadel, "Terrorism and the Novel, 1970-2001", *Poetics Today*, XXIX/3 (Fall 2008), 387, 395.

focalizer(s) of the story, the setting, the major incidents, the climactic action, as well as the terrorists, their tactics and their targets.[15] While the authors' sample chart based on these criteria provides a valuable overview of how (and from which perspective) terrorism was fictionalized at different points in time, scholars working in the field cannot stop here. For the more subtle differences between individual works only become apparent on closer analyses, through a consideration of the question of genre as well as – most importantly – the changing political and discourse-historical contexts. Such an investigation is the goal of this volume, which deliberately chooses a broad focus to include not only pre-9/11, but also non-English literature from across periods, genres, and national literatures.

II

Before we can embark on this project, one fundamental question needs to be addressed: what exactly is our object of study when we investigate the relationship between literature and terrorism? And what insights can be gained from such an analysis? If we follow Anthony Kubiak's short 2004 essay "Narrative Typologies of Terror", there are three possible answers to this question. Emphasizing that "terrorist writing is not all equal",[16] Kubiak distinguishes the following types of "terrorist narratives": first, "the writing of terrorist groups themselves", in which these groups formulate their political, religious, or ideological agendas, call for the use of violence, or prepare individual members for the execution of terrorist acts; second, "narratives *about* terrorism", including fictional explorations of terrorism, critical studies of such fiction, as well as all other academic literature related to the topic of terrorism; and third, "those forms of writing that we might, in the spirit of critical excess, describe as narrative terrorism: attempts to destabilize narrativity itself – disrupting linearity, temporality, plot, character or whatever conventions may be regarded as essential to the productions of stories, memories, dramas, or histories".[17] Kubiak's examples for the latter type of "terrorist writing" are the American authors Robert Coover, Donald Barthelme, Hunter S.

---

[15] See *ibid.*, Table 1, 412.
[16] Anthony Kubiak, "Spelling It Out: Narrative Typologies of Terror", *Studies in the Novel*, XXXVI/3 (Fall 2004), 295.
[17] *Ibid.*, 295-97.

Thompson, and William Burroughs, whose heterogeneous works do not thematically address terrorism.

According to Kubiak, then, the juxtaposition of literature and terrorism in the title of the present volume could theoretically refer to either terrorist literature (that is, literature by terrorists), terrorism in literature (that is. terrorism as a literary theme), or literary terrorism (that is, literature as a phenomenon analogous to terrorism in its challenge to established orders). Despite its brevity, Kubiak's essay is important in pointing out that the relationship between literature and terrorism can not only be described in terms of subject matter, but also in several other ways – with regard to such diverse aspects as author, narrative strategy, and mode. Not content with a "mere analysis of the thematics of terrorism in fiction",[18] Kubiak reinterprets the concept of "terrorist narrative" by extending the meanings of both "narrative"[19] and "terrorist". It is questionable, however, whether the category "terrorist" is really suited to describe a quality of fictional texts that are thematically unrelated to the phenomenon so described. What do we gain by choosing this adjective over, say, "deconstructive" or Kubiak's own "disruptive"?

In the short passage dedicated to "terrorist fiction", Kubiak fails to convincingly demonstrate the specific heuristic value of the term "terrorist" for a description of "attempts to destabilize narrativity", all the more because his extended concept of "narrativity" remains vague. "Terrorist" is itself notoriously difficult to define, not only because of the great variety of regimes and groups to which the attribute has been applied, but also because of the term's implicit delegitimization of the acts it describes. As a politically contentious, emotionally charged, and morally laden concept that cannot be abstracted from the various specific contexts of its use, it is difficult to metaphorize. Moreover, we

---

[18] *Ibid.*, 297.

[19] Kubiak opens his essay by reversing the common notion according to which language precedes narrative. In lieu of this, he proposes "that language itself represents the outcome of a prior operation of narration: that mind is narration first, is 'always already' narration". Referring to Roland Barthes' "Introduction to the Structural Analysis of Narratives", he conceptualizes narrative as a cognitive process underlying all perception, "a first principle, the means by which thought and memory come into being". From the perspective of this suggestive but ultimately speculative approach, even an extra-literary, physical act of terrorist violence may be described as "narrative" (*ibid.*, 295-96).

should be careful not to use it too carelessly: all things considered, experimental, disruptive storytelling is far removed from the extra-linguistic impact of an exploding bomb, even if we accept that our mind imposes (or, in such traumatic moments, fails to impose) a narrative structure on everything we perceive.

In the context of this volume we would like to reserve the adjective "terrorist" for politically, religiously, or ideologically motivated acts of violence or disruption that cannot be reduced to the level of dis-course – and that happen outside of the literary text, even if our own field of interest as literary critics is the discursivization of terrorism in literature (as the fictionalization, simulation, or staging of such events). Although non-literary texts frequently make use of narrative modes and the rhetorical strategies available to them, we would also suggest to limit the word "narrative" to "literature" in a more narrow sense. If our principal aim in this volume is to investigate the specific role of literature in the cultural response to terror, then we need to focus on those aspects of literary discourse that distinguish it from other modes: what can literature do that other modes of discourse can-not do? And how does this affect the relationship between literary and non-literary (political, academic, journalistic) discursivization of ter-ror?

A brief overview of the available literature on literary engagements with terrorism will allow us to outline more clearly the specific focus of our approach. In her pioneering 2001 study *Plotting Terror*, Marga-ret Scanlan (who is also among the contributors to the present volume) introduced the concept of the "terrorist novel",[20] which has since been taken up by – amongst others – Anthony Kubiak, Benjamin Kunkel, Francis Blessington, as well as Robert Appelbaum and Alexis Pakna-del.[21] While the available definitions of the terrorist novel are all centered on questions of content, they offer different descriptions of the relationship between literary narrative and terrorism. Margaret

---

[20] Margaret Scanlan, *Plotting Terror: Novelists and Terrorists in Contemporary Fiction*, Charlottesville and London: University of Virginia Press, 2001.
[21] Kubiak, "Spelling It Out"; Benjamin Kunkel, "Dangerous Characters", *The New York Times*, 11 September 2005: http://www.nytimes.com/2005/09/11/books/review/11kunkel.html (accessed 28 July 2009); Francis Blessington, "Politics and the Terror-ist Novel", *Sewanee Review*, CXVI/1 (Winter 2007), 116-24; Appelbaum and Paknadel, "Terrorism and the Novel".

Scanlan originally introduced the concept for an analysis of novels that confront – and compare – terrorists and novelists. Her paradigmatic example was Don DeLillo's 1991 novel *Mao II*, which contains the famous confession of fictional novelist Bill Gray:

> "For some time now I've had the feeling that novelists and terrorists are playing a zero-sum game .... What terrorists gain, novelists lose. The degree to which they influence mass consciousness is the extent of our decline as shapers of sensibility and thought. The danger they represent equals our own failure to be dangerous."[22]

According to Scanlan, texts such as *Mao II* or J.M. Coetzee's *The Master of Petersburg* (1994) both continue and subvert the romantic tradition of "the alliance between the writer and the revolutionary".[23] They cast "the terrorist as the writer's rival, double, or secret sharer";[24] but they also radically question the long-held view of the writer as a person endowed with the power to change human institutions. Although the bulk of Scanlan's study is dedicated to works from the end of the 1970s to the mid-90s, she begins with a short discussion of Dostoevsky, James, and Conrad. In her conclusion, she notes that "From James to Coetzee, novelists who imagine a bond between terrorist and writer assume that both are isolated and marginal, incapable of gaining a hearing in the ordinary language of civic life".[25]

Francis Blessington also traces the "terrorist novel" from Henry James to the present (which, in his case, is the post-9/11 present). His main focus lies on a different thematic aspect, however. Discussing recent novels such as Algerian writer Yasmina Khadra's *The Attack* (2005) and John Updike's *Terrorist* (2006), he observes:

> In these novels we are usually not focused on the victims but on the perpetrators, whose choices and acts we are asked to understand, even momentarily to sympathize with, though not necessarily to condone or forgive. The action hinges on three choices: the author's, a major character's, and the reader's. And each choice involves ... three parts ...:

---

[22] Don DeLillo, *Mao II* (1991), London: Vintage, 1992, 156-57.
[23] Scanlan, *Plotting Terror*, 4.
[24] *Ibid.*, 10.
[25] *Ibid.*, 155.

identity with the flawed establishment, identity with the idealistic and often naïve cause, or escape.[26]

Both Scanlan and Blessington develop their characterizations of terrorist fiction on the basis of a specific – and limited – corpus of exemplary texts. For that reason, their results are easily applicable to novels sharing the same thematic concerns, but less useful for an investigation of the full thematic range of terrorist fiction. The same applies to Anthony Kubiak's more general definition, according to which the main purpose of such fiction is "to explore the motives and ideas behind the sociopolitical and psychic act of terrorism".[27] This definition excludes large parts of post-9/11 literature, which is mostly not concerned with the perpetrators and their agenda, but with the impact of the September 11 incidents (or other, imaginary suicide attacks) on both individual characters and American or Western society at large. For the purpose of the present volume, the phrase "literature about terrorism" is therefore meant to apply to fictional explorations of both, the causes and motivations as well as the aftermath of terrorist attacks. To be sure, several other thematic aspects could be added to the list: the planning and execution of the terrorist act, the confrontation and interaction between the terrorists and their victims, as well as – not least – the political response.

In the great mass of academic writing on terrorism, the 1996 study *Terror and Taboo* by social anthropologists Joseba Zulaika and William Douglass has proved particularly suggestive for the purpose of literary studies. It sets forth the premise that insurgent "terrorism" – as it is publicly perceived and discussed – heavily relies on myth, making fact and fiction largely indistinguishable, and that it therefore calls for a specific method of critical analysis, which the authors term "a mythography of Terror".[28] The terrorist "myth", they argue, is produced collaboratively by the media, the academia, as well as the principal protagonists themselves: the violent activists on the one hand, the attacked government on the other. The latter employs the myth to legitimize counterterrorist measures and operations, exaggerating the

---

[26] Blessington, "Politics and the Terrorist Novel", 118.
[27] Kubiak, "Spelling It Out", 296.
[28] Joseba Zulaika and William A. Douglass, *Terror and Taboo: The Follies, Fables, and Faces of Terrorism*, New York and London: Routledge, 1996, x.

actual danger and creating over-generalized images of "the terrorists". In this context Zulaika and Douglass observe that, "regarding terrorism, the brandishing of stark facts goes hand in hand with great leaps into discursive fantasy" and that this raises the question as "to what extent all discourse on terrorism must conform to and borrow from some form of fictionalization". It should be noted that the authors here apply a very broad definition of "fiction" as "the crafting of a narrative",[29] so that their term "fictionalization" may be substituted by "narrativization". What they call "terrorism discourse" is explicitly said to encompass literary as well as non-literary "types of fictionalization – representation by the media, political manipulation, academic definitions, the imaginary archetype informing the thriller".[30]

In its emphasis on representation and narrativization, the approach laid out by Zulaika and Douglass seems to call for the expertise of literary studies. It is hardly surprising, therefore, that the first two book-length explorations of terrorism in late-nineteenth- and twentieth-century literature – Margaret Scanlan's *Plotting Terror* (2001) and Alex Houen's *Terrorism and Modern Literature* (2002) – both cite the study in their introductions, where they incorporate aspects of it into their own theoretical and methodological frameworks.[31] Zulaika and Douglass' approach also plays an important role in one of the most recent contributions to the field. In their 2008 article "Terrorism and the Novel" mentioned earlier, Robert Appelbaum and Alexis Paknadel ask in what ways fiction responds and contributes to the process of "mythification".

Their suggestion is that fiction

> ... add[s] its own coloration to the mythic identity of terrorism. Perhaps it challenges that mythic identity as well. Subjecting terrorism to its own conventions and aspirations, the novel makes terrorism into a phenomenon in the possible worlds it represents – an enabling phenomenon, lending itself to the construction of plot, character, and theme – and it makes terrorism at the same time into a symbolic function through which it pursues its various writerly and readerly ends,

---

[29] *Ibid.*, 4.
[30] *Ibid.*, 16.
[31] See Scanlan, *Plotting Terror*; Alex Houen, *Terrorism and Modern Literature, from Joseph Conrad to Ciaran Carson*, Oxford and New York: Oxford University Press, 2002.

generating suspense, sentiment, and even – yes – terror. What cultural work the novel thereby performs with regard to terrorism (or "terrorism") is one of the main issues in which we have been interested.[32]

We are particularly interested in what is here referred to as the "cultural work" of terrorist fiction. According to Appelbaum and Paknadel's conclusion, this cultural work is mainly concentrated on the issue of legitimacy. They write:

> [The] cultural work of the terrorism novel from 1970 to 2001 has been by and large to legitimate the position of innocence occupied by terrorism's victims and the political society to which they belong .... These novels tell us that terrorism is the violence of an Other; it is illegitimate violence perpetrated from an illegitimate position.[33]

This conclusion is especially interesting with regard to the novels that the authors do not discuss, because they were published after 2001: does the continuously growing body of post-9/11 fiction (possibly unintentionally) affirm the subject position assumed by the leaders responsible for the "war on terrorism" by clearly assigning the roles of victims and victimizers to "us" and "them"?

Although thought-provoking, Appelbaum and Paknadel's conclusion is not entirely satisfactory. In its one-sided focus on literary negotiations of legitimacy, it neglects other functions and dimensions of terrorist fiction. This may be due, in part, to an important conceptual and methodological limitation of Zulaika and Douglass' monograph itself, which fails to explain the specific contribution of "fiction" in the narrower meaning of the term. It is worth remembering that only fiction in the sense of "literary or cinematographic invention" has the discursive license to overtly fictionalize terrorism – independently of clearly defined didactic or tactical considerations. Whereas political, scholarly, and media representations are primarily concerned with actual terrorist and counterterrorist activities, the majority of narrative

---

[32] Appelbaum and Paknadel, "Terrorism and the Novel", 389. At this point, the authors misleadingly use the word "mythography" to describe the cultural production of the terrorist myth rather than its academic analysis. It is in this latter sense that the word was introduced by Zulaika and Douglass, who used it to describe their particular method or, rather, mode of writing, not the object of their analysis.
[33] *Ibid.*, 427.

texts that address the thematic complex of terrorism choose to depict imaginary perpetrators, conspiracies, attacks, and reactions thereto, even if the recent emergence of 9/11 as a subject and backdrop of fiction has slightly changed the picture. One of literature's specific potentials no doubt lies in its capacity to narrativize terrorism as fiction. Accordingly, one of our tasks in the following chapters will be to describe how (from what perspective and with which thematic priorities) literature fictionalizes terrorism – and what concrete forms of terrorism it takes into account.

III

Literature and Terrorism is divided into four parts. The chapters in the first section are united by their literary-historical perspective, exploring the emergence and development of terrorism narratives at various times and in different national literatures. With this comparative, diachronic framework in place, Part Two moves into the very recent past. Concerned with the continuities and breaks that have characterized fictional representations of terrorism since the late 1990s, it puts the postulation of 9/11 as a "cultural caesura" to the test. Part Three focuses on aspects of media, mode, plot, and form. The contributions in this section explore such questions as: how do literary representations of terrorism relate to other media? What strategies and techniques do authors employ while approaching the phenomenon in a fictional mode? And which aesthetic concerns play a role in the process? While this part is accordingly comprised of in-depth explorations of individual texts, the book's final section takes a step back to look at larger generic issues, comparing the forms of the novel and drama in terms of their respective capacities to create convincing portrayals of terrorism's impact on society and the individual.

The book opens with three chapters dedicated to the first appearances of the modern terrorist – then better known under such labels as "revolutionist", "nihilist", "anarchist", or "dynamiter" – on the literary scene. As early as 1872, Fyodor Dostoevsky's *The Devils* explored the psychological dimension of radical, violent movements organized in clandestine networks. Gudrun Braunsperger is mainly concerned with the historical contexts of Dostoevsky's novel. Her essay takes us back to the intellectual and socio-political situation of 1860s and 1870s Russia, in which some sections of the revolutionary student movement developed into anti-tsarist terrorism. Braunsperger traces several of Dostoevsky's historical references, laying particular emphasis on his fictionalization of the famous Nechaev case. Using this case as a basis for the plot of his novel, Dostoevsky demonstrated how political idealism can turn into fanaticism. In the words of Gudrun Braunsperger, *The Devils* portrays a "lost generation", some of whose members "develop monstrous imaginations of almightiness and omnipotence"; at the same time, Braunsperger adds, the novel's treatment of terrorism is timeless and prophetic, transcending its immediate historical context.

The two subsequent contributions both deal with the figure of the dynamite terrorist in British *fin-de-siècle* fiction. Michael Frank begins by calling to mind that the term "terrorist novel" was originally applied to Gothic fiction. Against this backdrop, he traces the semantic shift that the designation "terror" underwent from its usage in eighteenth-century aesthetic discourse through the French Revolution to the emergence of insurgent terrorism, showing how "Each new, historically determined understanding of 'terror' produced new types of terror narrative". Frank then goes on to discuss anarchist and dynamite novels of the late nineteenth and early twentieth centuries (most closely Robert Louis Stevenson and Fanny Van de Grift's *The Dynamiter* and Edward Douglas Fawcett's *Hartmann, the Anarchist*), which, as he argues, translate the terror of Gothic fiction into the new context of the late-Victorian metropolis of London. By relating the literary narrativization of terror to the forms of sub-state terrorism extant at the time, he reveals how the authors both tap into and shape what he conceptualizes as "the cultural imaginary of terrorism".

Hendrik Blumentrath approaches literary representations of the late nineteenth-century terrorist from a different angle. Focusing on the ways in which the new technology of dynamiting affected concepts of enmity, Blumentrath points to the difficulties in identifying potential or actual perpetrators – difficulties closely mirrored in the aesthetics of turn-of-the-century terrorism fiction, which is populated by "indistinguishable figures [and] enemies losing their shape". For Blumentrath, the "invisible enemies" who first appear in the works of Arthur Conan Doyle, Joseph Conrad, or Mary Richardson Lesesne are indicative of a "crisis of visibility" that triggered a reorientation towards statistical modes of inquiry. Diachronically linking these observations on late Victorian developments in Britain to 1970s Germany, the author identifies several analogies in both contexts. As he reminds us, the terrorism of the Red Army Faction (RAF) is more or less contemporaneous with the emergence of standardized data collection and electronic data processing in police work. These purely symbolic signifying techniques in turn affected the fictional representations of terrorists in novels by Friedrich Christian Delius and Rainald Goetz.

The book's second section, which looks at the impact of 9/11 on the way terrorism is represented in literature, opens with an analysis of Ann Patchett's *Bel Canto*. Published in the summer of 2001 and thus shortly before the September 11 attacks, the novel provides a remarkable example of how terrorists and their tactics were depicted in US fiction before terrorism had been identified as the primary concern of American politics. Eva Gruber shows that terrorism in *Bel Canto* is imagined and fictionalized in a manner that would have been inconceivable in the immediate aftermath of 9/11, namely, sympathetically and by giving its perpetrators a human face. Gruber also points out that the novel self-reflexively comments on its own representation of terrorism in what might be called a metadiscourse on the terrorist novel in general – a fact overlooked in critical reviews of the book. The reception history of *Bel Canto* suggests that 9/11 did indeed have a significant influence on the ways in which this particular terrorist text, and possibly terrorist fiction at large, has been (mis)read.

Martina Wolff's comparative reading of novels by two of the most renowned contemporary American writers – Philip Roth's *American Pastoral* (1997) and John Updike's *Terrorist* (2006) – bridges the periods before and after September 11, 2001. Her analysis suggests a thematic continuity rather than discontinuity: Wolff's focus is on the novels' adolescent protagonists, their search for identity, orientation, and stability in a superficial and ever-changing society; as she points out, both characters turn to (religious or, in Roth's case, quasi-religious) fundamentalism and terrorism in order to compensate for a perceived lack of transcendence in their secular, materialist society. Wolff consequently establishes a close link between religious fundamentalism, which in its rigorousness appears attractively reliable to the youths, and the disruptive force of terrorism, "the antithesis to our daily dream of an ordinary life, to an existence that is somehow whole, that makes sense".

In contrast, Roy Scranton's discussion of narcissism in American 9/11 novels seems to implicitly question the attacks' disruptive potential, at least in the way in which some of the texts look at them. Scranton diagnoses most novels with an inability to do justice to the event's impact "on individual lives, [to] seriously look at the political and economic forces at work, and still perform the aesthetic, personal, and psychological insights and satisfactions we traditionally expect". He ascribes this lack of apposite scope – as visible, for instance, in Claire Messud's *The Emperor's Children,* Jay McInerney's *The Good Life,* Jonathan Safran Foer's *Extremely Loud and Incredibly Close,* or Paul West's *The Immensity of the Here and Now* – largely to America's culture of narcissism, a willful ignorance towards global political developments. Scranton then proceeds to contrast the above-mentioned group of novels with texts that satirize and thus explicitly problematize the narcissism characteristic of both US politics and some post-9/11 fiction. His examples for this latter type of novel are Ken Kalfus' *A Disorder Peculiar to the Country,* Don DeLillo's *Falling Man,* and especially William Gibson's *Pattern Recognition.*

Interestingly, Scranton credits science fiction writer Gibson with the most successful attempt to (meaning)fully represent the impact of 9/11, despite the fact that the novel is not explicitly about the attacks. This assessment already points us toward Margaret Scanlan's approach to terrorist novels after 9/11. Scanlan reads Cormac McCarthy's dystopian novel *The Road* as a terrorist novel that transcends the literary realism characteristic of most fiction concerned with the attacks. Although set in mythic time, bare of direct political or historical references, and without recourse to post-9/11 rhetoric, *The Road*'s post-catastrophic scenario, Scanlan argues, clearly engages with the aftermath of 9/11, with American violence in general, and the Bush administration's war on terrorism in particular. Scanlan's reading contextualizes the novel with both popular and philosophical responses to 9/11. Building on the ideas of Slavoj Žižek and Jean Baudrillard, she observes that "*The Road* evokes the end times of an America where all the barbarians are native and where sending an army halfway around the world to extinguish terror is no longer feasible". Yet Scanlan also detects an undercurrent of idealism within McCarthy's text and considers this as a possible "model for how the novel can confront terrorism without giving in to the all too plausible despair it often engenders".

Turning from responses to 9/11 in American literature to recent German terrorism fiction, Michael König identifies these texts' main thematic, structural, and narrative components. In an argument that shows parallels to Scranton's comments on American narcissism, König finds that early German texts directly responding to 9/11 remain caught in the autobiographical. At best, such texts (for instance by Kathrin Röggla and Else Buschheuer) "highlight the tragic events as aesthetic and poetic caesura", whereas more "recent texts ... open the door for broader discussions about the social and cultural implications of terrorist disruptions". Early texts are marked by what König refers to as a "narrative crisis" to which the authors respond by composing highly self-reflexive and metafictional works. In contrast, later texts on terrorism, such as Ulrich Peltzer's *Teil der Lösung* re-politicize the topic by fictionalizing the impact of terrorism on social systems: paranoia, increased surveillance, and insurgence against growing state control. König concludes that German literature in this respect reflects a political shift away from ideological questions to what he identifies as a "culture of fear": a concern with counterterrorist security measures rather than with the roots of terrorism itself.

The third section of this book, with its focus on the formal and aesthetic dimensions of terrorism narratives, starts with Ulrich Meurer's reflections on an intriguing case of "double mediation". Meurer's contribution is devoted to Don DeLillo's short story "Baader-Meinhof", which features references to Gerhard Richter's *October 18, 1977* paintings, which are, in turn, based on iconic photographs (from wanted-posters to television stills) of RAF terrorists. Framing his analysis in theoretical discussions on the possibilities and limits of depicting terror, Meurer identifies a representational gap or "blind spot" in Richter's images as well as in DeLillo's text. Both refrain from any attempt at representing reality. Rather, Meurer contends, they "make something visible that was concealed by the mere technical reproduction" in the case of Richter's paintings or by mere direct reference in the case of DeLillo's text. The works, the author concludes, thus "create an interspace for the emergence of the unrepresentable", an interspace providing room for "an artistic alternative, an unthought-of sphere beyond replication".

The concepts of "unrepresentability", "invisibility", and "disappearance", already at the center of Hendrik Blumentrath's contribution, assume a different yet related meaning in Kirsten Mahlke's reading of Argentinian author Julio Cortázar's short story "Second Time Round". Like Meurer, Mahlke focuses on aesthetic modes of representing terror – in this case state terrorism – and finds the fantastic, against all odds, to be most suitable for narrativizing the case of Argentina's "Disappeared". The existence of this group of people, who went missing in 1970s and 1980s Argentina but were neither declared dead nor alive, runs counter to rational conceptualizations of reality. Mahlke finds that the fantastic, transcending the border between fiction and the real, constitutes a highly befitting mode for addressing this issue at once located in historical reality and strangely unreal. She approaches the phenomenon through Freud's ideas on the uncanny, Todorov's model of the fantastic, and Alazraki's definition of the neo-fantastic, and closely traces the linguistic, discursive, and structural strategies that mark Cortázar's story as a case of the fantastic.

In her analysis of Andre Dubus III's *The Garden of Last Days*, Georgiana Banita explores the relation between literature and terror with regard to "plotting". She suggests that Dubus' novel not only accomplishes what many other texts are accused of falling short of, namely to "elucidate the processes that allow terrorism to come into being"; it also critically reflects ideas of closure habitually imposed on 9/11, as Banita shows in her close scrutiny of the text's narrative strategies. Dubus' novel resists the sense-making functions and cohesiveness traditionally attributed to narrative, while all the same relying strongly on plot. This paradox, Banita explains, can be resolved by considering Dubus' text as a sort of "narrative anamnesis" of the characters' lives and their apparently random actions. In emphasizing the "middle" of the narrative – the minute details of its characters' trajectories – the novel refuses to be "end-determined" in the way most 9/11 novels are, hurling towards the attacks as the final and simultaneously most significant moment.

In the book's fourth and final section, the attention shifts to genre, with Marie-Luise Egbert and Herbert Grabes addressing the novel and drama as two alternative forms of representing terrorism. Asking "whether terrorism novels actually constitute a new paradigm within the genre of the novel", Egbert explores Don DeLillo's *Falling Man* and Patrick Neate's *City of Tiny Lights* by way of Jean Baudrillard's ideas of 9/11 as, simultaneously, a "resurgence of the real" and "fiction surpassing fiction". It is this paradoxical relationship between the fictional and the real, between reality and its representations, which informs Egbert's analysis, be it in her reading of the emotionally detached and therefore unreal protagonists of *Falling Man* or in the question of life imitating art in *City of Tiny Lights*. In a genre-theoretical approach that links the novel to the mode of realism, but also takes into consideration the crisis of this very link in postmodern fiction, Egbert critically scrutinizes potential analogies between the terrorist act and the creation of fiction in terms of their respective world-altering potential. Finding that the texts referred to as terrorism novels are marked by similar thematic concerns, but are usually rather conventional in terms of narrative form, Egbert concludes that "the question as to whether narratives of terror might constitute a new genre of fiction must be answered in the negative" – which is not, however, to devalue the important cultural work they perform in elucidating the phenomenon of terrorism.

Herbert Grabes also takes a brief excursion into narrative, offering a short look at *Falling Man*, the novel which incidentally has attracted most attention within this volume. Yet his main focus is on dramatic engagements with 9/11. Guided by the question of whether "9/11 literature" as *littérature engage*, burdened with all the ethical implications and complexities of writing about the attacks, can simultaneously fulfill the aesthetic demands posed to literary texts, he looks at a whole range of plays: Lavonne Mueller's *Voices from September 11th*, Ann Nelson's *The Guys*, Craig Wright's *Recent Tragic Events*, and Neil LaBute's *The Mercy Seat*. While Grabes attests a great qualitative heterogeneity to this field, he also observes shared tendencies in at least some of the plays, such as a leaning towards the patriotic, the centrality of the (auto)biographical, and a decline of the ironic or subversive that had marked postmodern literature. Comparing the genre-specific possibilities of drama and the novel for rendering the experiences of 9/11, he concludes that "the novel not only allows for a more comprehensive and detailed worldmaking but also leaves room for a broad unfolding of multiple plots and lengthy discussions of wider issues". In contrast, "dramatists have to be much more selective

... and their success depends more acutely on their ability to find 'tell-ing' incidents and render them in a way that makes for an intense theater experience".

While the articles collected in this volume are thus assigned to umbrella subjects, as this brief summary demonstrates, their inquiries are not restricted to each of the four parts' main topics, but create sev-eral productive overlaps. For instance, Georgiana Banita's analysis of Andree Dubus III's *The Garden of Last Days* parallels Eva Gruber's contribution on Ann Patchett's *Bel Canto* in its exploration of the role of terrorism as a plot device. Moreover, it shares Roy Scranton's and Herbert Grabes' aesthetic concerns and Martina Wolff's interest in terrorism's social implications. Similarly, both Michael Frank and Marie-Luise Egbert look at the specificities of novelistic representa-tions of terrorism before their (literary-)historical and generic back-grounds. And several other articles (such as those by Ulrich Meurer, Kirsten Mahlke, Marie-Luise Egbert, and Herbert Grabes, to name but the most obvious examples) devote their attention to the complex rela-tionship between fiction and the real in representations of terror. Despite these correspondences, the volume testifies to the importance of approaching the relation between literature and terrorism from var-ious angles and with differentiated analytical objectives. Roy Scran-ton's and Marie Luise Egbert's corpora of texts, for instance, overlap to a substantial degree, yet the conclusions the authors come to differ substantially. Furthermore, Egbert's and Margaret Scanlan's contribu-tions show that diverging ideas on what a new paradigm for the novel might look like lead to differing answers to the question of continuity and discontinuity in post-9/11 literature.

In its entirety, the volume therefore attempts to approach and – at least partly – map the complex field of literature and terrorism without imposing preconceived notions or hypotheses, but rather by close observation and perceptive analysis. In combination, the individual perspectives brought together in this book, like the pieces of a mosaic, will help render a larger picture. As editors, we hope that this open, multifaceted approach adds to the understanding of the intricate and changing relation between literature and terrorism.

*   *   *

We would like to thank the *Center of Excellence: Cultural Foundations of Integration* (EXC 16) at the University of Constance for generously supporting the conference on which this volume is based. Thanks are also due to Charlton Payne for his diligent proofreading and helpful suggestions.

The Emergence of the Terrorist in Fiction:
Literary-Historical Approaches

SERGEY NECHAEV AND DOSTOEVSKY'S *DEVILS*: THE LITERARY ANSWER TO TERRORISM IN NINETEENTH-CENTURY RUSSIA

GUDRUN BRAUNSPERGER

A number of interpretations explain Fyodor Dostoevsky's novel *The Devils* (published in 1872 and initially translated as *The Possessed*) in terms of an overwhelming prophecy. It is assumed not only to have predicted the further development of the nineteenth-century revolutionary movement in Russia, but also the 1917 upheaval and the subsequent triumph of Bolshevism. Although in this respect the novel has most often been related to the totalitarian movements of the twentieth century, one can find corresponding problems in other periods and societies as well. Thus, the historical background of Dostoevsky's novel shows several striking parallels to the student movement of 1968 and the terror of the RAF in Germany.[1] Moreover, the novel has gained new relevance during the last ten years with the threat of global terrorism.

And yet, *The Devils* is Dostoevsky's answer to the specific social conditions of his own time. More than any other of his works, *The Devils* cannot be understood without knowledge of the context of tsarist Russia and the Russian history of ideas during the second half of the nineteenth century. Otherwise, Dostoevsky's long dialogues seem to be no more than the verbose idle talk of a far-away past and the sunken social culture of "those crazy Russians", as German theater director Frank Castorf suggested in his 1999 staging of *The Devils* in Vienna. An appropriate analytical understanding of the novel requires

---

[1]   See Jan Philipp Reemtsma, "Lust an Gewalt", *Die Zeit*, 11, 8 March 2007: http://www.zeit.de/2007/11/RAF (accessed 12 February 2011).

an acquaintance with certain facts of Russian history that may not be common knowledge to the average Western reader.[2]

In March 1881, Tsar Alexander II was assassinated by a bomb thrown at him by two students who were members of a revolutionary organization called *Narodnaya Volya*, roughly translated as "The People's Will". This was not the first attack on the Tsar: there had been several attempts at his life during the 1870s. Alexander II was the successor to the despotic Nicholas I, and he was responsible for urgent liberal reforms, among them the liberation of the peasants. After his assassination, Alexander III succeeded him and avenged the murder of his predecessor with extreme reactionary policies.

More than a decade earlier, in 1870, Dostoevsky had begun to write his novel *The Devils*. It was published during 1871 and 1872 in the literary magazine *The Russian Herald*. The great novelist had been concerned over the issue of revolutionary movements in Russia for some while. His original intention had been to compose a pamphlet against "nihilism", a term then used to describe the revolutionary youth. But in the process of writing, the text evolved into what every one of Dostoevsky's great novels since *Crime and Punishment* had become: literary fiction with elements of a thriller, primarily addressing psychological and philosophical questions.

Dostoevsky had always been an avid reader of newspapers and he quite often made use of reported incidents as inspiring literary material. In 1869, he learned of a spectacular criminal case, the Nechaev case: the student Ivan Ivanov, a member of a clandestine revolutionary group who had opposed its leader, Sergey Nechaev, was murdered on the grounds of the Moscow School of Agriculture in November 1869 by Nechaev and other members of the group. Eighteen months later, when Dostoevsky had just returned from a long stay in Western Europe, the records of the trial against Nechaev's accomplices were published in their entirety. Meanwhile Nechaev had managed to leave the country and was not present at the trial.

After the publication of *The Devils*, Dostoevsky was severely criticized for his conservative position, not only by the Russian revolutionary youth but also by the liberal part of the Russian intelligentsia, both of whom reproached him for defaming youth in general. At this

---

[2]   See Abbot Gleason, *Young Russia: The Genesis of Russian Radicalism in the 1860s*, New York: Viking, 1980.

time, however, there was a considerable opposition within the revolutionary underground against the personality of Nechaev and his
radical methods, including violence and terror, which were widely
rejected. A large movement called *Zemlya i Volya* ("Land and Freedom") had developed. This group started out as an idealistic and
peaceful movement in the spirit of Russian populism, believing in the
power of enlightenment and in the opportunity to bring revolution to
the people. Thousands of young men and women – sons and daughters
of noble families who felt guilty for their privileged social status –
went to the countryside in order to experience the life of the peasants
and to spread socialist propaganda among them, while simultaneously
offering them medical help and trying to establish an educational
system through the Sunday schools. Although this movement was
initially founded as a peaceful answer to Nechaev's Machiavellian
radicalism, it ended up as a radical wing determined to employ
violence and terror against the government; it eventually developed
into "The Peoples' Will", the terrorist section responsible for the murder of Alexander II. The reason for this reorientation was despair: the
plain and humble people had no interest in revolution and even
denounced the students.

It was these "roots of revolution"[3] – to quote the title of historian
Franco Venturi's classic study of populist and socialist movements in
nineteenth-century Russia – which Dostoevsky had witnessed and
which he referred to in his novel. Literature played a major role in
Russian society at that time. In a country lacking freedom of press and
public discussion of social problems, the only way to express social
criticism in public was in literary magazines, in the "weighty tomes".
A series of Russian novels written in the middle of the nineteenth century deals with social and ideological issues, each responding to its
predecessor. Ivan Turgenev's *Fathers and Sons* is a reply to Alexander Herzen's novel *Who Is to Blame?*, which examines the category of
the superfluous aristocrat. This topic would soon gain in sociopolitical
significance as the younger generation started to accuse representa-
tives of the older generation of Russian intellectuals of being superfluous, that is to say, non-working noblemen, because during this

---

[3]   Franco Venturi, *Roots of Revolution: A History of the Populist and Socialist
Movements in Nineteenth Century Russia*, Chicago and London: University of Chicago Press, 1983.

period of Russian feudalism only members of the aristocratic class had access to higher education.

Generational conflict is the subject of Turgenev's novel *Fathers and Sons*, which was published in 1862. The children of the Sixties, the "nihilists", opposed their parents by rejecting their values. They rejected idealism, declared art and the ideals of aesthetics as superfluous, and used the slogan: "A pair of boots is more useful than Pushkin." Dissatisfied with their parents' abstract and theoretical social criticism, they also abandoned religion. They propagated as their main principle a purely utilitarian thinking in the name of reason and rationality in order to create a completely new social structure that would be fair and just. Turgenev was the first to describe this concept of nihilism, and he made the term "nihilism" a keyword of sociopolitical debates.

An inspiration and idol to the youth was Nikolay Chernyshevsky, a literary critic and the publisher of the most progressive Russian literary magazine, *The Contemporary*, which was always under suspicion by the authorities because of its social and political criticism. Chernyshevsky was venerated as the author of the novel *What Is to Be Done?*, which he wrote in 1862 in prison after *The Contemporary* had been banned. He was arrested, put on trial, and sent to Siberia. *What Is to Be Done?* became a Bible to the revolutionary youth of the Sixties. In this novel – which is striking in its idealism and remarkably modern spirit, if not in its literary quality – Chernyshevsky presents a far more sympathetic portrait of the "new people" than Turgenev, describing them as young people who put into practice a social utopia. He portrays an ideal life of these "new people", which includes alternative economic principles such as the fair distribution of living space, goods, and work following the principles of cooperatives, as well as women's liberation, on behalf of equal rights for men and women.

The progressive youth of the Sixties demonstrated their dissent by their eccentric appearance, showing that they belonged to a student culture of their own. They were dressed in black and smoked heavily, women did not wear corsets and kept their hair short, men had beards and long hair as symbols of freedom. Thus a visible culture of protest arose in the early Sixties in tsarist Russia, starting more generally with criticism of the prevailing social conditions, but later focusing on the search for modes of revolutionary subversion.

Why did disturbances and protest arise at this moment in Russian history, under the sovereignty of a liberal tsar, Alexander II, who was carrying out an ambitious project of reforms at the beginning of the Sixties, including the liberation of the peasants (Russia was the last European country having peasant-serfs)? Why did it arise at the moment of great educational reforms that included the liberalization of universities? Alexander II was the successor to Nicholas I, whose heritage, not in the least due to his reactionary policies, was an economically and technologically under-developed country. Russia's backwardness had its roots in the disastrous defeat in the Crimean War that ended 1856, a year after Alexander had come to the throne. While Nicholas had treated educational establishments such as seminaries and universities as if they were barracks and military camps, educating young people to be no more than obedient citizens, Alexander understood that education and intellectual capital expenditure was the only way to maintain industrial and technical standards and thus to redeem the failure in foreign policy. Alexander's reforms encouraged the populace to articulate its collective displeasure about suppression that had been piling up for decades. And Alexander's educational reforms included the opening up of universities, which until then had been reserved for the aristocracy. The reforms produced a new intelligentsia-class, the *raznochintsy*, literally "people of various ranks", or, people from different social classes. Not only the children of the nobility now had access to university, but also children of the bourgeoisie; and a striking number of revolutionary careers started from families of priests, such as Nikolay Chernyshevsky's. Thus the conflict of the generations was also a social conflict: it was the new generation of *raznochintsy* who labeled the elder noble intelligentsia-generation as superfluous.

Along with these reforms, new social problems emerged in the lives of the students. Many of them were very poor and dependent on the mutual help that was offered by students' associations. These supported organizations of everyday life, such as food kitchens and libraries, which soon gained political importance as places where revolutionary ideas could easily be spread. A revolutionary underground with various groups and circles appearing and disappearing developed out of the student milieu of the Sixties.

It is this atmosphere of youth culture that Dostoevsky refers to in describing the circle of "Our Group" in *The Devils*. This is a group of young people the wife of the governor Yuliya Michaylovna has chosen as her company in order to prove that she is very progressive and contemporary. She has great affection for them and especially admires their leader Peter Verchovensky. These people represent a mixture of revolutionary and riotous attitudes toward society, expressed in provocative actions mixed with fun and amusement. In fact, Peter Verchovensky is the commander of their inner core, a circle of conspirators, a group he has brought into being, leading them to believe that they are one of hundreds of secret groups of five which are part of a global secret network. Furthermore, there are mysterious fires in this novel, set by unknown arsonists and associated somehow with the protests and riots of factory workers who are blamed for the fires, though it seems that they have been falsely accused by the intriguer Peter Verchovensky.

Fire and arson refer to the history of the Sixties. In 1862, the nihilists were accused of arson, as there was a series of fires set by persons unknown in St. Petersburg and various provincial towns. The radicals blamed the authorities, for in their opinion this perfidious method would be used to denounce the nihilists in the court of public opinion. This led to the end of *The Contemporary* and to Chernyshevsky's arrest. As the St. Petersburg University had already been closed down at the end of the preceding year, because the authorities had been unable to gain control over student protests, this marked the moment when the government started to take repressive measures against the intelligentsia. In return, this was the moment when the critical youth started to form a revolutionary underground and when radical groups began to apply violent methods for the first time. The circle around Nikolay Ishutin discussed the possibility of killing the Emperor as well as the methods of Machiavellian conspiracy Nechaev would implement a few years later. During this time Dmitry Karakozov, a cousin of Ishutin, undertook the first attempt to assassinate the tsar in 1866. He failed and was executed. But the seeds for Nechaev's revolutionary career were sown.

Sergey Nechaev became the inspiration for Dostoevsky's Peter Verchovensky. But who was this protagonist of the exciting Nechaev case? To quote Vera Zasulich, who had been imprisoned in 1869 for several years because of her contact to Nechaev and who later became a female hero to the populist movement and the radical part of the Russian society when she wounded the governor of St. Petersburg in 1878 by a shot in a solo act of terror: "[Nechaev] was not a product of our world, of the intelligentsia. He was a stranger to us."[4]

Nechaev was of humble origins, born 1847 in Ivanovo, a small provincial town nearby Moscow that was about to develop into a kind of Russian Manchester, a center of textile industry. His father was a gilder and painter who later worked as a waiter and servant, while his mother was the daughter of peasant serfs. Nechaev was a man of the people who knew the brutal world so many populists were trying to enter, and in the words of Venturi: "he had painfully, deliberately and unaided, finally climbed up to the world of the intelligentsia, absorbed with astonishing speed all its most bitter elements; and then flung himself into action with an energy and ruthlessness which aroused admiration and fear in all around him."[5] There is a lot to be said about Nechaev's character and personality, about his fabulous energy, his extraordinary strength of will, his hatred, and his political life full of unknown facts and often deliberate mystification.[6] But although he served as Dostoevsky's model for Peter Verchovensky, the author's knowledge of the historic Nechaev was limited. All he knew was what he had learned from the records of the trial against Nechaev's accomplices printed in the newspapers.[7]

In his early youth, Nechaev was eager to learn, dreamed of studying and going to university in the capital. Although he found two paternal friends who supported his thirst for education by giving him the chance to attend a free school, he was to learn that his dream of going to university was beyond his grasp. Nonetheless, he went to Moscow in 1865 to become a schoolmaster, but he failed the exam. In April 1866, he left for St. Petersburg, the very month when Karakozov fired at Alexander II. Nechaev finally passed the exam and earned his

---

[4]   Vera Ivanovna Zasulič, *Vospominanija*, ed. Boris Pavlovič Koz'min, Moscow: Izdat. Politkatorzan, 1931, 57 (my translation).
[5]   Venturi, *Roots of Revolution*, 360.
[6]   See Philip Pomper, *Sergei Nechaev*, New Jersey: Rutgers University Press, 1979; Stephen T. Cochrane, *The Collaboration of Nečaev, Ogarev and Bakunin in 1869: Nečaev's Early Years* (Marburger Abhandlungen zur Geschichte und Kultur Osteuropas 18), Giessen: Wilhelm Schmitz, 1977.
[7]   *Moskovskie Vedomosti*, Moscow, 1869-70.

living as a schoolmaster, enrolling at the university as an external student. From then on he used his ambition not for his personal career and fortune but to influence the student movement in order to use it for a wider purpose, helping to direct the various movements into revolutionary channels. He had already read a lot on politics, was interested in the French Revolution and the predecessor of proletarian communism, Babeuf. He got into contact with radical revolutionary groups and made friends with the revolutionary Pyotr Tkachev, a theoretician of the Jacobin revolutionary tradition, with whom he wrote the *Program of Revolutionary Action.* The two fundamental points of the program were "union" and "insurrection", the primary aim being to achieve the necessary organization, to circulate clandestine pamphlets and proclamations, and to organize illegal meetings, demonstrations, and protests. Some of the *Program*'s items Nechaev would again take up later in his *Catechism of the Revolutionist,* and Dostoevsky seizes on some of them in his novel, for example Peter Verchovensky's mysterious hints at the exact time of the upcoming insurrection: "It will start in May and be all over in October."[8] Nechaev was sure about the fact of a revolt being near: The *Program of Revolutionary Action* predicts the expected outbreak of revolution for spring 1870, the end of the nine-year transitional arrangement after the peasants' liberation in 1861 and the final end of the reforms.

In spring 1869, a wave of arrests motivated Nechaev to invent the story of his "escape", an example of his inclination for creating an atmosphere of mystery and conspiracy around him. In fact, there was no need to escape from prison as he had not even been arrested. He left Russia by his own choice with the purpose of getting in contact with the elite of the Russian emigration in Europe. He went to Switzerland, introduced himself to the anarchist Mikhail Bakunin and to Nikolay Ogarev, and impressed the leading Russian *émigrés* at the age of twenty by claiming to be the delegate of a powerful secret society coming right from the very center of the revolutionary circles of Russia. During his stay, Nechaev shared Bakunin's home and a close relationship developed between the two men. The fifty-five-year-old Bakunin idealized the young man as a revolutionary prototype *par*

---

[8]   Fyodor Dostoevsky, *Devils* (1872), ed. and trans. Michael R. Katz, Oxford and New York: Oxford University Press, 1992, 394 (all subsequent references to this edition are indicated by page numbers in the text).

excellence, and there are speculations about Bakunin's homosexual inclination to explain his unusually naive trust in Nechaev. Ogarev wrote a poem devoted to Nechaev, entitled "Student", which was spread in pamphlets. In *The Devils*, Dostoevsky alludes to this in the form of a parodic poem, "A Noble Character", which plays a role in Peter Verchovensky's denunciation of Ivan Shatov as a traitor and his condemnation to death.

Before returning to Russia in autumn 1869, Nechaev sent a pile of proclamations both to friends and others, including complete strangers, and thus caused the arrest of many people – a procedure analogous to his unscrupulous methods of creating a revolutionary atmosphere. He brought with him the result of his theoretical considerations, a small booklet called *Catechism of the Revolutionist*, which contained the main traits of a revolutionary as Nechaev imagined him to be:

> The revolutionary is a doomed man. He has no interests of his own, no affairs, no feelings, no attachments, no belongings, not even a name. Everything in him is absorbed by a single exclusive interest, a single thought, a single passion – the revolution.[9]

As a result, Nechaev demanded that the revolutionary should give up all emotional ties to the outside world:

> Hard toward himself, he must be hard toward others also. All the tender and effeminate emotions of kinship, friendship, love, gratitude, and even honor must be stifled in him by a cold and single-minded passion for the revolutionary cause. There exists for him only one delight, one consolation, one reward and one gratification – the success of the revolution. Night and day he must have but one thought, one aim – merciless destruction. In cold-blooded and tireless pursuit of this aim, he must be prepared both to die himself and to destroy with his own hands everything that stands in the way of its achievement.[10]

---

[9]   Sergey Nechaev, "Catechism of the Revolutionist" (1869), in *The Terrorism Reader: A Historical Anthology*, eds Walter Laqueur and Yonah Alexander, New York and Scarborough, Ont: Meridian, 1987, 68.
[10]   *Ibid.*, 69.

The statement "to destroy with his own hands everything that stands in the way of its achievement" prefigures the end of Nechaev's own story: back in Russia he founded a secret society, *Narodnaya Raspra-va* ("The People's Revenge"), pretending that he was the representative of a mysterious committee supervising an enormous revolutionary organization. In reality there were but a few dozen members, yet Nechaev obscured the true number by means of a complicated system of membership recruitment. Each member had to found a new group of five, and each group was required to act independently and secretly, without knowing members of other groups, thus creating the impression of a large conspiratorial network. Most of Nechaev's adherents submissively obeyed his orders, but one of them, Ivan Ivanov, student of the Moscow School of Agriculture, spoke up against him; in response, Nechaev forced him to quit the society and decided to do away with him. He accused him of being a traitor and convinced the members closest to him to kill him. As in Dostoevsky's novel, the victim's body was disposed of in a pond. Dostoevsky's description of the murder of Ivan Shatov in one of the last chapters of *Devils*, "A Full Night's Work", is very close to what happened in the garden of the School of Agriculture. As in Dostoevsky's novel, the pretext of the murderers for calling a meeting there on 21 November 1869 was to dig up a typewriter.

A few days later, Nechaev left for St. Petersburg and shortly afterwards he went abroad. Meanwhile, a large number of people were arrested and, in Nechaev's absence, his accomplices were put on trial and sentenced to forced labor and exile in Siberia. Nechaev himself was arrested in 1872 in Zurich by a Russian agent and handed over to the authorities. He was put on trial in Moscow, received a life sentence, and died in 1882 in the deepest dungeon for political prisoners in the Peter and Paul Fortress in St. Petersburg.

Both the text of the *Catechism* and the transcript of the trial of Nechaev's accomplices in 1871 were published in Russian newspapers in full, and, as mentioned earlier, the latter provoked Dostoevsky to write a counter-revolutionary pamphlet attacking nihilism. Looking through the newspaper material, it is clear that the author studied it very carefully, for Dostoevsky used many historical facts, transferring them into literary fiction.[11]

But the Nechaev-Verchovensky line is not the only source of Dostoevsky's inspiration: *Devils* is both a religious and a philosophical tract. In the process of writing, spiritual and moral issues were given greater relevance, whereas the concept of the political pamphlet took a backseat. Dostoevsky had already for some time been planning a huge project called *Atheism*. While that *opus magnum* was never written, Dostoevsky took up the spiritual quest of this project and embodied it in the character Nikolay Stavrogin, the spiritual center of *Devils*. Dostoevsky himself regarded Stavrogin as the main character of his novel. According to the interpretation by the Russian philosopher Nikolay Berdyaev, the figures of Shatov, Kirillov and Verchovensky are possessed by fragments of Stavrogin's splintered personality. Ivan Shatov embodies belief, albeit an eccentric belief in extreme nationalism: He believes in Russia "as the only 'God-bearing-nation'", "destined to save the world in the name of a new God" (260). Aleksey Kirillov embodies atheism and rationalism. He undertakes self-annihilation out of an absurd individualism in order to prove his absolute freedom to himself, ignorant about the fact that he thereby allows the villain Verchovensky to co-opt his suicide to cover up a crime. And Peter Verchovensky embodies evil. He is the satanic principle, the true Mephisto. While Stavrogin pronounces the following words, it is Verchovensky who puts them into practice:

> All your bureaucracy and sentimentality – it's all good cement. But there's one thing that's even better: persuade four members of a circle to finish off a fifth on the pretext that he's an informer, and you'll immediately bind them together with the blood that's been shed. They'll become your slaves; they won't dare rebel or call you to account. (408)

Although Dostoevsky initially did not intend to make Verchovensky the novel's protagonist, the latter occupies the largest space of the book, and it is in this way that Dostoevsky returns to his primary

---

[11] See Gudrun Braunsperger, *Sergej Nečaev und Dostoevskijs* Dämonen*: Die Geburt eines Romans aus dem Geist des Terrorismus*, Frankfurt on Main *et al.*: Peter Lang, 2002.

purpose: to write a political pamphlet. In its social and political dimension, *Devils* may be read as an answer to Turgenev's *Fathers and Sons*, not least in the way that it draws a very nasty caricature of the writer in the unsympathetic figure of the elderly Karmazinov. But Dostoevsky goes one step further than Turgenev: his approach to the phenomenon of politically motivated violence is the approach of a psychologist, not only in terms of description but also in terms of explanation. Dostoevsky, the writer whom Friedrich Nietzsche would later call "the only psychologist from whom I had something to learn", explains the difference between two generations not only through their opposed values. He portrays a lost generation – children (Peter Verchovensksy and Nikolay Stavrogin) in deep despair, who, as they feel deserted by their biological and mental parents (represented by Nikolay Stavrogin's mother Warwara Petrovna Stavrogina and by his tutor Stepan Trofimovich Verchovensky, Peter Verchovensky's father), develop monstrous imaginations of immense power and omnipotence.

In this respect, *Devils* is a serious warning. Dostoevsky shows to what end the final line of Nechaev's *Catechism of the Revolutionist*, the Jesuit formula of "the end justifies the means", can lead. And he demonstrates the process of the voluntary submission of weak characters to a leader in the name of an idea, especially when this leader turns out to be an intriguer. As Peter Verchovensky, who calls himself a "scoundrel", puts it:

> We'll proclaim destruction... .... We'll spread fires... We'll spread legends... Every mangy little group of five will prove useful. I'll find you such devoted followers in these groups that they'll be willing to shoot at anyone and will even be grateful for the honour. Well, sir, then trouble will begin! There'll be an upheaval such as the world has never seen... (446-47)

Many of the protagonists in the novel are murdered. Two commit suicide and one dies for his ideals, being exploited for the "common cause". The devils that haunt the mind of Stavrogin also haunt the youth of his time. In this respect, Dostoevsky's novel can be understood as a prophecy in the original sense of the prophets of the Old Testament: not forecasting the future but telling people how they must not live. Or, as Sergey Bulgakov, another Russian philosopher, put it:

Devils is a novel "not about the Russian Revolution but about the disease of the Russian soul".[12]

Dostoevsky's psychological approach can still be regarded as valid and useful for the analysis of the outpouring of political violence and terror in our times. Observing how young people get in touch with radical Islam and looking at the origins of their extremism from a psychological point of view, Dostoevsky, were he still around, would perhaps write a stunning up-to-date version of *Devils*.

---

[12]   Quoted in Roland Opitz, "Die Herausbildung des Gestaltensystems in Dostojewskijs schwierigstem Buch", in *Das Prophetische in Dostojewskijs* Dämonen, eds Olga Grossman and Roland Opitz, Weimar: VDG, 1998, 36 (my translation).

PLOTS ON LONDON:
TERRORISM IN TURN-OF-THE-CENTURY BRITISH FICTION

MICHAEL C. FRANK

From Gothic "terror" to terrorist "terror"

In a 1797 journal essay written in the form of a letter to the editor, an anonymous reviewer deplored the vogue of "terrorist novel writing" that dominated the literary scene at the close of the eighteenth century. For the unknown author, a "terrorist novel" was a text in the tradition of Horace Walpole's *The Castle of Otranto*, a tradition now better known under Walpole's own term, "Gothic". The critique specifically aimed at the "great quantity of novels" produced in the wake of Ann Radcliffe's successes of the early 1790s, "in which it has been the fashion to make *terror* the *order of the day*, by confining the heroes and heroines in old gloomy castles; full of spectres, apparitions, ghosts, and dead men's bones".[1] This fashion is closely related to a revaluation of affect in the latter part of the eighteenth century. One of the most influential aesthetic writings of the period, Edmund Burke's *Philosophical Enquiry into the Origin of Our Ideas of the Sublime and Beautiful* (1757), famously argued that sublimity appeals to the passions relating to self-preservation and that it therefore causes stronger

---

[1]   Anonymous, "Terrorist Novel Writing" (1797), in *The Spirit of the Public Journals for 1797: Being an Impartial Selection of the Most Exquisite Essays and Jeux d'Esprits, Principally Prose, That Appear in the Newspapers and Other Publications. With Explanatory Notes and Anecdotes of Many of the Persons Alluded to*, London: R. Philipps, 1798, I, 223 (emphases in original). In the same year, another anonymous letter drew a direct connection between the Gothic tradition in Britain and recent events in France, arguing that British novelists had developed their own "system of terror" in response to the Jacobin atrocities; see Anonymous, "The Terrorist System of Novel-Writing" (1797), in *Gothic Readings: The First Wave, 1764-1840*, ed. Rictor Norton, London and New York: Leicester University Press, 2000, 299-303.

emotions than beauty. Against this background, Burke identified terror
as "the ruling principle of the sublime",[2] which he in turn described as
"the strongest emotion which the mind is capable of feeling".[3] For
Burke, the "delight" in terror was restricted to those frightful and
potentially dangerous objects or situations that cannot actually harm
us, because we perceive them from a safe distance[4] – for instance, as
viewers of art or as readers of poetry. The literary tradition of Gothic
romance inaugurated by Walpole in 1764/65 gives expression to precisely this positive understanding of terror as a prime source of aesthetic enjoyment.

The noun "terror" and its derivative adjective "terrorist" were soon
to undergo a dramatic semantic shift, however – a shift that had
already begun when the essay "Terrorist Novel Writing" was first
published. In the context of the Reign of Terror during the French
Revolution, the term *"la terreur"* acquired a markedly different meaning, used by the protagonists themselves to describe the Jacobin policy
of intimidation.[5] The earliest appearance of the neologism *"terrorisme"* in French occurred in 1794.[6] After Maximilien Robespierre
was deposed and executed, the Thermidorians used the term with
unambiguously pejorative intent, in order to differentiate themselves
from the Jacobin "terror". As early as 1795, the English lexicon had
adopted this new meaning of "terrorism". "Thousands of those Hell-
hounds called Terrorists … are let loose on the people",[7] Edmund

---

[2]   Edmund Burke, *A Philosophical Enquiry into the Origin of Our Ideas of the Sublime and the Beautiful: And Other Pre-Revolutionary Writings*, ed. David Womersley,
London: Penguin, 2004, II, ii, 102.

[3]   *Ibid.*, I, vii, 86.

[4]   See *ibid.*, I, xv, 94, and I, xviii, 97.

[5]   On the history of the concepts of "terror" and "terrorism" before and after the
"Reign of Terror", see the meticulous reconstructions by Gerd van den Heuvel, "Terreur, Terroriste, Terrorisme", in *Handbuch politisch-sozialer Grundbegriffe in Frankreich 1680-1820*, vol 3: *Philosophe, Philosophie; Terreur, Terroriste, Terrorisme*, eds
Rolf Reichardt and Eberhard Schmitt, Munich: R. Oldenbourg, 1985, 89-132; Rudolf
Walther, "Terror, Terrorismus", in *Geschichtliche Grundbegriffe: Historisches Lex-
ikon zur politisch-sozialen Sprache in Deutschland*, eds Otto Brunner, Werner Conze,
and Reinhart Koselleck, Stuttgart: Klett-Cotta, 1990, VI, 323-444.

[6]   See Heuvel, "Terreur, Terroriste, Terrorisme", 120, 124; Walther, "Terror, Terrorismus", 348.

[7]   Edmund Burke, "Fourth Letter on the Proposals for Peace with the Regicide Di-
rectory of France: Addressed to the Earl Fitzwilliam. 1795-7", in *The Works of the*

Burke wrote in a letter of that year. The same Burke who had so greatly contributed to the prestige of "terror" as an aesthetic category in the
middle of the eighteenth century was among the first to condemn
revolutionary "terror".

Gothic fiction writers quickly responded to the events in France. In
the climactic riot scene towards the end of Matthew Lewis' *The Monk*
(1796), an incensed populace lynches the prioress of St. Clare, before
invading and burning down the convent[8] – in a scenario that, regardless of its medieval Spanish setting, is clearly meant to evoke the
storming of the Bastille.[9] Patrick Brantlinger comments that from
1789 onward "Gothic terror often reflects revolutionary terror".[10] Despite such metaphorical references, however, the concept of terrorism
itself had not yet entered the literary stage. Outside of literature, the
term "terrorism" remained inextricably linked with Robespierre and
his followers. According to the *Oxford English Dictionary*, all instances of the word from the first half of the nineteenth century refer
to the Jacobins.[11] What the *OED* does not say is when exactly this
usage of "terrorism" was superseded by the more general one that we
still primarily associate with the word today – and that encompasses
state or top-down terrorism as well as the bottom-up terrorism of sub-
state groups.

It is exclusively in this latter sense that twenty-first century critics
apply the term "terrorism" to literature. While today the description of
Gothic fiction as "terrorist novel writing" seems curiously obsolete,
the phrase "terrorist novel" itself has gained new currency.[12] Two

---

Right Honorable Edmund Burke, rev. edn, Boston: Little, Brown, and Company,
1866, VI, 70.

[8]   Matthew Lewis, *The Monk* (1796), ed. Howard Anderson, Oxford and New York:
Oxford University Press, 1998, 355-58.

[9]   See Ronald Paulson, "Gothic Fiction and the French Revolution", *English Literary History*, XLVIII/3 (Spring 1981), 534-35.

[10]   Patrick Brantlinger, *The Reading Lesson: The Threat of Mass Literacy in Nineteenth-Century British Fiction*, Bloomington, IN: Indiana University Press, 1998, 51.

[11]   See the entries on "Terror", "Terrorism", and "Terrorist" in *The Oxford English
Dictionary*, 2nd edn, prepared by J.A. Simpson and E.S.C. Weiner, Oxford: Clarendon Press, 1989, XVII, 820-21.

[12]   Margaret Scanlan, *Plotting Terror: Novelists and Terrorists in Contemporary
Fiction*, Charlottesville and London: University of Virginia Press, 2001; Anthony
Kubiak, "Spelling It Out: Narrative Typologies of Terror", *Studies in the Novel*,
XXXVI/3 (Fall 2004), 294-301; Benjamin Kunkel, "Dangerous Characters", *The New*

hundred years after the rise of Gothic fiction, the term is now applied
to a novelistic sub-genre that only emerged in the late nineteenth century, that was temporarily discontinued in the context of the two world
wars, and that has increasingly gained in importance since the 1970s,[13]
with notable booms in the 1990s and the years following the 9/11
attacks. When Margaret Scanlan re-introduced the phrase "terrorist
novel" in 2001, she traced the history of the genre to Fyodor Dostoevsky's *Devils*, Henry James' *Princess Casamassima*, and Joseph
Conrad's *Under Western Eyes*.[14] These works, she argued, set the pattern for late twentieth-century terrorist fiction. Other diachronically
oriented approaches to terrorism in literature have followed Scanlan's
example.[15]

    What these various studies have in common is that they consider
turn-of-the-century terrorism fiction as the starting point of a new literary form. As the example of post-revolutionary Gothic indicates,
however, the "terrorist novel" has a much longer (pre)history. It is
perhaps helpful in this context to think of the narrative of terror not in
terms of a "fixed genre" but as a transgeneric "mode".[16] As such, it
has repeatedly changed with the concept of "terror" itself. Each new,
historically determined understanding of "terror" produced new types
of terror narrative. Thus the present article will demonstrate that the
anarchist and dynamite novels of the late nineteenth and early twentieth centuries adapted the conventions of Gothic terror to the new
phenomenon of "terrorist terror" by complementing or substituting the

---

York Times, 11 September 2005: http://www.nytimes.com/2005/09/11/books/review/
11kunkel.html (accessed 28 July 2009); Francis Blessington, "Politics and the Terrorist Novel", *Sewanee Review*, CXVI/1 (Winter 2007), 116-24; Robert Appelbaum and
Alexis Paknadel, "Terrorism and the Novel, 1970-2001", *Poetics Today*, XXIX/3
(Fall 2008), 387-436.
[13] See Appelbaum and Paknadel, "Terrorism and the Novel", 395-96.
[14] See Scanlan, *Plotting Terror*, 7-11.
[15] In what was then only the second monograph entirely devoted to the topic, Alex
Houen similarly juxtaposed Victorian and Edwardian fiction with later twentieth-
century literature, and the same holds for a more recent essay by Francis Blessington,
which expands the focus to also cover post-9/11 fiction. See Alex Houen, *Terrorism
and Modern Literature, from Joseph Conrad to Ciaran Carson*, Oxford and New
York: Oxford University Press, 2002; Blessington, "Politics and the Terrorist Novel".
[16] I am thinking here of Fredric Jameson's definition of "mode" as "a formal possibility which can be revived and renewed". Fredric Jameson, "Magical Narratives:
Romance as Genre", *New Literary History*, VII/1 (Autumn 1975), 142.

genre staples of "old gloomy castles, ... spectres, apparitions, ghosts, and dead men's bones" with new settings and motifs: the late-Victorian metropolis of London, anarchist conspiracies, dynamite explosions, and the contradictory images of inept would-be-terrorists who accidentally blow themselves to pieces and futuristic scenarios of a London laid waste by modern weaponry. This is not to say that turn-of-the-century terrorism novels merely updated the Gothic tradition. As will become apparent, they rather combined Gothic elements with various other modes, incorporating the phenomenon of "terrorist terror" into a host of narrative genres – with very different effects.

This multiple narrativization of terror cannot be investigated independently of what the social anthropologists Joseba Zulaika and William Douglass term "terrorism discourse".[17] Even if the late twentieth-century situation examined in their study is radically different from the ones in earlier decades, many of the tendencies described by Zulaika and Douglass may be traced to the very beginnings of public interest in terrorism. This is particularly true for the observation that, "regarding terrorism, the brandishing of stark facts goes hand in hand with great leaps into discursive fantasy".[18] To achieve its defining effect – collective fear of (more) violence to come – terrorism has always relied on the belief that the next attack is impending, and that it could happen anywhere, anytime. As the recent example of 9/11 has shown, this belief is, seemingly paradoxically, underpinned by counterterrorist rhetoric, which insists that the "question is not if, but when".[19] In this sense, the phenomenon of terror is located in the interstice between the real (actual attacks and their tangible aftermath) and the imaginary (speculations about possible future assaults), a fact reinforced by the perception of the perpetrators as being both invisible and in our very midst, omnipresent in public discourse but still elusive in person.

---

[17] See Joseba Zulaika and William A. Douglass, *Terror and Taboo: The Follies, Fables, and Faces of Terrorism*, New York and London: Routledge, 1996, "Part One: Fashioning Terrorism Discourse", 1-119. See also the Introduction to the present volume.

[18] *Ibid.*, 4.

[19] See Frank Furedi, *Invitation to Terror: The Expanding Empire of the Unknown*, London and New York: Continuum, 2007; Joseba Zulaika, *Terrorism: The Self-Fulfilling Prophecy*, Chicago and London: The University of Chicago Press, 2009.

The fantastic dimension of terror may be one of the reasons why writers of fiction were quick to respond when insurgent terrorism first emerged – in various guises – on the stage of history. From its beginnings in the last two decades of the nineteenth century, novels dealing with terrorism have predominantly depicted imaginary attacks, perpetrators, and conspiracies, answering real plots with invented ones. Accordingly, I will put forward the thesis that such novels give insight into the "cultural imaginary" of terrorism, which may be defined as the period-specific repertoire of images and stories pertaining to terrorism in both its actual and its potential forms. Combining the available historical knowledge with the counterfactual, this imaginary is shaped not only by the respective period's public discourse on terrorism (the often hyperbolic pronouncements of politicians, the media, as well as the terrorist groups themselves) but also by the literary traditions that lend themselves to the narrativization of terror. By focusing on the emergence of the theme of terrorism in late-Victorian fiction, the following analysis will be concerned with the earliest manifestations of the cultural imaginary of terrorism in British literature.

Three forms of insurgent terrorism at the close of the nineteenth century

The first comprehensive account of terrorism in *fin-de-siècle* fiction has been provided by Barbara Melchiori. Apart from outlining the variations of the dynamite theme in British novels of the period, Melchiori offers a helpful historical contextualization. Two general observations from her introductory chapter are particularly relevant for what follows. The first concerns the diversity of terrorist groups and causes at the close of the nineteenth century. Melchiori distinguishes three "subversive movements", which were active in different countries and had specific aims: the Russian Narodnaya Volya, or "People's Will" (better known in the West as "Nihilists"), the Irish and Irish-American Fenians, as well as the pan-European anarchists. According to Melchiori, each of these movements directed its violence at a specific type of target: public figures, public buildings, or the public at large.[20] While this distinction is too clear-cut – since neither group can be reduced to just one type of target – it is nevertheless helpful: the ques-

---

[20] See Barbara Arnett Melchiori, *Terrorism in the Late Victorian Novel*, London, Sydney, and Dover, NH: Croomhelm, 1985, 6-8.

tion as to whom or what terrorists aimed their bombs at played a significant role in the public perception of the phenomenon. For this reason, I want to begin by elaborating on Melchiori's point.

In 1879, ninety years after the outbreak of the French Revolution, the Russian Nihilists adopted the term "terrorism" to characterize their own revolutionary practice in the struggle against the autocratic regime in Russia.[21] A "terrorist revolution" carried out by a small group was lauded in pamphlets as a preferable alternative to a broadly based popular uprising, as it would entail fewer victims, and the victims it claimed would be almost exclusively just. Henceforth, despots were to be in a state of constant fear for their lives.[22] Consequently, the efforts of Narodnaya Volya were almost exclusively focused on assassinating Czar Alexander II.[23] Yet the type of terrorism pioneered by the Nihilists was not limited to the removal of despots; it could also be applied to members of the police, the military, or other officials. Martin Miller points out that what differentiates the political assassinations of the nineteenth century from earlier regicides is the fact that "the objects of attack expanded": violence was now also directed against "individuals *associated* with the unjust authority".[24]

Although members of a Fenian splinter group, the Irish National Invincibles, stabbed the Chief Secretary for Ireland and his Under-Secretary in Phoenix Park, Dublin, in 1882, the Fenians' chief strategy in the 1880s was to plant bombs in public buildings. This strategy was advanced by the American branch of the movement. Between 1881 and 1885, Clan na Gael and its breakaway faction, the Skirmishers, ran parallel operations in Britain, sending small groups of American-Irish men equipped with explosives to the country. Several attempts

---

[21]   See Walther, "Terror, Terrorismus", 389.
[22]   See Nikolai Morozov, "The Terrorist Struggle" (1880), and G. Tarnovski, "Terrorism and Routine" (1880), in *The Terrorism Reader: A Historical Anthology*, eds Walter Laqueur and Yonah Alexander, rev. edn, New York and Scarborough, ON: Meridian, 1987, 72-78 and 79-84.
[23]   See Yves Ternon, "Russian Terrorism, 1878-1908", in *The History of Terrorism: From Antiquity to Al Qaeda*, eds Gérard Chaliand and Arnaud Blin, trans. Edward Schneider, Kathryn Pulver, and Jesse Browner, Berkeley, Los Angeles, and London: University of California Press, 2007, 147-50.
[24]   Martin A. Miller, "The Intellectual Origins of Modern Terrorism in Europe", in *Terrorism in Context*, ed. Martha Crenshaw, University Park, PA: The Pennsylvania State University Press, 1995, 30-31.

failed because the bombs were discovered when their fuses were still burning or because they did not detonate, but despite these setbacks thirteen attacks were successfully executed in London alone.[25] As the historian Kenneth Short notes at the beginning of his study *The Dynamite War*, the British capital "for almost five years daily faced the threat of gunpowder and dynamite explosions occurring in the City of London, the street of Westminster, the Tower of London, the House of Commons, under London Bridge, in the railway stations' left luggage rooms, and the tunnels of the underground".[26] The sustained campaign (the first of its kind in the history of terrorism) culminated on January 24, 1885 with near-simultaneous explosions at the Tower of London, Westminster Hall, and the House of Parliament.

The Fenian bombs were not primarily directed at civilians, even if they caused severe injuries among bystanders (especially when they were detonated on underground trains). While it is notable that the whole campaign of the 1880s did not cause as many fatalities as the December 1867 attack on Clerkenwell prison – a failed attempt to free a Fenian prisoner by blasting the wall of the prison yard during which six people were instantly killed and more than a hundred injured[27] – this fact alone does not indicate that the American-Irish terrorists deliberately avoided civilian deaths. As Lindsay Clutterbuck notes, the use of dynamite in the public space rather suggests that "At best, the perpetrators were reckless or careless to the potential loss of innocent life or at worst, they considered it of little or no consequence to their objective."[28]

Despite this qualification concerning the supposedly discriminate character of Fenian operations, Clutterbuck would probably agree that

[25] For a concise account of the operations run by Jeremiah O'Donovan Rossa (1881-83) and Clan na Gael (1883-85), see the section "The Dynamite Campaign" in Séan McConville, *Irish Political Prisoners, 1848-1922: Theatres of War*, London and New York: Routledge, 2003, 330-56.

[26] K.R.M. Short, *The Dynamite War: Irish-American Bombers in Victorian Britain*, Dublin: Gill and Macmillan, 1979, 1.

[27] For a brief account of the Clerkenwell prison attack, see *ibid.*, 7-12.

[28] Clutterbuck continues: "To infer from the low level of actual casualties that *Clan na Gael* ... actually attempted to minimise them is to confuse their failure to kill anyone with a desire not to do so .... [O]nly good fortune prevented casualties occurring as an inevitable consequence of their actions." Lindsay Clutterbuck, "The Progenitors of Terrorism: Russian Revolutionaries or Extreme Irish Republicans?", *Terrorism and Political Violence*, XVI/1 (Spring 2004), 166, 169.

of all dynamite terrorists of the late nineteenth century, only anarchists purposefully attacked the public at large. In 1892, two people died after the Véry restaurant in the Boulevard de Magenta, Paris, had been blown up. The attack was supposed to avenge the incarceration of notorious dynamiter Ravachol, who had spoken too freely about anarchism to a waiter of the restaurant and subsequently been arrested there.[29] The following year, a Spanish anarchist threw two bombs into the audience at the Liceu Opera House in Barcelona, causing the death of more than twenty. This deed was committed to retaliate the execution of an anarchist assassin, but neither the targeted people nor the place of the attack were in any way related to that event.[30] Another year later, Émile Henry bombed the Café Terminus near the Saint-Lazare railway station in Paris, injuring more than twenty and killing one. He acted in response to severe government measures against anarchists. However, Henry was less interested in the possible secondary effects of his attack – the pressure that it might put on the government to reconsider its measures – than in its immediate consequences: the punishment of the "bourgeoisie", which Henry held collectively responsible.[31] Taken together, these three bombings signal the rise of indiscriminate terrorism – terrorist violence aimed at whole social groups and populations.[32]

The second important observation made by Barbara Melchiori in her study on late-Victorian terrorism fiction concerns the choice of villains. Historian Bernard Porter notes that "between 1823 and 1906

---

[29]   See Olivier Hubac-Occhipinti, "Anarchist Terrorists of the Nineteenth Century", in *The History of Terrorism: From Antiquity to Al Qaeda*, eds Gérard Chaliand and Arnaud Blin, trans. Edward Schneider, Kathryn Pulver, and Jesse Browner, Berkeley, Los Angeles, and London: University of California Press, 2007, 127.

[30]   See *ibid.*, 120.

[31]   See *ibid.*, 129.

[32]   In his recent study of Henry and the anarchist circles in Paris, John Merriman describes the Café Terminus bombing as "a defining moment in modern history": "It was the day that ordinary people became the targets of terrorists." John Merriman, *The Dynamite Club: How a Bombing in Fin-de-Siècle Paris Ignited the Age of Modern Terror*, London: JR Books, 2009, 5. It would be gravely misleading, however, to simply identify anarchism with indiscriminate terrorism. Not all anarchists endorsed violence and even fewer participated in it. And even among the latter, the targeting of civilians was the exception rather than the rule. At the turn of the century, the greatest number of political assassinations was committed by alleged anarchists.

no refugee who came to Britain was ever denied entry, or expelled".[33]
As a consequence of this policy, Victorian Britain and especially its
capital became an asylum for both Russian dissidents and anarchists
from all over Europe, including some of the Paris *dynamitards*. There
were various political refugee clubs in the city, with the "Autonomy
Club" serving as the "unofficial headquarters of the informal network
of foreign anarchists".[34] As a hub of international anarchism, London
played a pivotal role in the dissemination of radical journals and
pamphlets, many of which were printed there. Because in 1880 the
country "did not have a secret political police force of any kind, and
had not had one for more than twenty years", as Porter adds in another
study, "revolutionaries of all political and national complexions
enjoyed more liberty of action in Britain than they had anywhere
else".[35] Some extremists used this liberty to continue plotting against
their home governments. Britain itself, however, was spared.

While the campaigns of the People's Will were naturally concentrated on Russia, only one anarchist bomb detonated on British soil: in
1894 Martial Bourdin, a French tailor who was well-known in London's anarchist circles, accidentally blew himself up while carrying
explosives through Greenwich Park – in what was apparently a failed
attack on the Royal Observatory. As Melchiori emphasizes, all terrorist attempts that were successfully executed within the British Isles
were organized by the Fenians. The Fenian "outrages", as they were
then called, were Britain's only direct encounter with terrorist
violence. All the more surprising is the fact that "the dynamite novelists of the 1880s and 1890s for the most part were inclined to attribute
their fictional attempts to rather vaguely defined anarchists or, occasionally, Nihilists or socialists". Notably absent from the majority of
turn-of-the-century terrorism novels is the figure of the American-
Irish dynamiter. "The reason", Melchiori believes, "can only be the
wish, conscious or otherwise, to keep the condition of Ireland question

[33] Bernard Porter, *The Refugee Question in Mid-Victorian Politics*, Cambridge:
Cambridge University Press, 1979, 8.
[34] Merriman, *The Dynamite Club*, 123.
[35] Bernard Porter, *The Origins of the Vigilant State: The London Metropolitan Police Special Branch before the First World War*, London: Weidenfeld and Nicolson,
1987, 1, 9.

out of the novel *qua* media".[36] Did English novelists or their publishers not wish to provide a platform for radical Irish nationalism and its agenda? Or were the London circles of anarchists from Russia, France, and other continental European countries simply considered a more exotic and therefore literarily more attractive subject? What is certain, in any case, is that the Victorian cultural imaginary of terrorism was dominated by the image of the foreign anarchist.[37]

Robert Louis and Fanny Van de Grift Stevenson's *The Dynamiter* (1885)

Despite the dominance of the alien anarchist in late-Victorian fiction about terrorism, the "condition of Ireland question" did appear in at least one novel by a well-known non-Irish author: *The Dynamiter*, co-authored by the Scottish writer Robert Louis Stevenson and his American-born wife Fanny Van de Grift, is the earliest literary response to the Fenian campaigns of the 1880s. The majority of the stories in the collaborative novel date back to the winter of 1883, when the couple resided in Hyères in southern France. According to a 1923 "Prefatory Note", they were first conceived as bedside stories for Robert Louis Stevenson, who, among other ailments, had caught an eye disease that threatened him with blindness. To entertain her husband, Fanny Stevenson took on the role of "Scheherazade"[38] and invented one new story every day. The news from England about the Fenian attacks provided her the material for a frame narrative. As she recalls, "There had been several dynamite outrages in London about this time, the most of them turning out fiascos. It occurred to me to take an impotent dynamite intrigue as the thread to string my stories on" (xi-xii). Only a year

---

[36] Melchiori, *Terrorism in the Late Victorian Novel*, 8.

[37] In an essay on newspaper representations of anarchism in late-Victorian Britain, Hana Shpayer-Makov demonstrates that the various forms of terrorism distinguished above were often conflated, "anarchism" becoming the umbrella term for all disruptive activities, including those of the Fenians. See Haia Shpayer-Makov, "Anarchism in British Public Opinion 1880-1914", *Victorian Studies*, XXXI/4 (Summer 1988), 487-516.

[38] Robert Louis [and Fanny Van de Grift] Stevenson, *More New Arabian Nights: The Dynamiter* (1885) (The Works of Robert Louis Stevenson: Tusitala Edition, III), 2nd imp., London: William Heinemann, 1924, xi. Unless specified otherwise, all subsequent references are to this edition.

later did the couple begin to write down these stories. Finding themselves short of money, they decided to publish the collection as a
sequel to the 1882 volume of *New Arabian Nights*.

Bearing the main title *More New Arabian Nights*, the stories are
modern fairy tales, set in a London that is presented, in the very first
sentence, as "the city of encounters, the Bagdad of the West" (1). The
tales are loosely tied together by a frame narrative that relates the adventures of three impecunious young gentlemen: Challoner, Desborough, and Somerset, "three futiles" (4) lacking the training for any
useful occupation. When the men accidentally meet in a cigar divan at
the beginning of the narrative, Somerset persuades his friends that
they should "hunt down [a] miscreant" (6) sought by the police. The
role of amateur detective, he is convinced, is the only one suitable for
men in their position. Accordingly, Somerset prompts his friends to
unhesitatingly embrace "the next adventure that offers itself" (7).

What follows is a surreal sequence of chance encounters. During
their adventures, Challoner and Desborough unwittingly meet members of the conspiratorial group associated with the man wanted by the
police. In the meantime, Somerset shares a house with the wanted man
himself, who turns out to be the bomb-builder "Zero". Apart from
Zero, only two terrorists play a significant role in the story. One is the
Irish-American Patrick M'Guire; the other is Clara Luxmore, a young
English lady who ran away from home (so her mother tells Somerset)
because "Some whim about oppressed nationalities – Ireland, Poland,
and the like – ha[d] turned her brain" (81). In the course of the novel,
Clara appears in various exotic guises. Her imaginary life-stories are
the subject of two of the inset narratives. Located in the Mormon
community of Utah and in a Cuban slave plantation, respectively, they
are romantic tales of escape involving Destroying Angels, voodoo
witches, slave traders, and pirates. Apart from a brief reference to a
Mormon scientist's experiments with a life-elixir that causes accidental explosions, the stories' only connection to the overall theme of
dynamite terrorism is the motif of camouflage: as they suggest, to be a
terrorist means to play a perpetual game of false appearances and to
erase one's true identity.

This is confirmed by the chief terrorist of the group, who lives a
life of constant dissimulation – to the extent that he has almost become a non-entity, as his preferred alias "Zero" indicates. He has as

many pseudonyms as he keeps wigs, artificial beards, suits, and over-coats in his bedroom closet (see 114, 116). The alias "Zero" alludes to a documented Fenian practice: that of assigning members letters of the alphabet or numbers. During the trial following the Phoenix Park murders of 1882, James Carey, who had played a crucial part in the Irish National Invincibles' conspiracy, surprisingly turned Queen's witness. Among other things, he provided a description of the current commandant of the society, known only by his pseudonym, "Number One". Following Carey's testimony, there was wild speculation in the press as to who that mysterious person might be. This case provides a striking example of the imaginary appeal of terrorism, as one contemporary account illustrates:

> [T]he newspapers increased the number of individuals who in their estimation might have been the owner of this peculiar *nom de guerre,* some mythical and some in the flesh …. It eventually became such a mystery that the general public began to pronounce "Number One" a myth and the creature of Carey's brain.

According to the same source, "'Number One' would have remained … the greatest mystery of the nineteenth century" had he not been identified through a photograph and forced to escape to the United States.[39]

In *The Dynamiter*, the masquerading of Clara Luxmore, the woman terrorist, has an additional function apart from shielding her from police identification: it also helps her to win the sympathy of the self-declared detectives and to trick them into inadvertently assisting her. Both Challoner and Desborough readily take on the role of "knight-errant" (52, 57, 183), helping the case of radical Irish republicanism in the naïve belief that they are serving a lady in distress. To Clara's great amusement, Challoner agrees to travel all the way to Glasgow, where he delivers a warning note and money at M'Guire's hideaway

---

[39] The quotations are from Chapter XXXIII of the book written by Number One (alias Robert Tynan) himself. This particular chapter allegedly has a different author, however; it is signed Patrick Kinsella, who is identified as the man in charge of the Dublin faction of the Invincibles during Number One's absence: P.J.P. Tynan, *The Irish National Invincibles and Their Times: Three Decades of Struggle against the Foreign Conspiracy in Dublin Castle*, New York: The National Invincible Publishing Co., 1894, 469.

in a derelict part of town. The younger Desborough – who falls in love with Clara, believing her to be a "fair Cuban" – is even more gullible. This time, Clara feels remorse, however. When Desborough carries a box containing a bomb to Holyhead (in a plot to blow up a steamer to Dublin), she follows him and reveals the truth – eventually abjuring terrorism and becoming his wife.

At first sight, terrorism as such seems to play a marginal role in the Stevensons' novel. Once the scattered passages dealing with the political uses of dynamite are considered together, however, two recurring themes emerge from them: that of the indiscriminate character of dynamite terrorism; and that of the unreliable bomb. Both are closely connected with Zero, whose origins remain obscure. All we know for sure is that he is a foreigner (see 137), probably from a non-English speaking country (since he mispronounces the word "bomb" as "boom" [121] and uses stilted language), who is ready to risk his life for the sake of "green Erin, green Erin" (197). This deliberately ludicrous phrase suggests that Zero is driven by a vague romantic attachment to Ireland rather than a genuine political agenda. Here as elsewhere in the novel, the Stevensons have little to say about the causes and goals of Irish republicanism. Zero himself merely states that his motivation for becoming a terrorist was his outrage at seeing the "liberty and peace of a poor country desperately abused" (116).

Other passages suggest less altruistic reasons. After his utterly pointless destruction of the – empty – mansion in which he had rented a room, Zero, the "author of the outrage of Red Lion Court" (119), prides himself on also being "the author of the Golden Square Atrocity" (198). As with "report", the Stevensons' preferred designation for explosions,[40] the word "author" is carefully chosen: terrorists were indeed "authors" of outrages to the degree that journalists turned the "reports" of their bombs into newspaper reports, immortalizing them under such names such as "the Outrage at Salford Barracks". Zero makes it clear that the aspiration to this kind of "anonymous, infernal glory" (116) is one of the main driving forces behind his terrorism. By suggesting that the attention-seeking of terrorists is related to an egotistical desire for fame, the Stevensons call into question the political basis of terrorist violence.

---

[40] On this pun, see also Houen, *Terrorism and Modern Literature*, 29.

But Zero is nevertheless given space to develop his threatening vision of "the fall of England, the massacre of thousands, the yell of fear and execration" (118) – a vision that is much closer to the mass-casualty terrorism of our own times than it is to the Fenian attacks of the late nineteenth century. *The Dynamiter* seems well informed about the functioning of terrorist tactics: "Whatever may strike fear, whatever may confound or paralyse the activities of the guilty nation, ... imperial Parliament or excursion steamer, is welcome to my simple plans" (119), Zero explains, admitting that he endorses an "indiscriminate" type of terrorism (118-19). This terrorism is illustrated in a tale about an abortive plot to blow up a statue of Shakespeare – a satirical response to a real incident in May 1884, when an unexploded device was found at the foot of Nelson's Column in Trafalgar Square:[41]

> Our objective was the effigy of Shakespeare in Leicester Square: a spot, I think, admirably chosen; not only for the sake of the dramatist, still very foolishly claimed as a glory by the English race, in spite of his disgusting political opinions; but from the fact that the seats in the immediate neighbourhood are often thronged by children, errand-boys, unfortunate young ladies of the poorer class, and infirm old men – all classes making a direct appeal to public pity, and therefore suitable with our designs. As M'Guire drew near, his heart was inflamed by the most noble sentiment of triumph. Never had he seen the garden so crowded; children, still stumbling in the impotence of youth, ran to and fro, shouting and playing round the pedestal; an old, sick pensioner sat upon the nearest bench, a medal on his breast, a stick with which he walked (for he was disabled by wounds) reclining on his knee. Guilty England would thus be stabbed in the most delicate quarters; the moment had, indeed, been well selected ... (121-22)

In accordance with current definitions of terrorism, this passage neatly distinguishes between the immediate targets (the effigy of Shakespeare and innocent civilians), their symbolic values (Shakespeare as a supposed supporter of Elizabeth I and her Irish policies; the old, the poor, the sick, and the young as objects of public pity), as well as the intended message (the punishment of England, the great imperial nation). Significantly, the wounding of civilians is an essential part of

---

[41] See Melchiori, *Terrorism in the Late Victorian Novel*, 18.

the scheme. Victims are selected not so much because they are held responsible for the oppression of Ireland (as citizens of a "guilty" nation) but because their deaths are likely to stir a public outcry – and thereby to increase attention to the terrorists' cause. The Stevensons are more than explicit about the callousness of this strategy, which purposely targets the weak and the helpless to achieve its aims and, in doing so, far exceeds even the most ruthless Fenian and anarchist bombings.

On 14 January 1881, the first explosion of the Fenian "dynamite war" occurred at Salford Barracks near Manchester. During a densely foggy afternoon, two men removed a ventilation grid from the outer wall and lowered explosives into what they presumably thought to be the armory. Instead, the dynamite exploded in "the building set apart for butcher's meat". The partial destruction of the butcher's shed would almost have been comical had it not killed a seven-year old "workman's son" who happened to be passing by in the street when the explosion took place.[42] It is quite obvious that the Stevensons had in mind this particular attack when they devised "the outrage of Red Lion Court", an incident with a similar outcome: Somerset remembers that the bombing merely destroyed "[a] scavenger's barrow and some copies of the *Weekly Budget*" (119), to which Zero proudly adds that it also injured a child.

Although considered a *"fiasco"* by Somerset, the outrage of Red Lion Court is the only "success" of Zero's entire career (119). For once, the bomb did not misfire; and it even went off at the desired place and time, which is not the case with Zero's other contrivances. When the first explosive device that is mentioned in the novel deto-nates "thirty hours too soon", producing a thud, a hiss, and ill-smelling vapors but no major explosion, the reader learns that this was just the last in a series of failures (10, 61). As the failures continue, Zero grows increasingly despondent. After another of his bombs has burned "like tobacco" (195), he decides to resign. Now that he has "fallen to be a laughing-stock and mockery", he feels that he can no longer pur-sue his occupation, that he is "extinct" as a terrorist (193, 194). Zero's many failures give his alias an unintended new meaning. And so does the conclusion of the Zero subplot: when the terrorist's bag full of

---

[42]   "The Outrage at Salford Barracks", *The Times*, 27 January 1881, 11.

explosives knocks against a bookstall at a train station, he is literally "expunged" (201).

Even though accidental explosions such as this one demonstrate the great destructive power of dynamite in the hands of terrorists, they nevertheless suggest that dynamite primarily endangers those who carry it around London. This impression is reinforced by the fact that the Stevensons' terrorists are themselves more terrified than their potential victims. With the exception of Clara Luxmore, who performs her role in a light-hearted and playful manner, all terrorists in *The Dynamiter* are described as conspicuously nervous and pale. M'Guire is the very personification of the terrified terrorist. His pathological susceptibility to "terror" manifests itself in various scenes, and he himself is fully aware of it (see 59, 110-11). In the end, it comes as no surprise that M'Guire – who is revealed to have undergone treatment "for sleeplessness, loss of appetite, and nervous depression" – dies without any apparent cause. His doctor concludes that he must have "died of fear" (204). Unlike Zero, then, M'Guire is not killed by explosives. Yet he, too, falls victim to his own terrorism: the permanent fear of being caught by the police and, worse still, of being destroyed by dynamite proves too much for him to bear.

Terrorist invasions: *Hartmann, the Anarchist* (1893)
One year after the publication of *The Dynamiter*, John Most, the infamous German socialist dissident and founding editor of the journal *Die Freiheit*, reminded revolutionaries that the effective employment of weapons required intense training. "[The] actual possession of arms is only half the story", he wrote, adding that "one must also know how to use them." More often than not, bombs either failed to detonate or were planted in such a way that they did not cause the desired amount of damage: "Numerous incidents – notably in England – have shown just what a fool one can make of oneself if one does not know how to handle these substances properly."[43] Most understood that the primary

---

[43] John Most, "Advice for Terrorists" (1884-86), in *The Terrorism Reader: A Historical Anthology*, eds Walter Laqueur and Yonah Alexander, rev. edn, New York and Scarborough, ON: Meridian, 1987, 108.

purpose of terrorist violence was to create terror and that, accordingly, terrorists who failed to produce this effect did not deserve that name.[44]

It is certainly significant in this context that *The Dynamiter* chose to describe terrorist failures rather than successes, refusing to be intimidated by terrorists and even to take them seriously. The impotence and mishaps of the Stevensons' would-be-bombers stand in stark contrast to the omnipotence and technological prowess of later fictional dynamiters. Writing in a utopian (or, depending on the perspective adopted, dystopian) mode, several contemporary novelists used real-life terrorist plots to imagine spectacular attacks. Some of these are reminiscent of the notion of "Skirmishers" developed by Fenian leader Jeremiah O'Donovan Rossa in the mid-1870s. In 1875, New York newspaper publisher Patrick Ford asked his readers to donate to a "Skirmishing Fund" which would be used to purchase explosives and to recruit fighters:

> The Irish cause requires Skirmishers. It requires a little band of heroes who will initiate and keep up, without intermission, a guerrilla warfare – men who will fly over land and sea like invisible beings – now striking the enemy in Ireland, now in India, now in England itself, as occasion may present.[45]

Literary responses to the dynamite war were frequently closer to Ford's projected image of heroic Skirmishers than to the actual bombers, who committed all kinds of blunders. Note that Ford's vision of "men who will fly over land and sea like invisible beings" is strongly indebted to the Burkean sublime: these imaginary fighters possess superhuman powers, they remain shrouded in obscurity, and they produce the emotion of terror.

The same applies to several of the period's fictional terrorists, men who literally "fly over land and sea". *A Modern Dœdalus* by the Irish doctor Tom Greer describes how the first-person narrator invents

---

[44] To assist terrorists in the construction of explosives and other weapons, Most had published a how-to manual in 1885. See Johann [aka John] Most, *Science of Revolutionary Warfare: A Handbook of Instruction Regarding the Use and Manufacture of Nitroglycerine, Dynamite, Gun-Cotton, Fulminating Mercury, Bombs, Arsons, Poisons, etc.*, no translator cited, El Dorado, AR: Desert Publications, 1978.

[45] *The Irish World*, 4 December 1875; quoted in Short, *The Dynamite War*, 38.

mechanical wings that enable him to fly.[46] In an air strike *avant la lettre*, he and his squadron, a "flying brigade" of fifty men, drop dynamite on the British forces in Ireland and free the country from foreign rule.[47] In another utopian narrative, *The Dynamite Ship* by Irish-American writer Donald MacKay (1888), three men – one Irish, one American, one English – reach the same aim with the help of a steam-yacht that has been transformed into a military vessel, propelled by petroleum and equipped with compressed-air guns able to shoot dynamite projectiles as far as eight miles.[48] Having anchored below London Bridge, the three assailants and their Irish-American crew send an ultimatum to the British Parliament, before reducing several landmark buildings to rubble and setting fire to the city.

Their method is identified as open warfare, in explicit contrast to the clandestine terrorism of the Fenians. In a similar vein, the flying Irishman in Greer's novel distances himself from the tactics of radical Irish republicans, eventually starting his own campaign. Even though the attack is in each case conducted by a non-state group that uses dynamite in an asymmetric conflict, both novels describe acts of war rather than the kind of bombing that the British public witnessed in the 1880s. They belong to a genre inaugurated by George Chesney's "The Battle of Dorking", an 1871 short story describing how, in the near future, a technologically and strategically superior German army successfully invades and subjugates Britain.[49] Between 1871 and 1914 several dozen similar future-war stories emulated the "Chesney formula",[50] constituting a distinct genre that I.F. Clarke, the leading expert in the field, has named the "tale of the war-to-come".

The destruction of London, the Victorian metropolis, is frequently at the center of these tales. In 1893, the English writer and adventurer

---

[46] Tom Greer, *A Modern Dædalus*, London: Griffith, Farran, Okeden and Welsh, 1887 (rep. New York: Arno Press, 1974).

[47] Greer, who lived in London, began his novel by emphasizing his own sympathies for England and his support of the Union, presenting his book as an admonitory tale.

[48] Donald MacKay, *The Dynamite Ship*, New York: Manhattan Publishing House, 1888. I would like to thank Hendrik Blumentrath for sharing his microfiche copy of this extremely rare book with me.

[49] George Tomkyns Chesney, *The Battle of Dorking: Reminiscences of a Volunteer*, Edinburgh and London: William Blackwood, 1871.

[50] I.F. Clarke, *Voices Prophesying War, 1763-1984*, Oxford and New York: Oxford University Press, 1966, 38.

Edward Douglas Fawcett presented his own version of the future-war story in response to the recent wave of anarchist violence in Europe. Fawcett's *Hartmann, the Anarchist; or, The Doom of the Great City* is set in an imaginary future, "after the late Continental wars",[51] in 1920. The first-person narrator, Stanley, is himself a moderate socialist subscribing to the watchword "Not revolution, but evolution" (5). He is friendly with a radical anarchist, however, who openly endorses terrorism and who is in contact with the anarchist leader Hartmann. Ten years before the events of the novel, Hartmann tried to blow up the German Crown Prince and his suite during their visit to London by placing a bomb on Westminster Bridge. After the failure of the assassination attempt, which killed fifty to sixty bystanders, Hartmann escaped and was generally believed to have drowned on his way to Holland. As Stanley soon learns, Hartmann really fled to Switzerland. Not only is he still alive, but he has also made plans for a major anarchist revolution – together with his "tutor in vice" (43), the "obnoxious German" Michael Schwartz (38) – that is to take place in several European capitals and to begin in London. For this purpose, Hartmann, an engineer of genius, has developed the prototype of a flying-machine, the "aëronef". Constructed out of a new ultra-light material, the aëronef (also referred to as "aëroplane") is electrically powered, driven by propellers, and buoyed up by surrounding envelopes filled with hydrogen.

The narrator is on board the aëroplane when Hartmann and his crew of international anarchists begin their devastating attack. Hovering above London, the terrorists drop dynamite, the new, more powerful explosive forcite, and incendiary oil, seeking to destroy buildings – the Houses of Parliament, the entire City, St. Paul's Cathedral, and many other edifices – as well as civilians (the illustration reproduced on the cover of the present volume shows the collapse of the Big Ben clock tower). In the meantime, bands of anarchists and rioters continue the work of destruction on the ground. The novel's climactic scene contains one of the rare instances in which the aims and strategies of the terrorists are described in more detail. From our own present-day

---

[51] E. Douglas Fawcett, *Hartmann, the Anarchist; or, The Doom of the Great City*, London: Edward Arnold (rep. New York: Arno Press, 1974), 5. Unless specified otherwise, all subsequent references are to this edition.

perspective, its vision of a strike against the network of global capitalism seems strikingly prescient, as does the terrorists' choice of targets:

> [Hartmann's] aim was to pierce the ventricle of the heart of civilization, that heart which pumps the blood of capital everywhere, through the arteries of Russia, of Australia, of India, just as through the capillaries of fur companies in North America, planting enterprises in Ecuador, and trading steamers on African rivers. "Paralyze this heart", he has said, "and you paralyze credit and the mechanism of finance almost universally." (148)

After the first raid, the appalled (though fascinated) narrator is allowed to leave the aëronef. He parachutes into the city and searches for Hartmann's mother, only to discover that she is among the numerous victims of the attack. Stanley finds her last letter, in which she condemns her son's actions, and conveys it to Hartmann, who steers his ship away from the city and blows it up with himself in it.

Throughout the novel, Fawcett's narrator is more interested in Hartmann's invention than in his plans for an anarchist revolution. Large parts of the book are dedicated to either Stanley's exhilaration at flying or to descriptions of the aëroplane in all its technical details. These sections combine Jules Verne-type science fiction with elements of the late-Victorian adventure story. The ideology behind the terrorist attacks remains vague. Hartmann merely tells Stanley that his object in launching attacks on London and other major cities is "to wreck civilization", and that he and his men are "Rousseaus who advocate a return to a simpler life" (84). The novel is therefore not a book about anarchism; rather, it is a book that uses anarchism in accordance with certain generic conventions: it casts terrorists in the role that would later be played by other invaders (for example, H.G. Wells' Martians).

Coda: Turn-of-the-century novelists and their terrorist plots
For Barbara Melchiori, the various literary engagements with the theme of dynamite terrorism at the close of the nineteenth century constitute a "new genre", the dynamite novel.[52] Apart from the dynamite theme, however, the novels in question often have little in com-

---

[52] Melchiori, *Terrorism in the Late Victorian Novel*, viii.

mon. The examples of *The Dynamiter* and *Hartmann, the Anarchist*
are a good case in point. Melchiori herself has demonstrated that in
the 1880s and 1890s, the dynamite theme was taken up – and adapted
– by various pre-existing literary forms, from the social novel through
popular romance to science fiction. Each of these forms, I would add,
influenced the respective representation of terrorism in specific ways.
In this sense, the emergence of the terrorist in fiction did not produce a
new literary genre, characterized by unique structural features, but
was rather itself shaped by the specific narrative patterns of the genres
involved. These genres produced a wide range of – often conflicting –
images of terrorism, its causes, its perpetrators, its motivations, and its
dangers to British society.

Margaret Scanlan's observation that "terrorist novels" often hint at
the tacit "affinities ... between literary and terrorist plots"[53] is suggestive in this context. The novels investigated by Scanlan feature writer-
protagonists, which is not the case in the examples discussed here.
However, the figure of the writer may also be located elsewhere: in
the implied author, who is responsible for the terrorist plots conceived
and sometimes executed in the novel and who frequently marks his
presence behind the story in the form of a paratext. From this angle,
the pun in Scanlan's felicitous title – *Plotting Terror* – seems even
more appropriate, for the plotting of the fictional conspirators is merely a structural ingredient of the author's plot, which sets the terrorist
tale in motion.

To illustrate this point, I would like to briefly turn to the best
known and most widely discussed English-language novels about late
nineteenth-century terrorism, Henry James' *The Princess Casamassima* (1886) and Joseph Conrad's *The Secret Agent* (1907). In both
works we may recover traces of actual events (as mediated by contemporary newspaper reports). Whereas in the case of Conrad's novel,
the link to the Greenwich Bomb Outrage of 1894 is well established,[54]
James did not model his story on one particular incident. Yet he, too,
wrote his novel against the backdrop of intense media interest in
international terrorism, and he made extensive use of contemporary

---

[53]   Scanlan, *Plotting Terror*, 2.
[54]   See in particular Norman Sherry, "The Greenwich Bomb Outrage and *The Secret
Agent*", *The Review of English Studies*, XVIII/72 (November 1967), 412-28.

accounts.[55] The parallel does not end here. Both James and Conrad later wrote autobiographical accounts of the origins of their respective novels (James in a lengthy Preface to the 1909 New York Edition, Conrad in his "Author's Note" of 1920), offering strikingly similar narratives.

James begins his Preface by asserting that "this fiction proceeded quite directly, during the first year of a long residence in London, from the habit and the interest of walking the streets". During his late-evening perambulations through the Victorian metropolis, James continues, his imagination was "assault[ed] directly by the great city", and this is how the idea for his story and its characters came to him:

> ... to a mind curious, before the human scene, of meanings and revela-
> tions the great grey Babylon easily becomes, on its face, a garden bris-
> tling with an immense illustrative flora. Possible stories, presentable
> figures, rise from the thick jungle as the observer moves, fluttering up
> like startled game, and before he knows it indeed he has fairly to
> guard himself against the brush of importunate wings. He goes on as
> with his head in a cloud of humming presences ...[56]

At first sight, James seems to picture himself here as a mere receptacle of stories. The basic elements of his novel, he writes, only had to be collected from the streets of London, where the main protagonist and would-be-terrorist Hyacinth Robinson virtually "sprang up for me out of the ... pavement".[57]

In *The Princess Casamassima*, James appears to suggest, London wrote itself through him. Yet the novel itself tells a different story. The vast terrorist conspiracy at the core of the text is unmistakably the author's free invention, as is his protagonist's vision of a London that is literally undermined by secret revolutionary activities. "Nothing of it appears above the surface", Hyacinth tells the Princess, "but there's an immense underworld, peopled with a thousand forms of revolutionary passion and devotion .... In silence, in darkness, but under the

---

[55] See Wesley H. Tilley, *The Background of* The Princess Casamassima, Gaines-
ville, FL: University of Florida Press, 1961.
[56] Henry James, *The Princess Casamassima* (1887), ed. Derek Brewer, London:
Penguin, 1987, 33.
[57] *Ibid.*, 34.

feet of each one of us, the revolution lives and works."[58] This topo-
graphical motif is conspicuously inconsistent with the image of the
flâneur evoked in James' belated Preface, since neither a secret conspiracy nor an underground revolution would be visible to even the
most perceptive of city strollers. As a closer examination of the cited
passage reveals, James does not deny his use of poetic license. In the
author's careful phrasing, his London walks provided him with "possible stories": what was there in the streets of London was not an actual
but a potential plot – and it was up to James to realize this potentiality.
Significantly, the London depicted in the Preface is clearly marked as
being already literary, shaped by the classical topos of Babylon as
well as by the more recent discourse of late-Victorian London as an
"urban jungle".[59] The London that inspired James, then, was not a
geographical and historical given that preceded his fiction, but a city
belonging to the cultural imagination. It is in the context of this imaginary that James' plotting of a terrorist conspiracy has to be read.

The London of Conrad's "Author's Note" is even more obviously a
projection. Like James, Conrad evokes "the memories of my solitary
and nocturnal walks all over London in my early days".[60] But he also
portrays the city as a "Dark Continent", echoing the frame narrative of
his earlier novel *Heart of Darkness* as well as the Assistant Commis-
sioner's experience of Soho as a "jungle",[61] in Chapter Seven of *The
Secret Agent*:

> ... the vision of an enormous town presented itself, of a monstrous
> town more populous than some continents and in its man-made might
> as if indifferent to heaven's frowns and smiles; a cruel devourer of the
> world's light. There was room enough there to place any story, depth

---

[58] *Ibid.*, 330.
[59] For a detailed reconstruction of this discourse, see Joseph McLaughlin, *Writing the Urban Jungle: Reading Empire in London from Doyle to Eliot*, Charlottesville and London: University Press of Virginia, 2000.
[60] Joseph Conrad, *The Secret Agent: A Simple Tale* (1907), ed. John Lyon, Oxford and New York: Oxford University Press, 2004, 231. The quotation is from the "Author's Note", which was first published in 1920 and which is reprinted in *ibid.*, 228-33.
[61] Conrad, *The Secret Agent*, 110.

enough for any passion, variety enough there for any setting, darkness
enough to bury five millions of lives.[62]

Everything is possible in the Victorian metropolis, and this fact allows
the author of a London fiction to "place any story" in "any setting".
Conrad himself made ample use of this freedom by concocting a complex conspiracy narrative centering on an informer who works for
both the Russian embassy and the London police. Verloc, the half-
French "secret agent" of the novel's title, runs a pornography shop in
Soho, where he attempts to infiltrate London's revolutionary community by organizing clandestine meetings for an anarchist group in the
apartment above his shop. These anarchists are portrayed as ineffec-
tual shams who are parasitically dependent on the social system they
set out to eradicate. Their actions are limited to talking and pamphle-
teering, and even the "Professor" – the only truly threatening character
in the book – never makes use of the bomb that he is constantly carrying in his coat. It is one of the narrative ironies of Conrad's novel that
the only instance of terrorist violence that occurs in the book is really
a perverse act of counterterrorism. The odious Ambassador Vladimir
uses Verloc as an *agent provocateur*, hoping that the explosion at the
Greenwich Observatory will prompt the British government to reconsider its policy of granting political asylum to foreigners.

In James and Conrad, London – the "grey Babylon" and "cruel
devourer of light" – is alluring to political subversives as well as to
novelists, in whom it inspires ominous visions of revolutionary under-
grounds and terrorist plotting. As in the examples discussed above, the
plots that the novels ascribe to terrorists are really products of the
imagination. Because both terrorism and counterterrorism involve
clandestine operations, only spectacular occurrences such as attacks or
arrests become visible to the general public. The rest remains in the
dark, offering a world of possibilities to the imagination. Drawing on
and combining various literary traditions, late-Victorian terror narratives exploited the peculiar status of terrorism as real (past) and imagined (future) violence for their own purposes, neglecting for the
most part the political and social issues at stake. Thus decontextua-
lized, "terror" became a fantastic element in the novels' plots.

---

[62]   Conrad, "Author's Note", 231.

ENMITY AND THE ARCHIVE: AESTHETICS OF DEFIGURATION IN LITERATURE AND CRIMINOLOGY, 1900/1970

HENDRIK BLUMENTRATH

When in 1898 the International Anti-Anarchist Conference was held in Rome to find new means of controlling the seemingly rising threat of anarchist terrorism, this threat had already been framed as a serious crisis of visibility. Rendered possible by the invention of dynamite by Alfred Nobel, a previously unknown concept of enmity evolved at the close of the nineteenth century, and with the emerging figure of the dynamiter, nothing less than the disappearance of the visible enemy seemed to have set in. No longer limited to the old model of regicide or political assassination, this new threat affected theatergoers, strollers, and subway passengers alike; and since even small amounts of the dangerous substance were said to generate highly destructive effects, narratives of a mobile and invisible danger immediately emerged. "It is an unpleasant reflection", *The Times* wrote in 1881, "that one of the clearest consequences of civilization is that it has armed folly and crime with terrible powers, and that it enables any one to carry out the threat contained in the famous letter to Lord Monteagle touching the Gunpowder Plot – 'they shall receive a terrible blow, this Parliament, and yet they shall not see who hurt them' – in a way which was but lately impossible."[1]

Equipped with clock mechanisms, the bombs referred to as "infernal machines" were presumed to explode any minute and any place. This kind of war was feared to break out anywhere, and, as United States Army Officer Philip Henry Sheridan suggested in 1884 with respect to recent threats in Europe, it could be waged by "infuriated people with means carried with perfect safety to themselves *in the*

---

[1]   Editorial in *The Times*, 26 July 1881.

pockets of their clothing".[2] British police complained that in the massive crowds of London, the observation of suspects was doomed to failure, and even the identification of well-known offenders posed serious problems.[3]

A narrative of disappearance hence pervaded the discourse of the dynamite threat, and this narrative was not restricted to the problem that policemen working on the streets failed to identify the bombers: it was also turned into a diagnosis of society. Foreigners were held responsible for the explosions, and they were now said to be irretrievably mixed up with the law-abiding British population: "They come", *The Times* quoted a high official of the Metropolitan Police in 1910,

> ... into this country – whether in increasing numbers or not I cannot tell; a few thousand aliens, more or less, are soon absorbed in London – prepared to do any desperate job for money. Murder is nothing to them; and burglary, rather than political machination, is their real aim. They are, of course, chiefly anarchists, and they follow respectable callings, if at all, only as a cover for their lawlessness.[4]

The invisibility of possible enemies and undiscovered dangers in the midst of society seemed to require continuous vigilance on the part of authorities and populace alike: "we must not allow ourselves", *The Times* warned after one of the explosions in London, "to forget the presence among us of reckless enemies of social order".[5] Turn-of-the-century fiction negotiated, in numerous variations, the anxiety that such enemies could no longer be identified. Whether in Doyle's "That Little Square Box", in which the narrator fails in his attempts to "classify and label" his fellow-passengers on a boat where he suspects an infernal machine;[6] or in the Preface of Lesesne's *Torpedoes; or,*

---

[2]   *The Alarm*, 15 November 1884, as quoted in Jeffory A. Clymer, *America's Culture of Terrorism: Violence, Capitalism, and the Written Word*, Chapel Hill and London: The University of North Carolina Press, 2003, 7 (emphasis in original).

[3]   On the observation of suspected anarchists and Fenians, see Bernard Porter, *The Origins of the Vigilant State: The London Metropolitan Police Special Branch Before the First World War*, London: Weidenfeld and Nicolson, 1987, 122-24.

[4]   "Anarchists in London: High Explosives and Crime", *The Times*, 29 December 1910, 8.

[5]   Editorial in *The Times*, 6 November 1894.

[6]   "They presented the usual types met with upon these occasions. There was no striking face among them. I speak as a connoisseur, for faces are a specialty of mine. I

Dynamite in Society, in which society is represented as an aquatic zone with "under-water hostilities" and an unreliable order of signs;[7] or in Conrad's *The Secret Agent*, with the police diagnosing a collapse of demarcations and classifications,[8] again and again, the figure of the disappearing enemy flashes up against the background of a society that is itself represented as inscrutable, as a zone in which signs have lost their reliability and dangers elude the eye until the very moment of their outbreak.

The aesthetics observable in these texts – aesthetics of indistinguishable figures, of enemies losing their shape, and of failing identification attempts – point to more than what is often understood merely as features of an artistic modernism. They refer to a specific history of enmity, a history, one might argue, that is bound to the imaginary of dynamite and the infernal machine; to the notion of risk and the concept of the "dangerous individual" in criminal anthropology,[9] and to the ever-expanding networks of communication that substitute any processed suspicion with a new one. Most notably, however – and this is what the present article will focus on in what follows – this history of enmity is also bound to its media. What the vanishing figures refer to is the rise of a new cultural technique, a shift in the mode of representation.

---

pounce upon a characteristic feature as a botanist does on a flower, and bear it away with me to analyse at my leisure, and classify and label it in my little anthropological museum" (Arthur Conan Doyle, "That Little Square Box", in *The Captain of the Polestar and Other Tales*, Leipzig: Bernhard Tauchnitz, 1891, 144). First published in *London Society: An Illustrated Magazine of Light and Amusing Literature for the Hours of Relaxation*, Christmas Number, 1881, 52-64.

[7]   "Under-water hostilities are carried on in society to a fearful extent, and many schools engaged in drilling in deadly work are without signs of their true character" (Mary Richardson Lesesne, *Torpedoes; or, Dynamite in Society: A Story Founded on Fact*, Galveston, TX: Shaw and Baylock, 1883, 5).

[8]   "But those people were as denationalised as the dishes set before them with every circumstance of unstamped respectability. Neither was their personality stamped in any way, professionally, socially or racially" (Joseph Conrad, *The Secret Agent: A Simple Tale* [1907], eds Bruce Harkness and S.W. Reid, Cambridge: Cambridge University Press, 1990, 115).

[9]   See Michel Foucault, "About the Concept of the 'Dangerous Individual' in 19th-Century Legal Psychiatry", trans. Alain Baudot and Jane Couchman, *International Journal of Law and Psychiatry*, I/1 (February 1978), 1-18.

Bertillon and the crisis of visibility

The declared crisis of visibility is, as Alan Sekula has described it, a
"crisis of faith in optical empiricism".[10] This crisis accompanied the
emergence of archival, statistical knowledge, a gaze directed at charts
and statistics. It can be observed both in individual police identification as well as in questions concerning demographic phenomena.
Implemented on a grand scale in the statistical bureaus at the end of
the nineteenth century, techniques that initially aimed at encyclopedic
compilation shifted their focus more and more to the generation of
operationalizable data suitable for extrapolations and prognoses.[11]
Remarkably, the celebration of the new statistical knowledge was frequently accompanied by a staging of failing visual observation and a
declared loss of distinct demarcations and reliable signs, as portrayed,
for example, in the texts of Conrad, Doyle, or Lesesne. This rhetorical
framing can already be noticed in an exemplary description of the
British census from the middle of the nineteenth century. What is presented here is a society that has been turned into a battlefield, into a
zone where the observer can neither discern differences nor structures
and where he eventually loses track of his own movements:

> A vast and busy swarm, pent up in a compass unequal to its numbers,
> and still more unequal to its genius and ambition, with its ancient
> bonds and institutions gradually dissolving, we are in daily jeopardy
> of losing all principle of order. We are becoming an immense host in
> heat of battle. The common observer discerns only a chaos of men,
> and horses, and smoke, and engines of war. He sees them roaming
> over the plain, and scattered in ravines. He understands nothing of
> what he sees and hears – not even his own movements. Without
> knowledge of the field, without continual and exact reports from every
> member of his armament, the commander is bewildered, and, as a
> matter of course, immediately defeated. The British nation is engaged
> in a great and arduous struggle for life and sustenance, in which whole
> classes have been miserably worsted. We have a great conquest to
> achieve over the difficulties of nature, and the not less obstinate impe-
> diments of human creation. So, the first thing to be done is to ascertain
> the present state of the battle-field; – what flank is gaining ground,

---

[10]   Alan Sekula, "The Body and the Archive", *October*, XXXIX (Winter 1986), 16.
[11]   On the transformation of statistics in the nineteenth century, see Ian Hacking, *The
Taming of Chance*, Cambridge: Cambridge University Press, 1990.

what is hard pressed, where is the strength of the foe, where our reserve, what is the state of our ammunition, the nature of the ground,
and so on .... Neither tall chimnies, nor continuous canopies of
smoke, nor miles of wavy corn, seduce or frighten its [i.e. the Occupation Abstract's] researchers. Without theory or interest, it coolly analyses and subdivides its enormous field, and measures all that comes
in its way with a nicely graduated scale.[12]

The social world is depicted as an opaque and uncertain sphere, as a
chaotic aggregation of things, actors, and events offering no hold for
the eyes of the observer. According to this early argumentation in
favor of mass data collection, the struggle of the nation can only be
won by means of continuous and thorough registration, and hence by a
fundamental change in perspective. It is the gaze of the statistician that
takes over the commander's perspective in the battleground of society:
operating with numbers and charts, not even the most elusive conditions, changes, and transitions can escape his attention. Government
concern demonstrated in such praise of statistical knowledge – the
attempt to prevent possible future dangers and disturbances of any
kind – is chiefly directed at long-term developments. Nonetheless,
great expectations were placed on the emergent statistical practices in
light of the recent enmity. As early as 1884, the utopian hope was to
precalculate and therefore predict the next possible detonation:

> Mysterious explosions now-a-days occur in London with that regular
> irregularity which tempts the statistical mind to strike an average, and
> thus bring them in some sort under the reign of law. The chance of an
> explosion in any given month will shortly be calculable, and after a
> time the data may even accumulate to such an extent as to enable us to
> fix the probable locality of the next catastrophe.[13]

This vision was by no means going to be fulfilled as hoped. For the
discourse of dynamite scares at the end of the nineteenth century, the
statistical registration of the population rather gained relevance in
terms of its rhetorical framing. Its praise came, as the example from

---

[12] Editorial in *The Times*, 4 September 1844.
[13] Editorial in *The Times*, 27 February 1884; see also Alex Houen, *Terrorism and Modern Literature: From Joseph Conrad to Ciaran Carson*, Oxford and New York: Oxford University Press, 2002, 25-26.

The Times shows, as the reverse side of a declining authenticity attributed to the optical. However, while this mode of writing – or, rather,
counting – affected the literary negotiation of a society turning
opaque, more direct consequences of archival knowledge about the
new enmity are to be found in the field of individual identification and
the police work on the streets.

The identification system recommended by the 1898 International
Anti-Anarchist Conference in Rome,[14] the *portrait parlé*, was a technique that relied on a complex combination of both optical and statistical elements. Invented by Alphonse Bertillon, French criminologist
and director of the Identification Bureau of the Paris police, it was
based on his best-known system of identification, the Bertillonage,
which increasingly gained importance during and after the 1880s. In
order to overcome the unreliability of eyewitness accounts for identifying criminals and to register what might escape the eye, Bertillon
relied heavily on photography. Nonetheless, the criminologist was
highly skeptical of the supposed objectivity of the camera. Entirely
different pictures of the same person could be produced, he argued,
and while the face aged, the picture taken remained the same for all
time.[15] Thus, his efforts aimed to control the treacherous image always
suspected of betraying the correct identification of the criminal body.

For that purpose, Bertillon combined the visual gaze with the results of Quetelet's statistical works: photography with a set of bodily
measurements. Besides a massive standardization of the measuring
methods as well as of the photographic techniques (such as exposure
time, pose, lighting, etc.), this meant the introduction of a highly for-
malized symbolic system consisting of numerals rather than words:

> ... we find in the common languages no terms which can denote the
> numerous fine points and graduations of nuances as well as numerals

---

[14] See Mathieu Deflem, "International Police Cooperation – History of", in *The
Encyclopedia of Criminology*, eds Richard A. Wright and J. Mitchell Miller, New
York and London: Routledge, 2005, 795. Britain initially objected to new treaties
concerning international police cooperation; a version of the Bertillonage was used
after 1895: see Richard Bach Jensen, "The International Anti-Anarchist Conference of
1898 and the Origins of Interpol", *Journal of Contemporary History*, XVI/2 (April
1981), 323-33.
[15] See Simon A. Cole, *Suspect Identities: A History of Fingerprinting and Criminal
Identification*, Cambridge, MA and London: Harvard University Press, 2001, 48.

can do .... While common language first and foremost aspires to be precise and short, only in very special cases are specific terms at its disposal. A description that claims high accuracy ought to be formed of numerical language, and one should never disregard the progressive gradation of words in order to acquire transitional terms by which language can move from one extreme to the other.[16]

Bertillon's consideration that a numerical system is superior to "the most complete catalogue of words"[17] relates to his efforts to get beyond an encyclopedic accumulation of knowledge. It alludes to a function that does not aim at direct representation but rather at the necessary incorporation of objects into the routines of the archive. For with regard to the 75,000 photography cards which the Paris police had already collected by 1880, Bertillon could only wonder who would examine every single card successively every time a suspect had to be checked.[18]

Therefore the purpose of a standardized symbolic system lay in the operationalization of data – and the process of standardization necessary for that did not spare the images themselves: "It is without doubt", the criminologist wrote, "that the uniformity of the portraits stored in the archives of the court repositories is almost a material necessity that considerably alleviates comparison and identification".[19] Bertillon's system hence not only integrated the visual into a symbolic system instituted in order to efface any trace of subjectivity from the process: by means of standardized photographs, identification cards, and, most importantly, a highly formal numerical system, it also aimed at establishing a filing system with locatable addresses and objects.

It is these dynamics that structure the discourses of identification at the end of the nineteenth century and accompany the emergence of the figure of an invisible enemy. The rise of statistical knowledge goes hand in hand with a decline of faith in the optical gaze: what is made evident by the production of the image is at the same time suspected

---

[16] Alphonse Bertillon, *Die gerichtliche Photographie: Mit einem Anhange über die anthropometrische Classification und Identificirung*, Halle-on-Saale: Wilhelm Knapp, 1895, 89-90 (my translation).

[17] *Ibid.*, 91 (my translation).

[18] See Cole, *Suspect Identities*, 43.

[19] Bertillon, *Die gerichtliche Photographie*, 3 (my translation).

of leaving space for further interpretation, or even – a line of argument to be found both in aesthetic as well as in police discourse – of systematically concealing some hidden truth underneath. Thus, even though contemporary discourses such as physiognomy and phrenology emphatically embraced the concept of photographic realism as a completely reliable means for the identification of the criminal body, the image was from the beginning inserted into a dispositive of different non-optical practices and techniques seeking to assure this alleged reliability. By means of extensive standardization, objects are then turned into operational, archival data and produce a combined knowledge not accessible before. "In short", Sekula writes with regard to the use of identification techniques by the police at the end of the nineteenth century,

> ... we need to describe the emergence of a truth-apparatus that cannot be adequately reduced to the optical model provided by the camera. The camera is integrated into a larger ensemble: a bureaucratic-clerical-statistical system of "intelligence". This system can be described as a sophisticated form of the archive. The central artifact of this system is not the camera but the filing cabinet.[20]

Herold's electronic archive

The success of the Bertillonage was only short-lived. Too complex and at the same time not dependable enough, it soon had to make way for the more effective system of fingerprinting. But the dynamics of representational and operational functions that – in their different forms – become apparent both in the statistical examination of the population and in the police identification practices at the end of the nineteenth century were to become crucial for the discourse of terrorism half a century later. Under the wholly new conditions of new media technologies, the gaze at the individual and the gaze at the population were combined in a system of standardized data seeking to fulfill the dream of predictability which *The Times* had already experienced facing the dynamite scares in the 1880s. Now, the battleground formed within the sphere of statistics and data mining: from now on, the search for the internal enemy more than ever took place in

---

[20]   Sekula, "The Body and the Archive", 16.

registers, columns of statistics and piles of data before switching to another ground.

The new police system I am referring to is inextricably linked to the work of Horst Herold, President of the German Federal Criminal Police Office in Germany (BKA) from 1971 to 1981. Its famous context is the then emerging terrorism of the Red Army Fraction (RAF). Again, and with even more emphasis on the lack of prominent characteristics and features, an enemy is declared whose "modus operandi is environmentally congruent" and who "attempts to go into hiding in the anonymity of mass society".[21] According to the press, one might now encounter terrorists in a wide variety of civilian masks: appearing to be students, civil servants or insurance agents.[22] Now, while millions of wanted posters displaying faces of RAF terrorists circulated throughout German cities, Herold questioned the usefulness of photographs and identikit pictures. "For an extremist", he commented, a photograph "rather provides indications of what he must, by any means, not look like if he does not want to attract attention"; therefore, he continued, the police had started to supplement the unreliable system of photos with a new method of tracing and identification, a system of "electronic data processing" operating solely with "elements and features translated into numerics" and designed to be the center of a "closed system of objectivation".[23]

Herold here refers to the introduction of computers and the extensive implementation of data processing by the German police since the

---

[21] Stephan Wanner, *Die negative Rasterfahndung: Eine moderne und umstrittene Methode der repressiven Verbrechensbekämpfung* (Rechtswissenschaftliche Forschung und Entwicklung 69), Munich: Florentz, 1985, 18 (my translation). Wanner refers to Günter Ermisch, "Fahndung und Datenschutz aus Sicht der Polizei", in *Möglichkeiten und Grenzen der Fahndung: Arbeitstagung des Bundeskriminalamtes Wiesbaden vom 12. bis 15. November 1979*, ed. Bundeskriminalamt, Wiesbaden: Bundeskriminalamt, 1980, 63-77.

[22] See, for example,"Eigentlich müsste jeder verdächtig sein. Das Dilemma der Terroristen-Fahndung: Untergrund in Bürgermaske", *Der Spiegel*, 12 September 1977, 22-33.

[23] Horst Herold, "'Der Computer nicht Fetisch, sondern große Hilfe bei der Fron der Routinearbeit'", *Frankfurter Allgemeine Zeitung*, 27 October 1978, 8 (my translation). See also Michael Fehr, "Die 'Authentizität der Fotografie': Kommentare zu einem strapazierten Begriff", in *Wie seh' ich denn da aus?! Unheimliche Begegnung mit der zweiten Dimension.*, eds Herbert Bardenheuer, Hartmut Beifus, and Michael Fehr, Munich: Heinz Moos, 1979, 148.

late 1960s. "The objective of all informational efforts", Herold stated in retrospect,

> ... was to accelerate the solving of criminal activities and to increase the quality of data until prognoses were possible, up to the extrapolation and early diagnosis of danger. Terrorism itself was to provide the data for its overcoming. At the end of 1976, our objective to gain informational superiority over the RAF was reached, prognoses became possible. At the end of 1976, we knew more about the perpetrators than they knew about themselves. At the end of 1976, we knew the persons who in 1977 became terrorists.[24]

This project of a cybernetic police, a project in which development, action, and strategy became part of a self-regulatory system and police work was to be directly regulated by information feedback and crime data, eventually proved to be a phantasy.[25] Nonetheless, Herold's concepts became crucial for the history of combating terrorism and formed the basis for various later types of data mining. The shift in the media used in the search for known criminals was not just a question of quantity or speed – rather, it was one of the constitutive preconditions for a new concept of police, focusing on possible threats, searching for yet unknown dangers, and hence generating a new kind of enemy figure.

On numerous occasions, Herold characterized the specific perspective of the new police system as a perception of hidden structures. "Even for the most qualified policemen", he complained in 1973, "it is often difficult to see the real historical forces beneath the surface of

---

[24] Wolfgang Kraushaar and Jan Phillip Reemtsma, "'Die entscheidende Triebkraft besteht in einem unbändigen, alles ausfüllenden Hass': Interview mit dem ehemaligen Präsidenten des Bundeskriminalamtes Dr. Horst Herold", in *Die RAF und der linke Terrorismus*, ed. Wolfgang Kraushaar, Hamburg: Hamburger Edition, 2006, II, 1372 (my translation).

[25] On Herold's project of a cybernetic police force, see Lea Hartung, *Kommissar Computer: Horst Herold und die Virtualisierung des polizeilichen Wissens*, Diploma Thesis, University of Weimar: http://edocs.fu-berlin.de/docs/receive/FUDOCS_document_000000005003 (accessed 21 September 2010); Lea Hartung, "Horst Herolds kybernetische Polizei und die RAF: Überlegungen zur Ent-Politisierung eines Konflikts", in *Politisierung und Ent-Politisierung als performative Praxis*, eds Sabine Berghahn, Detlef G. Schulze, and Frieder O. Wolf, Münster: Dampfboot, 2006, 181-86.

events".[26] According to the President of the Federal Police, only by means of a formal system is it possible for the police work to "seismographically indicate what transformations go on or develop unnoticed, subliminally, but notably".[27]

However, the metaphor of depth is more than a recourse to the topical conjunction of depth and truth. It follows a topology of knowledge linked to the introduction of the new data processing system. For Herold, it is the latency of regulatory and control information that has been neglected for too long. The computer is able not only to draw attention to this previously disregarded information, but to "abruptly lift it from its latency".[28] But how is this knowledge made accessible? Herold illustrates the need for the electronic revolution of the archive: prior to the introduction of the computer, the Federal Criminal Police Office alone could call 28 million fingerprints, 3.5 million photographs, 2.8 million criminal files and more than 6 million records with diverse contents its own.[29] But instead of finding usable information, the officers constantly ran the risk of getting lost in piles of paper. If, as Herold summarizes the failure of the common search processes, a young officer was sent into the archives at the beginning of his career with a simple question, he would not come out again until right before his retirement.[30]

Hence, one aim of the reorganization process was to establish addresses and locatable data. Furthermore, as Herold again and again explained, it is not just the speed of electronic data processing, but rather its potential for seemingly limitless comparison and combination that renders it indispensable. "Computers", Herold states, "are capable of connecting data, which in principle lie far apart, in any

---

[26]   Horst Herold, "Gesellschaftlicher Wandel – Chance der Polizei?", in *Kriminalstrategie und Kriminaltaktik* (Grundlagen der Kriminalistik 11), ed. Herbert Schäfer, Hamburg: Steintor, 1973, 26 (my translation)

[27]   *Ibid.*, 13 (my translation).

[28]   Horst Herold, "Information und Staat", in *Festschrift für Rudolf Wassermann zum sechzigsten* Geburtstag, eds Christian Broda *et al.*, Darmstadt: Luchterhand, 1985, 361 (my translation).

[29]   See Horst Herold, "Rationalisierung und Automation in der Verbrechensbekämpfung", *Universitas: Zeitschrift für Wissenschaft, Kunst und Literatur*, XXXI/1 (1976), 63.

[30]   See Horst Herold, "Elektronische Datenverarbeitung im Dienste der Polizei", in *Symposium Innere Sicherheit in den 80er Jahren*, ed. Ministerium des Innern, Mainz: Ministerium des Innern, 1980, 60.

possible combination and in surprising new ways".[31] Thus, when a system of paperwork and records is replaced by a system of electronically searchable data sets, relations may become apparent that had previously been imperceptible.

Most notably, however, this "multidimensionality of processing"[32] not only allows data processors to examine combinations selected according to the officer's suspicion, but, inversely, to postpone any suspicion until the end of the process, indeed, to establish this suspicion in the first place. Automated search runs will draw attention to any correlation that seems worthy of further inspection, be it,

> ... for instance, the correlation of body height and crime. I do not know if such a correlation exists, but maybe it is possible. We do not know. Or the correlation of fingerprint and heredity. Is there such a correlation? We do not know. Or the correlation between divorce and frequency of criminal activities.[33]

It is worth noting that these examples do not hint at any interest in common criminal typology: Herold's police concept does not attempt to identify the "nature of the terrorist", it does not search for essences or eternal truths. What Herold is interested in is relations and statistical correlation.

A series of relays
"Needless to say, you have to prepare the machine for this task – it does not feed and chew on all food":[34] Braudel's comment from 1958 regarding the use of tabulating machines and early computers in historiography also applies to police work under the conditions of electronic data processing. Herold's aim was to establish a system of universal comparability in order to generate relational knowledge that allows for

---

[31] Horst Herold, "Konstruktive Sicherheit – eine Gegenthese", in *Der Traum der Vernunft, vom Elend der Aufklärung: Eine Veranstaltung der Akademie der Künste, Berlin*, Darmstadt: Luchterhand, 1986, 258-59 (my translation).

[32] *Ibid.*, 259 (my translation).

[33] Herold, "Elektronische Datenverarbeitung im Dienste der Polizei", 60 (my translation).

[34] Ferdinand Braudel, "Die lange Dauer [La longue durée]" (1958), in *Theorieprobleme der Geschichtswissenschaft*, eds Theodor Schieder and Kurt Gräubig, Darmstadt: Wissenschaftliche Buchgesellschaft, 1977, 190 (my translation).

both long-ranging trends and short-term control information. But before such a system can commence its work, the first step must be to generate machine-readable and, particularly, -processable data – a regulated circulation of signs. And if, as Herold rephrases Marx, the "machinal being determines the police consciousness",[35] it is not the system of electronic data processing that has to be adapted to the institution of the police, but it is the police that rather have to adapt its routines to the technical ones. Bertillon had already worked on a system of numbers and signs, as well as on highly standardized routines of photography, in order to generate processable data for his archives: The standardization processes of the German BKA were to surpass his efforts by far.

Fingerprints, photographs, handwriting, ballistic evidence, not to mention documents and files – everything has to be translated into digital code. Emphasis is also placed on the training of the officers entering data: they "have to be able to think in formulas, abstractly, quantitatively and analytically".[36] The registered information must not be interpreted, but translated into formulas, into calculi, symbolic markers circulating in the system. When, for example, case reports are to be analyzed, one faces the problem that the papers are based upon descriptions that do not allow any further processing. Not a lack of quality in observation, but differing modes of representation make further use impossible. For if different policemen "equipped with divergent abilities in observation and expression"[37] describe their observations as realistically as possible, one might gain a detailed picture of whatever happened, but no comparable data. Therefore, case reports must strictly follow the same structure. Data that does not conform is automatically rejected, and the newly conceived blanks and questionnaires are all designed to "stimulate the necessary data-compatible way of thinking".[38] Before the material is, in a very last step, made evident either by visualization or its embedding in a coherent narra-

---

[35] Horst Herold, "Organisatorische Grundzüge der elektronischen Datenverarbeitung im Bereich der Polizei: Versuch eines Zukunftsmodells", in *Taschenbuch für Kriminalisten*, 18 (1968), 240 (my translation).

[36] *Ibid.*, 246 (my translation).

[37] Horst Herold, "Künftige Einsatzformen der EDV und ihre Auswirkungen im Bereich der Polizei", *Kriminalistik*, IX (1974), 389 (my translation).

[38] Herold, "Organisatorische Grundzüge der elektronischen Datenverarbeitung", 246 (my translation).

tive, every desire for representation has to be subordinated to a process of operationalization: everything centers around the setting of the archive itself.

"What is good form in living nature is bad form in the symbolic", Lacan writes when trying to describe the difference between the imaginary order and radically symbolic systems.[39] Common narratives are objects too bulky for the information flow required by the police; narratives, that is, are not a fit basis for an operation. Accordingly, what Herold's police system aims at is not the representational effect of the sign but its connectivity, its ability to circulate in a formal system. It is bound to a continuous symbolic operation which does not just refer to "language" or "discourse", but to the concept of the symbolic formulated by Lacan in his engagement with cybernetics: "The one thing which cybernetics clearly highlights is the radical difference between the symbolic and the imaginary orders."[40] Any machine, he states, can be "reduced to a series of relays which are simply pluses and minuses" – a registering of presence and absence that his concept of the symbolic is based on: "Everything, in the symbolic order, can be represented with the aid of such a series."[41]

The symbols themselves can therefore no longer be seen as fixed landmarks, but, on the contrary, are permitted "to fly with their own wings".[42] What Lacan points to is an independent symbolic order that is no longer tied to the real, the emergence of a symbolic system that does not belong to the realm of semantics or the imaginary order. And while that does not mean the end of the imaginary, while enemies still have to be represented and the search for invisible enemies triggers what can be called an excess of the imaginary, these attempts to represent, to visualize and shape the figure of the enemy henceforth take place in the vicinity of a calculus system based on strictly formal symbolic operations.

---

[39]   Jacques Lacan, "Psychoanalysis and Cybernetics, or On the Nature of Language", in *The Seminar of Jacques Lacan II: The Ego in Freud's Theory and in the Technique of Psychoanalysis, 1954-1955*, ed. Jacques-Alain Miller, trans. Sylvana Tomaselli, New York and London: W.W. Norton, 1988, 306.

[40]   *Ibid.*

[41]   Jacques Lacan, "Odd or Even? Beyond Intersubjectivity", in *ibid.*, 185.

[42]   Lacan, "Psychoanalysis and Cybernetics", 300.

Fading figures

This epistemological shift in police work is not without effect on literary constructions of the corresponding enemy figure, the terrorist. In Friedrich Christian Delius's *Himmelfahrt eines Staatsfeindes*, for instance, one of the police officers suffers from a migraine attack and can barely see anything but flickering dots from which "faces are formed, faces from well-known mosaics, the old familiar friends from the wanted posters. They disappear again, but they disappear too fast; he regrets that, for it gives comfort to see human shapes at least for a moment."[43] What this scene shows is the astonishment of an investigator bereft of his opponent's familiar shape. In *Himmelfahrt eines Staatsfeindes*, the figure of the enemy has dissolved into dots and numbers;[44] in Rainald Goetz's *Kontrolliert* (1988), every stable image of the opponent is lost and Goetz's writing style even seems to evoke the symbolic operations of a calculus system.[45]

These aesthetics of defiguration, however, can not only be observed in narratives dealing directly with the new forms of tracing techniques that came into being when searching for RAF terrorists. This is evidenced by the debates about the aesthetics of other German novels on terrorism in the late 1970s and 1980s. Literary critics usually consider the novels to be impersonal fictionalizations of terrorism; they note an ostensible failure of the attempts to give terrorists or investigators a face; they criticize a lack of figural form, a lack of character formation in favor of pure function.[46] Another text by Delius, *Ein Held der inneren Sicherheit*,[47] a novel which does not directly address the media of police tactics, is criticized for presenting silhouettes

---

[43] Friedrich Christian Delius, *Himmelfahrt eines Staatsfeindes*, Reinbek near Hamburg: Rowohlt, 1992, 360 (my translation).

[44] See *ibid.*, 241-49.

[45] I here refer to Goetz's excessive use of negative prefixes that again and again lead to the invention of new terms that establish a strictly formal binary system – leaving the reader with visibility and "nonvisibility", madness and "nonmadness", policemen and "nonpolicemen". Rainald Goetz, *Kontrolliert*, Frankfurt-on-Main: Suhrkamp, 1988, 171, 234, 242 (my translation).

[46] See Gerrit-Jan Berendse, *Schreiben im Terrordrom: Gewaltcodierung, kulturelle Erinnerung und das Bedingungsverhältnis zwischen Literatur und RAF-Terrorismus*, Munich: Edition Text + Kritik, 2005, 186-87.

[47] Friedrich Christian Delius, *Ein Held der inneren Sicherheit*, Reinbek near Hamburg: Rowohlt, 1981.

of characters, for presenting a protagonist who does not qualify as a literary figure and even less as a "hero".[48]

The diagnosis of fading figuration in the dynamite novels around 1900 and in the narratives of terror in the 1970s has alternately been described as a result of a lack of historical distance, language falling silent in the light of an overwhelming excess of violence, or, even more generally, as respectively modern or postmodern aesthetics. But this aesthetic constellation might also – and this has been the main focus of the present essay – be traced back to the history of media and the corresponding concepts of enmity. It is no coincidence that the literary figures of the German "autumn of terror" constantly oscillate between figuration and defiguration. But this oscillation points to the change of perspective in the gaze of the police. The problematic status of the vanishing figure is not just a motif: it is a structural effect of literature engaging with the question of enmity under conditions of electronic tracing. Narrativizations of terror take place in the immediate vicinity of cultural techniques that operate strictly formally and syntactically, and in an epistemic space characterized not only by the mimetic effects of the sign but by a formation of series and syntactic operations. From the 1970s on, the precarious state of the terrorist figure points to a system of tracing and searching that rests upon a dissolving of mimetic effects into discrete sets of calculi, a system that consequently operates in the realm of the symbolic.

The specific constellations of the signifying practices and techniques that I have described incite the categorical unstableness of the terrorist figure. Their symbolic markers quickly glide from one object to the next in the prognostics of probable or possible delinquents, turning stable differences between friends and enemies into transitional probabilities. In doing so, they evoke a concept of enmity that leaves behind Carl Schmitt's famous notion of the opponent defining his adversary. "The enemy stands on my own plane", Schmitt writes: "For that reason I must deal with him in battle, in order to gain my own measure, my own limit, my own gestalt."[49] What Schmitt describes is the logic of constructing entities through difference. While the

---

[48]   See Volker Hage, "Als Held eine Charge", *Frankfurter Allgemeine Zeitung*, 21 February 1981, BuZ 5.
[49]   Carl Schmitt, *Theorie des Partisanen: Zwischenbemerkung zum Begriff des Politischen*, Berlin: Duncker und Humblot, 1963, 87-88 (my translation).

declared enemy (at least in theory) has the same rights as his opponent, the terrorist becomes an enemy who is suspected to lurk behind
the mask of any friend and who, without further ado, might become
the object of security measures and military-police operations.

Delius' *Himmelfahrt eines Staatsfeindes* ends with the dissolving
of the enemy into clouds, clouds which not only allude to the religious
connotations of the "Himmelfahrt", the ascension, but also to the
probability clouds of the statistical systems installed to search for
possible future enemies. And when in the course of the novel the president of the German Federal Police Office grieves for the dissolved
faces and shapes of his enemies, he does so not only because he is
losing his personal adversaries. What in the light of probability clouds
and risk management can only be restored in a romanticized retrospective is the concept of enmity that rests upon the reflective image of the
other: In the dispersing figurations of the terrorist arises the identikit
picture of an enemy that has become a variable in the archival management of risks.

Pre- and Post-9/11
Representations of Terrorism in Fiction:
Continuities and Breaks

NARRATING TERRORISM ON THE EVE OF 9/11: ANN PATCHETT'S *BEL CANTO*

EVA GRUBER

Since September 11, 2001, terrorist novels have moved to the center of attention – although it was only after a certain time lag that the genre actually produced texts addressing the event. The following analysis will take a closer look at a terrorist novel published shortly before the attacks, in May 2001 to be precise: *Bel Canto* by Ann Patchett. The main questions to guide the inquiry are: firstly, how is terrorism and are terrorists depicted in this novel, and which literary and narrative strategies are being employed? And secondly: how does the reception history of the novel figure against the background of the historical and cultural developments immediately following its publication, that is, the attacks on the Pentagon and the World Trade Center? Based on the answers to these questions, the third and final part of the article will present a reading of the novel that uncovers a layer of meaning not taken into consideration by previous interpretations.

Depicting terrorism and terrorists in *Bel Canto*
At first sight, *Bel Canto*'s plot appears paradigmatic for a terrorist novel and is quickly summarized: in an unspecified South American country, a group of international guests – mostly businessmen and diplomats – attend a birthday party for a rich, Japanese electronics mogul everyone hopes will invest in the country. But Mr. Hosokawa has no intention whatsoever of doing so and has to be bribed into accepting the invitation by the promise of a private performance that night by his favorite opera diva. The party, taking place at the vice president's home, is hijacked by terrorists planning to kidnap the president, who had decided at the last minute not to attend, preferring to stay at home to watch his favorite soap opera. The terrorists take the guests hostage instead, and what follows is an account of the lengthy internment in which the opera singer – the only woman among the

hostages – and the music she performs come to play a crucial role in the events by providing a platform for communication and rapprochement between hostages and terrorists. On closer examination of its seemingly transparent story, however, the novel's representation of terrorism and terrorists consists of several complex, even contradictory or jarring strategies, two of which will subsequently be discussed in greater detail.

Terrorism as real event, fictional tool, and metafiction
In contrast to many of the terrorist novels that appeared in response to 9/11 and were concerned mainly with the aftermath of the attacks,[1] *Bel Canto* presents what Appelbaum and Paknadel refer to as "full coverage" of a terrorist incident from beginning to end, from cover to cover.[2] The novel's plot is in fact loosely based on an actual terrorist incident, the raid of the Japanese ambassador's residence in Lima, Peru, during a gala celebration on the occasion of the emperor's birthday in December 1996. As in Patchett's fictional scenario, the actual siege lasted over four months and ended with the Peruvian military's assault on the residence, killing one hostage and all of the guerrillas. And while Patchett changes several details – the host is not the Japanese ambassador but the vice president of the country, the occasion is different, and an opera diva is among the hostages[3] – the terrorist group itself, named "La Familia de Martin Suaréz" (LFMS), is clearly modeled on the Marxist MRTA, the *Movimiento Revolucionario Tupac Amaru*. Accordingly, the fictional terrorists qualify as such according to most established definitions (although they probably conceive of themselves as "freedom fighters" rather than terrorists, a fact already pointing to the relativity of such definitions): first of all, they use strategic violence or at least the threat of violence to generate fear in order to advance their political agenda, "to free the workers through revolu-

---

[1]   See Ann Keniston and Jeanne Follansbee Quinn, "Introduction: Representing 9/11: Literature and Resistance", in *Literature after 9/11*, eds Ann Keniston and Jeanne Follansbee Quinn, London and New York: Routledge, 2008, 4.
[2]   Robert Appelbaum and Alexis Paknadel, "Terrorism and the Novel, 1970-2001", *Poetics Today*, XXIX/3 (Fall 2008), 391.
[3]   Roxanne Coss is an invented character, but she is modelled on Karol Bennett, an opera singer and personal acquaintance of Patchett's (see interview with the author: http://www.bookbrowse.com/author_interviews/full/index.cfm/author_number/645/Ann-Patchett [accessed 25 February 2011])

tion" (53[4]), to "do something for the people" (61), and "to see [their] brothers released" (136[5]) – causes which they "believe ... to be altruistic and serving to better society";[6] and, secondly, their actions are clearly intended to achieve an effect in a particular audience, namely the people and government of their country, and possibly the international community. Their appearance – "dirt-smeared" and each "sporting several weapons" (33) – supports this impression, as does the description of the group's seizure of the residence, which calls up familiar scenes from respective Hollywood genre films (such as Daniel Petrie's *Toy Soldiers* from 1991):

> the edges of the room seemed to push forward, yelling. Heavy boots and gun butts pounded through vents, stormed in through doors. People were thrown together and then just as quickly broke apart in a state of animal panic. The house seemed to rise up like a boat caught inside the wide arm of a wave and flip onto its side. (12)

All the same, some readers might not be able to help noticing that, as far as the story is concerned, a terrorist attack and ensuing siege are as good a starter as any for uniting an unlikely group of characters in a confined space. Indeed, as the novel progresses further, the terrorist seizure itself moves more and more to the background and appears to become but a prop for the novel's main plot: the expounding of the complicated relationships between and among the hostages and terrorists during the four-month internment. So not only does the novel start with an opera recital rather than the terrorist attack itself – which is recounted sparingly (the passage just quoted is as detailed as it gets) partway into the novel; even subsequently, *Bel Canto* remains a char-

---

[4]   Ann Patchett, *Bel Canto* (2001), New York: HarperPerennial, 2002, 53 (unless specified otherwise, all subsequent references to this edition are indicated by page numbers in the text).

[5]   The passage continues: "For General Benjamin, of course, this meant both his philosophical comrades and his literal brother, Luis. Luis, who had committed the crime of distributing flyers for a political protest and was now buried alive in a high-altitude prison" (136). This constitutes another real-life parallel: in addition to the release of all imprisoned members of the organization, Néstor Cerpa Cartolini, who had commanded the attack on the Japanese embassy in Lima, also fought for the release of a particular prisoner: his wife.

[6]   Clifford E. Simonsen and Jeremy R. Spindlove, *Terrorism Today: The Past, the Players, the Future*, Upper Saddle River, NJ: Prentice Hall, 2000, 17.

acter study verging on romance and an homage to opera rather than granting terrorism center stage. The only violence committed by the terrorists is a blow with the butt of a rifle to the vice president's cheek at the beginning of the siege (19), which causes a minor wound requiring some stitches. The only shots fired are at the ceiling to command attention, or go off accidentally when one of the terrorists mistakes a pearl-handled pistol collected from a lady's evening bag for a lighter (21). And while the terrorists' readiness to kill is repeatedly invoked (26, 38, 279, 301), they never do any harm.[7] Even immediately after the takeover, "terror" seems an inadequate description for the atmosphere prevailing in the novel, as the vice president notes that the terrorists "did not smile but there was nothing particularly threatening in their faces either" (21). "What initially look[s] like a frightening situation becomes instead a peculiarly entrancing one", observes Janet Maslin.[8] Despite being based on a real event, *Bel Canto* is therefore more an abstract parable than a historically grounded exploration: "a story that takes place out of real time. Out of real space too."[9]

Is terrorism in *Bel Canto*, then, simply "handy subject matter for the composition of plots, the invention of psychological conflict, the discovery of interesting locales, the devising of timely themes"?[10] The novel's self-reflexive and metafictional aspects, which highlight the "constructed nature of terrorist plots",[11] seem to suggest so. The text starts with an implicit comment on the intricacies and instabilities of representation and perception: it postulates an event as fact – the first sentence reads "When the lights went off, the accompanist kissed her" – only to question its actuality immediately afterwards:

---

[7]   In fact, these invocations receive an ironic twist through Ishmael's (the youngest and smallest of the terrorists) claim that he "shot men over less than an eggplant" (191), which, coming out the mouth of a fourteen-year-old, definitely sounds like a joke rather than a threat.

[8]   Janet Maslin, "Uninvited Guests Wearing You Down? Listen to Opera", *The New York Times*, 31 May 2001: http://www.nytimes.com/2001/05/31/books/books-of-the-times-uninvited-guests-wearing-you-down-listen-to-opera.html (accessed 26 February 2011).

[9]   Daniel Mendelsohn, "Ransom Notes", *New York Magazine*, 18 June 2001: http://nymag.com/nymetro/arts/books/reviews/4804/ (accessed 26 February 2011).

[10]   Appelbaum and Paknadel, "Terrorism and the Novel", 388.

[11]   Margaret Scanlan, *Plotting Terror: Novelists and Terrorists in Contemporary Fiction*, Charlottesville and London: University of Virginia Press, 2001, 15.

> ... every person in the living room would later remember a kiss. They did not *see* a kiss, that would have been impossible. The darkness that came on them was startling and complete. (1)

This dual strategy of employing, yet simultaneously undercutting, a realistic narrative mode (and thus putting it on display) also informs the novel's tendency to emphasize its alleged veracity by giving absurdly detailed information (see, for example, 20), while concurrently stressing the presence of a narrative voice which at times intrusively provides corrections to the narrative: "Clarification: All of the women were released except one" (69). This intrusive narrative voice comments on the novel's phrasing – "One would think the sentence should read ..." (86), complete with subsequent alternatives to previous statements – as well as on its plot, announcing: "to rejoin the story a week after Mr. Hosokawa's birthday party ended seems as good a place as any" (106). Moreover, both the discourses of musical performance (which, just like terrorism, is directed at an audience with the intent of evoking a reaction) and of translation (which, with its emphasis on mediation and language, just like narrative becomes virtually transparent when it goes smoothly; see 222) serve as metadiscourses on the terrorist novel. I will, however, leave the novel's metafictional aspects for now and turn instead to a second aspect of the representation of terrorism and terrorists in *Bel Canto*.

Terrorism-at-a-distance and terrorists-up-close
Bel Canto is set in an unnamed South American country, and relies on familiar processes of Othering. References to the country by foreigners, specifically by the hostages, are to "this dismal jungle" (31), "this godforsaken country" (36, 315), "this wretched country" (174), and, in allusion to Joseph Conrad, even "the Heart of Darkness" (187). With regard to infrastructure, the country is obviously underdeveloped. When at the beginning of the seizure the lights go off:

> No one was frightened by the darkness .... The people who lived in other countries assumed that things like this must happen here all the time. Lights go on, go off. People from the host country knew it to be true. (2)

Economically, the country is shown to be in dire need of Mr. Hosokawa's electronics plant for "creating the illusion of a country moving
away from the base matter of cocaine and heroin, so as to promote
foreign aid and make trafficking of those very drugs less conspicuous"
(3) – a description that oozes with allegations of political corruption.

Depictions of the story's setting in this fashion are symptomatic of
the way terror had been conceptualized in the United States previous
to 9/11. Despite such incidents as the 1993 World Trade Center bombing and the 1995 attack on the Oklahoma City Federal Building, terrorism was usually relegated to unstable banana republics – something
to be followed on world news on the TV screen, not something happening in your own backyard.[12] *Bel Canto* subscribes to this view of
"terrorism-at-a-distance",[13] to what Jeffory Clymer characterizes as a
"sense that terrorism is inevitably the work of foreigners".[14] It is the
unspecified country itself which seems to breed terrorism, as is evidenced by Mr. Hosokawa's remark that "he believed his daughters
were not old enough to date and yet clearly *by the standards of this
country* they were old enough to be members of a terrorist organization" (117, emphasis added). This mode of locating terrorism in the
Other, as Zulaika and Douglass point out in their critical study of terrorism discourse, is in turn predicated on "a definite world view that
opposes countries and cultures within a hierarchy of values in which
'we' are at the top and the practitioners of terrorism at the bottom".[15]
Highly compatible with ideas of American exceptionalism and bene-
volence, such a conceptualization basically ethnocentrically attributes
terrorism to a lack of civilization and democracy – allowing Ameri-

---

[12]   Jeffory Clymer diagnoses this as "America's amnesia concerning its history of
terrorist violence" and observes that despite the marked presence of domestic terrorism in the 1990s Americans tend to speak of 9/11 as the "first" attack on American
soil (Jeffory Clymer, *America's Culture of Terrorism: Violence, Capitalism, and the
Written Word*, Chapel Hill and London: University of North Carolina Press, 2003, 3,
9-10).
[13]   Beau Grosscup, "Terrorism-at-a-Distance: The Imagery That Serves US Power",
in *Global Terrorism*, eds Brenda J. Lutz and James M. Lutz, London: Sage, 2001, I,
10-25. (First published in *Global Dialogue*, II/4 [Fall 2000], 74-87.)
[14]   Clymer, *America's Culture of Terrorism*, 11; see also Grosscup, "Terrorism-at-a-
Distance", 11.
[15]   Joseba Zulaika and William A. Douglass, *Terror and Taboo: The Follies, Fables,
and Faces of Terrorism*, New York and London: Routledge, 1996, 13.

cans to retain a high opinion of their own society, political system, and way of life.[16]

In *Bel Canto*, this lack of civilization is played out through aspects such as literacy or food culture, but most obviously through music: Western style opera, to be precise.[17] In his search for an accompanist for Roxane Coss, one of the hostages "skip[s] over their captors on the assumption that piano lessons were an impossibility in the jungle" (125-26). The local music is described as consisting of "high-pitched pipes and crude drums" (133) that give Mr. Hosokawa a headache. And when Roxane Coss discovers that the terrorist Cesar has a beautiful singing voice and begins to train him, she thinks to herself: "It would have lived and died in a jungle, this voice, if she hadn't come along to rescue it" (308) – implying an inherent hierarchy between cultures. All the more astonishing are the changes affected through Roxane Coss' singing. Coming from a world where a girl's beautiful voice is attributed to her having swallowed a bird, the rugged terrorists melt at the soprano's every note (see 128), are moved to tears (see 150), or "confused ... to the point of senselessness", no longer able to "hold on to [their] convictions" (153). While starting out as an illiterate, uncultured bunch of roughnecks who rely on action rather than persuasion to achieve their goals, over the course of the internment the terrorists take to learning languages, reading and writing, singing, playing chess, cooking refined cuisine, or tending the gardens. The hostages display similar tendencies now that they have so much free time on their hands, one of them quipping: "Who knew that being kidnapped was so much like attending university?" (249). Critics have thus rightly spoken of a "new impromptu civilization [being] born

---

[16]   See Grosscup, "Terrorism-at-a-Distance", 10, 13. It is therefore not very surprising that Roxane Coss, a famous American soprano, in her only confrontation with the terrorists invokes her nationality and her creed with an astonishing aplomb: "You've kept one woman, one American, and the one person that anyone in the world has ever heard of before, and if you kill me, and make no mistake, you will have to – ... the very wrath of God will come down on you and your people" (84).

[17]   In the only extended scholarly article on the novel to date, Jane Marcus-Delgado capitalizes on this issue and stresses the role of Western music in this process. See Jane Marcus-Delgado, "The Destructive Persistence of Myths and Stereotypes: Civilization and Barbarism Redux in Ann Patchett's *Bel Canto*", *Letras Hispanas*, II/1 (Spring 2005), 51-53.

under the vice president's roof"[18] or an "ascent from chaos to culture",[19] pointing to the novel's strong emphasis on art's redemptive
potential. If they had been given an education and the opportunity to
witness and appreciate the beauty found in high culture, the novel
idealistically seems to suggest, these people would not have turned
terrorists in the first place. Their chance to partake in such cultural
discourses during the internment triggers a process of emancipation
from cultural naivety to a state in which some of them would gladly
forsake their initial political goals if only they could keep on learning
and practicing in their "culture-filled idyll".[20]

   This turn of events only becomes possible by bringing the terrorists
up close, that is, by temporarily suspending or even reversing the
processes of othering just outlined. The text employs various strategies to accomplish this. Initially, the terrorist army of unknown
strength is presumed to belong to "La Dirección Auténtica", a thinly
disguised version of Peru's extremely violent terrorist organization
Sendero Luminoso. Soon after, however, readers and hostages alike
come to learn that the three generals and fifteen recruits belong to "La
Familia de Martin Suarez" (LFMS). This correction, with its replacement of "family" for "revolutionary army", has important implications. Not only do the members subsequently repeatedly contrast their
group with *La Dirección Auténtica*'s brutality,[21] thereby capitalizing
on LFMS's alleged "reasonableness", the group is, as readers are told,
"named for a boy of ten who had been shot dead by the government's
army while passing out flyers for a political rally" (13) – circum-

---

[18]   Maslin, "Uninvited Guests".
[19]   Mendelsohn, "Ransom Notes".
[20]   *Ibid.*
[21]   See 13, 42, 61, and 199. Once more, Patchett draws inspiration from the actual
event. During the 1996/97 internment, MRTA assumed the role of the "warm, gentle
partisans of the people. There was almost no shouting, or waving of guns. The terrorists chatted, joked, and permitted hostages such remarkable freedoms as use of cellu-
lar phones. In extended political discussions and speeches, they repeatedly under-
scored supposed differences between themselves – as 'politicians' – and the more
violent, apocalyptic Shining Path, notorious for its mass murders of villagers and its
use of dynamite. By such words and actions, and by frequent releases of some of the
hundreds of hostages, the group conveyed reasonableness and established an atmosphere in which negotiations might succeed, making MRTA the diplomatic equal of the
elected government of millions of Peruvians. This solicited some embarrassingly generous remarks from hostages grateful to MRTA for being freed early" (Christopher C.
Harmon, *Terrorism Today*, London: Frank Class, 2000, 203-204).

stances evoking sympathy for the terrorists rather than the government. What is more, the group turns out to be a family replacement for many of the young terrorists – and young they are indeed. Apart from the generals, they range from the age of fourteen to their early twenties, their bare faces afflicted by acne rather than traces of combat, and their bodies curved by the weight of the weapons they carry. They are frequently referred to as "boys" (for example, 24, 33, 95) or even "children" (166, 230) rather than "terrorists", and this characterization is reinforced when one of them admits to having "come to think of [the people around him] as the grown-ups rather than the hostages" (224). The youngsters are shown to childishly frolic about the unfamiliar luxury of the vice president's mansion, jumping on the soft beds and "flush[ing] the toilets again and again for the pleasure of watching the water swirl away" (111). They take to watching too much television, play soccer, and are altogether presented as sometimes moody but surprisingly innocent teenagers – an annoyance rather than a threat, as visible in one of the hostages' advice to one of them to "Go and play for a while" (243). Along with another hostage, readers cannot but wonder: "Could these be the same men who burst into their party, the same marauding animals?" (111).

In the course of the novel, the generic terrorists are provided with names – "Paco and Ranato and Humberto and Bernardo" (128) – and gendered identities (two of the boys part-way into the novel turn out really to be girls, and one of them falls in love with a hostage). This transforms them from an indistinguishable mass of dirty fatigues, boots, and guns into discernible individuals, well-rounded characters endowed with detailed traits, personal histories, idiosyncrasies, talents, even humiliating physical ailments. And once again, rather than simply doing so without drawing the reader's attention to the process, the novel implicitly comments on its own strategy. Gen, Mr. Hosokawa's translator, thinks to himself:

> That was something Gen had never considered, that General Benjamin had children, that he had a home or a wife or any kind of existence outside of the group that was here. Gen had never stopped to think about where they lived, but wouldn't it be in a tent somewhere, hammocks strung between the muscular limbs of jungle trees? Or was it a regular job to be a revolutionary? Did he kiss his wife goodbye in the morning, leave her sitting at the table in her bathrobe drinking coca

> tea? Did he come home in the evening and set up the chessboard while
> he stretched his legs and smoked a cigarette? (184)

This passage does not simply provide a fuller picture of General Benjamin, a former grade school teacher, it also causes readers to reflect
on the discursive construction of terrorism or terrorists, on their representation (for instance in the media) and general perception – a
process by which "terrorist" and "regular human being" clearly become mutually exclusive categories.

   With regard to narrative technique, a major means of creating such
occasions for reflection on terrorism's conceptualization is the novel's
shifting focalization. For the most part the novel is told from the point
of view of a variety of characters, which, next to the hostages, also
include the terrorists and the Swiss negotiator. Through the terrorists'
refraining from violence, their reasonable agendas and increasing
offers for identification (as perceived through the eyes and minds of
their hostages as well as the negotiator), readers cannot but reconsider
their initial sympathies.[22] They are increasingly led to regard not the
internment of the hostages but the government's detainment and killing of LFMS activists and their rescue policy in the current case as
forms of terror.[23] By redirecting the readers' allegiances, the shifting
focalization implicitly highlights an issue already briefly addressed –
the fact that definitions of terrorism are by necessity subjective.
H.H.A. Cooper succinctly summarizes this point: "What I do, however unpleasant, is not terrorism; what you do is terrorism."[24] As the

---

[22]   Despite the negotiator's repeated assertion of the terrorists' lack of professional-
ism – "He had never seen such an unprofessional group of terrorists. It was a complete and utter mystery to him how they ever managed to overtake the house" (136) –
I disagree with Appelbaum and Paknadel's observation that "Our sympathies can be
drawn to the terrorists since, while they have many grievances that we can acknowledge and a courage to fight for their convictions that we can admire, they are not
really dangerous" (Appelbaum and Paknadel, "Terrorism and the Novel", 306). In my
view, it is not their lack of dangerousness but their humanity that readers are drawn to.
[23]   As in the case of the actual siege, in the novel the government forces' eventual
raid on the occupied vice presidential mansion is represented as the willful, indiscriminate, and cruel execution of the mostly unarmed terrorists rather than the liberation
of the hostages – symbolized in the shooting of Ishmael, the youngest of the terrorists,
whose hands hold a spoon for digging planting holes in the garden (312).
[24]   H.H.A. Cooper, "Terrorism: The Problem of Definition Revisited", in *Essential
Readings on Political Terrorism: Analyses of Problems and Prospects for the 21st
Century*, ed. Harvey W. Kushner, Lincoln, NE: Gordian Knot Books, 2002, 4.

boundaries between terrorists and hostages – or, as they are increasingly referred to, between the "boys" and the "guests" – blur and both sides comes to actually cherish the confinement, readers with "the desperate unreason of a reader seduced"[25] hope that everything might still end well or even, as one reviewer mockingly put it, experience "a strange yearning to be kidnapped".[26]

Are we to take Patchett's text at face value, then, as a "paean to art and beauty"[27] celebrating human potential? Or are readers indeed merely "seduced" in the sense of "deceived"? Much is at stake with this question. In the first case, the novel asserts – as John Updike assumes – "that everybody is nice, given half a chance. In the pessimistic halls of literary fiction, [Patchett] speaks up, gently but firmly, for human potential."[28] In the second case, however, the novel is a self-reflexive exercise in demonstrating the powers of fiction to manipulate reader sympathies – and, implicitly, terrorism discourse. Terrorism's true impact, after all, lies beyond the immediate damage: it "resonates in the halls of the collective imagination", as Zulaika and Douglass point out[29] – fiction's home ground. The novel allows for either reading, and I would argue that what readers take away from it depends on their perceptiveness for the text's metacommentary, which in turn is a function of their particular needs. It is therefore instructive to take a brief look at the novel's reception in relation to the events following its publication.

Bel Canto's reception history: returning to the *status quo ante*?

Bel Canto was published in May 2001. A success with critics, the novel won the PEN/Faulkner Award as well as the British Orange Prize. Still, hardcover sales were slow and the novel mostly remained on the shelves until the end of 2002, when the paperback edition (which had come out in April 2002) climbed the bestseller lists and became an absolute book club favorite in 2003. It has since sold over a million copies and has been translated into more than thirty languages.

---

[25]   David Kipen, "Hostage Novel Ropes You In", *San Francisco Chronicle*, 13 June 2001, E 1.
[26]   John Updike, "A Boston Fable", *The New Yorker*, 1 October 2007, 98.
[27]   Maslin, "Uninvited Guests".
[28]   Updike, "A Boston Fable", 98.
[29]   Zulaika and Douglass, *Terror and Taboo*, 11.

Does this development, one might wonder, correlate in any way with changing ideas about terrorism in the United States? While I only have reviews and sales numbers at my disposal, I want to venture into some hypotheses.

Bel Canto presents its terrorists as "idealists pure and simple [whose] choice of terrorism is only a choice of tactics".[30] It locates terrorism far from the US, and by familiarizing the terrorists deconstructs and minimalizes rather than conveys the terror which terrorism aims to elicit. Yet on September 11, Americans (allegedly) for the first time were faced with immense collective terror up close. In addition to terrorism literally being too-close-to-home a topic for fiction in general right after the attacks, *Bel Canto* conveys an image of terrorism that was irreconcilable with what Americans had just experienced. Also, as more concrete forms of spreading Western democratic ideals among what were called "rogue" states were envisaged, spreading world peace through opera, haute cuisine, reading Gabriel García Márquez, and learning to play chess must have appeared too otherworldly a scenario. Most importantly, the novel gives terrorism a human face and tells the story sympathetically, partly from the terrorist's point of view.[31] Such a text was indeed highly unlikely to become a bestseller at the time of its publication.

Why, then, the success one and a half years later, at a time when the immediate shock of 9/11 had somewhat worn off? One possible explanation is that readers nostalgically longed for a return to former conceptualizations of terrorism. *Bel Canto*'s terrorism to a large extent presents the *status quo ante*: it is a phenomenon of the non-West (and since LFMS is a communist-inspired group, it appears almost as a remnant of the Cold War era); it is a terrorism that cannot possibly elicit any allegations of an American lack of empathy and lack of interest in world politics – as were directed at the United States within days of

---

[30]   Appelbaum and Paknadel, "Terrorism and the Novel", 306.
[31]   Martin Amis' "The Last Days of Muhammad Atta" from 2006 to my knowledge was the first attempt to do so with regard to 9/11, and it can hardly be said to be sympathetic. Benjamin Kunkel observes about terrorist novels after 2001: "Of course novelists will go on writing about terrorism; the subject weighs light or heavy on every day. What seems unlikely is that many will continue writing about the actual doers of the deeds from the inside, and with the same sympathy (however much ambivalence was always involved, however little endorsement ever implied)" (Benjamin Kunkel, "Dangerous Characters", *New York Times*, 11 September 2005: http://www.nytimes.com/2005/09/11/books/review/11kunkel [accessed 28 July 2009]).

the attack;[32] and it is a terrorism that can still serve as a projection screen for American exceptionalism,[33] described by Beau Grosscup as "the combined imagery of America 'the innocent and benevolent' and America victimised by terrorism-at-a-distance". Grosscup observed as early as 2000 that

> ... projecting the imagery that terrorism and terrorists plague only people of 'lesser' societies sustains public confidence in the 'special circumstance' of the American experience. As a result, terrorism remains a non-divisive, non-partisan issue, used with great effect to create the 'us-versus-them' mentality so crucial to US domestic and foreign policy success.[34]

When would asserting that mentality be more important to Americans than when, due to the Bush administration's increasingly visible "war on terror" and its legitimizing of preemptive strikes, their role as world police and arbiter came under serious attack and anti-Americanism became rampant? Most reviews read the novel as a sometimes overly idealistic, or far too beautiful, but overall convincing literary tribute to the redemptive powers of high culture and love.[35] Being exposed to art and beauty as well as human affection,

---

[32] See Martin Amis, "2001: Fear and Loathing", *The Guardian*, 18 September 2001: http://www.guardian.co.uk/world/2001/sep/18/september11.politicsphilosophyandsoci ety (accessed 26 February 2011); and Susan Sontag, "The Talk of the Town", *The New Yorker*, 24 September 2001: http://www.newyorker.com/archive/2001/09/24/010 924ta_talk_wtc (accessed 26 February 2011). In fact, in the real incident, "it was in American newspapers that MRTA saw the most progress in its declared desire to improve conditions for its comrades in Peruvian jails – where some 400 members are confined as compared to less than a hundred still active in Peru. Stories by American columnists blossomed, especially in January 1997 in the third week of the siege, describing the dungeon-like conditions and freezing cold in which several thousand MRTA and Sendero convicts are held. Readers' letters printed by a major US paper said that Peru's prison conditions were evidence of 'state-sponsored terrorism'" (Harmon, *Terrorism Today*, 203-204).

[33] See Clymer, *America's Culture of Terrorism*, 11.

[34] Grosscup, "Terrorism-at-a-Distance", 24.

[35] Examples are Maslin, "Uninvited Guests"; Mendelsohn, "Ransom Notes"; Laura Miller, "Review of *Bel Canto* by Anne Patchett", Salon.com, 22 June 2001: http://dir.salon.com/books/review/2001/06/22/patchett/index (accessed 09 October 2010); Ruth Scurr, Review of *Bel Canto* by Ann Patchett, *New Statesman*, CXXX/4548 (30 July 2001), 43. The most blatant yet simultaneously scathing evaluation in this direction comes from Jane Marcus-Delgado: "It is a story of the triumph of civilization

the novel was assumed to suggest, "brings out the best in every-body".[36] *Bel Canto* would thus clearly subscribe to a view of the Unit-ed States as a beacon of culture and civilization, indeed a "city upon a hill", shining to all those far off countries beleaguered by the malaise of terrorism.

It is such an interpretation, I would suggest, that attracted readers by the end of 2002 and in 2003, at a time when terrorism was no long-er a taboo area, when there was in fact a need for fiction to address the issue, and yet 9/11 was still too uncomfortable a subject to broach openly. With hardly any 9/11 novels on the market yet – and those that did appear later hardly ever dealt with the incident itself but chronicled its aftermath – *Bel Canto* might have served as both a sur-rogate text for coping with September 11 in a microcosmic setting and a reassurance of America's role in the world. Yet interpreting the nov-el this way, as I suggest most readers did, might say more about American readers at the time than about the text itself. It might be a historically conditioned misreading, or at least an incomplete reading, as it turns a blind eye to the novel's metadiscursive aspects.[37] These are the aspects that I now want to return to in lieu of a conclusion, of-fering an alternative reading of Patchett's text.

Bel Canto as metadiscourse on literature and terrorism

Yoking together two subjects as distant as opera and terrorism, the novel takes its title from *bel canto* singing, a musical style represented in the works of Donizetti, Rossini, and Bellini, marked by long lines and complex vocal ornaments. Literally "beautiful singing", it is about pure sound, and the title therefore appears to provide a fitting paratex-tual frame to the novel itself: *Bel Canto* in sum seems to be as much about the aesthetic beauty and the ensuing cultural potential of art and literature as about terrorism. Not only is the novel's lyrical prose often curiously at odds with the subject of terrorism, as exemplified by sen-tences such as: "It was during that performance of *Rigoletto* that opera imprinted itself on Katsumi Hosokawa, a message written on the pink

---

over barbarism, in which the allegedly culturally superior Westerners illuminate the lives of the Latin American 'terrorists' – and eventually walk away unscathed after witnessing their massacre" (Marcus-Delgado, "The Destructive Persistence", 48).

[36] Kipen, "Hostage Novel", E1.

[37] Ironically, Roxane Coss' response to a Russian hostage's request that she think like a Russian seems to anticipate the novel's one-dimensional reception when she flippantly admits: "Americans have a bad habit of thinking like Americans" (222).

undersides of his eyelids that he read to himself while he slept" (4). At a closer look, the text suggests that readers, along with the characters, experience a secondary form of Stockholm syndrome (describing an inexplicable attraction and solidarity between captives and captors). When one of the hostages feels "an unaccountable fondness" (228) for his captors and another reflects –

> How had he come to want to save all of them? The people who fol-
> lowed him around with loaded guns. How had he fallen in love with
> so many people? (303)

– readers by analogy have to ask themselves how they, in turn, have come to the point of falling for the text and its characters. What, moreover, could be the motivation for giving away the tragic ending on page thirteen and then proceeding to turn the characters that readers now know will get killed into the ones they sympathize with, if not to demonstrate the seductive workings of fiction and possibly also to comment on the way society conceptualizes terrorists as inhuman, disembodied, and illegitimate in their aims?

The novel both demonstrates and comments upon its characters' collective willful amnesia with regard to their situation (see 304-305), both captives and captors "work[ing] as hard at forgetting as [they] had ever worked to learn" (304). Concurrently, it draws a veil over its readers' eyes – a veil, however, that to the alert reader is semi-transparent because of the novel's metafictional aspects. As I argued especially in the first part of this analysis, the entire text displays a marked critical awareness of its own fictional status, its use of genre conventions, and its recourse to terrorism discourse. The novel's ending is no exception: while the focalization of the omniscient narration remains strictly within the confinements of the vice-presidential mansion throughout the main body of the text, it eventually returns to the real world beyond the walls in the novel's Epilogue. This severing of all of the previously formed attachments probably feels as abrupt to most readers as to the surviving hostages. Interpreted as awkward and unconvincing by some critics, it is only the final and least subtle call to re-evaluate the enchanting internment as exceptional, something out of this world, illusory – fiction.

Bel Canto accordingly testifies to Benjamin Kunkel's observation that "the terrorist novel [is always] also a kind of metafiction, or fiction about fiction"[38] – and, as one could add in view of this particular novel, a kind of metadiscourse, a discourse on the discourse of terrorism. In addition to the instances pointed out earlier, this becomes most apparent in Roxane Coss's assessment of the siege as a "failed social experiment" (153) and in the negotiator Joachim Messner's response to a hostage's claim that they no longer mind the internment as it has developed:

> What do you think, that they'll keep the wall up and pretend this is a zoo, bring in your food, charge money for tickets? 'See defenseless hostages and virtuous terrorists live together in peaceful coexistence.' It doesn't just go on. Someone puts a stop to it and there needs to be a decision as to who will be in charge of the stopping. (303)

Clearly, it is also Patchett's literary experiment and its degree of contrivance that are discussed in this passage, and it is up to her to end it – which she proceeds to do a few pages later. The passage consequently reflects on fiction's potential to enter into the discursive construction of terrorism by re-encoding the accustomed images and roles of terrorists conveyed predominantly through the media (which are attributed a conspicuously low profile in this novel). Yet at the very moment it has succeeded in this re-encoding, it bursts the beautiful bubble and snaps readers out of the dreamlike scenario, breaking the spell. In doing so, it aligns itself with, yet exceeds, what Margaret Scanlan regards as characteristic for terrorist novels: that they "elucidate the process that allows militants, journalists, and politicians to construct terrorism as a political reality".[39] *Bel Canto* also elucidates the process that allows fiction to construct terrorism as a phenomenon literally capturing our imagination. When analyzed against the background of reactions to the events of September 11, its mostly one-dimensional interpretation seems clearly impoverished by the narrow needs of American readers in the extended, not the immediate aftermath of the attacks. It remains to be seen whether in time further layers of meaning will receive wider attention.

---

[38]   Kunkel, "Dangerous Characters".
[39]   Scanlan, *Plotting Terror*, 2.

SELF, IDENTITY AND TERRORISM
IN CURRENT AMERICAN LITERATURE:
AMERICAN PASTORAL AND *TERRORIST*

MARTINA WOLFF

> When the Old God leaves the world, what
> happens to all the unexpended faith?[1]

This article explores the representation of terrorism and its impact on
the formation of self and identity of two young literary characters:
Merry Levov, a middle-class daughter turned terrorist in Philip Roth's
novel *American Pastoral* (1997) and Ahmad (Ashmawy) Mulloy, the
central character in John Updike's *Terrorist* (2006). Both novels por-
tray terrorism as a means of constructing an independent identity in
surroundings the characters experience as superficial, egocentric and
lacking in transcendence. In both texts religious fundamentalism and
terrorism are presented as closely intertwined issues, at times even
interchangeable, fulfilling identical functions within the construction
of adolescent identity. In linking the subtexts of both novels, religion
emerges as a key element in interpreting literary representations of
terrorism. The decisive link between terror and fundamentalist religion in these texts is the promise of certainty, a concept at odds with
the project of modernity.

Terror and the daughter: *American Pastoral*
American Pastoral is the story of Seymour Levov, also known as the
Swede. A star athlete at Weequahic High, a predominantly Jewish
neighborhood in Newark, New Jersey, during World War II, Seymour
is loved for his achievements in sport as much as for his character.
After having done "the right thing" by joining the Marines during the
war and then dutifully taking over his father's business, Seymour for

---

[1]   Don DeLillo, *Mao II*, New York: Penguin, 1991, 7.

once defies his dominant family by not taking a Jewish wife but instead marrying Dawn Dwyer, a beauty of Irish extraction and recent Miss New Jersey. In the following years, Seymour manages a rare thing: the switch from being perceived as the son of third-generation Jewish immigrants to a successful business man and a respected member of the rural WASP gentry of Old Rimrock. Dawn now spends her time raising prize-honored bulls and Meredith, their beloved daughter, ironically nicknamed Merry. This bright girl, in trying to develop a personality independent from her overwhelming parents, runs through the typical phases of an American youth, ranging from an infatuation with Audrey Hepburn to astronomy, the 4H Club and a Catholic phase inspired by her Irish grandmother. What sets Merry apart from her peers is her stuttering and her mother's efforts to accept a daughter, who, in the throes of her speech impediment and a puberty-induced weight-gain, is so strikingly different from her attractive and successful parents. And while Seymour and Dawn's interest in politics do not exceed the by then well established middle-class combination of socially liberal with economically conservative views, Merry gradually develops a thorough hatred of everything American for which her parents stand.

After puberty, she modifies her self-concept once again, coming to the conclusion that "what was deforming her life wasn't the stuttering but the futile effort to overturn it".[2] Like many at that time, she is politicized by protests against the Vietnam War, and it is Lyndon B. Johnson who infuriates her most:

> And the impediment became the machete with which to mow all the bastard liars down: "You f-f-fucking madman! You heartless mi-mi-mi-miserable m-monster!" she snarled at Lyndon Johnson whenever his face appeared on the seven o'clock news.[3]

From then on, Merry focuses her political activism on her surroundings. Inspired by the radical Weathermen, she continually argues with her ever-patient father, gives up on her mother, and goes on a political mission at her high school. And then, in 1968, "after turning their living room into a battlefield, after turning Morristown High into a

---

[2]   Philip Roth, *American Pastoral*, London: Vintage, 1997, 101.
[3]   *Ibid.*, 100.

battlefield, she went out one day and blew up the local post office",[4] killing Old Rimrock's doctor Fred Conlon in the process.

After the assault, Merry lives underground for five years, pursuing her revolutionary aims with various groups and from places all over the United States, even Cuba. In 1973, Seymour finally tracks her down near home, in a derelict area of Newark, where she lives under hideous conditions. Merry has again switched identity and has "deconstructed her militant persona",[5] echoing her uncle Jerry's statement that "personal philosophies have a shelf life of about two weeks".[6] The former violent revolutionary has become a Jain, a follower of a small Indian religious sect whose most salient feature is its strict non-violence. She, who lost her stutter over the intense concentration necessary for bomb-building and who, during her time underground, killed three more people, is now wearing a veil, so as not to destroy with her breathing the micro-organisms in the air.

Avoidance and repression

When Seymour finds his daughter in these conditions, filthy, half-starved, obviously on the brink of collapse, he is devastated. His means of grasping Merry's development prove inadequate. What until the bombing had taken him through a successful and rewarding life – his rational and modest ways of thinking, his set of values, his love of America and his sustained belief in the American Dream – are useless in the face of terror and where his daughter is concerned. Seymour's unconditional wish to understand, to make sense of what has happened, cannot be fulfilled because he has to realize that things do not make any sense.

The novel refrains from offering closure on the question of cause and reason for Merry's deeds and instead focuses on their consequences. Suddenly, Seymour finds himself confronted with the very same questions concerning identity and conformism which trouble his antagonistic daughter and which he always eluded or dodged. Seymour is "awakened, in middle age to the horror of self-reflection".[7] It

---

[4]   *Ibid.*, 113.
[5]   Elaine B. Safer, *Mocking the Age: The Later Novels of Philip Roth*, New York: New York State University Press, 2006, 84.
[6]   Roth, *American Pastoral*, 276.
[7]   *Ibid.*, 85.

is his resentful brother Jerry, "a heart surgeon with a scalpel for a tongue",[8] who expresses this in a key scene of the novel, when he rants about Seymour's inappropriate perception of the country he loves, especially its political state which has little in common with the Johnny-Appleseed-Dream-America of Seymour's boyish fantasies:

> You longed to belong, like everybody else to the United States of America? Well, you do now, big boy, thanks to your daughter. The re-ality of this place is right up in your kisser now. With the help of your daughter you're as deep in the shit as a man can get, the real American crazy shit. America amok! America amuck![9]

But even Jerry cannot refrain from applying reason where there is none, when he explains Merry's atrocities with her superficial, hypo-critical and all too lenient upbringing.

And though Seymour realizes the futility of causal thinking where his terrorist daughter is concerned, he still finds himself unable to incorporate this insight into his existence. Seymour's train of thought, which ends the scene in the novel, leads to his favorite modes of deal-ing with conflict, avoidance and repression:

> Causes, clear answers, who there is to blame. Reasons. But there are no reasons. She is obliged to be as she is. We all are. Reasons are in books. Could how we lived as a family ever have come back as this bizarre horror? It couldn't. It hasn't. Jerry tries to rationalize it but you can't. This is all something else, something he knows absolutely noth-ing about. No one does. It is not rational. It is chaos. It is chaos from start to finish. "I don't want that," the Swede tells him. "I can't have that."[10]

The novel's lack of closure with respect to its engagement with terror and its consequences is further exacerbated through its narrative per-spective: a first-person narrator who is not the focalizer of the story. This narrative situation suggests a clearer separation of character and narrator than the reader actually gets. Nathan Zuckerman, Roth's narr-ative alter ego of several novels, stays in the background so decidedly

---

[8]   Mark Shechner, *Up Society's Ass, Copper: Rereading Philip Roth*, Madison: Uni-versity of Wisconsin Press, 2003, 156.
[9]   Roth, *American Pastoral*, 277.
[10]   *Ibid.*, 281.

that the reader forgets that most of what he or she reads about is purely the speculation of a first-person narrator, not the omniscient third-
person perspective the reader supposes:

> I pulled away from myself … and dreamed …. I dreamed a realistic
> chronicle. I began gazing into his life – not his life as a god or a demi-
> god whose triumphs one could exult as a boy but his life as another
> assailable man.[11]

I hesitate to connect this narrative construction too tightly with the
topic of terror, because Roth is too postmodern an author for that.
Blurring the boundaries between reality and fiction within the narrated
world has always been part and parcel of his writing. But both terror
and metafictional musings go well together here, because both are
rooted in ambiguity, and Levov, this "assailable man", can be read as
the reader's representative, caught in the tangles of this ambiguity.
With respect to Swede Levov, the focalizer of the story, Derek Parker
Royal observes: "Much like Fitzgerald's Jay Gatsby, who refuses to
see the more sordid reality behind the green lights of Daisy's dock,
Swede Levov … attempts to live an idealized American life."[12] Moreover, he fails to realize (or chooses to ignore) the sordid sides of
America in the Sixties. Represented in this way, terror becomes the
antithesis to our daily dream of an ordinary life, to an existence that is
somehow whole, that makes sense. The terrorist pits his (singular)
convictions about society against the pursuits of those surrounding
him. The resulting discrepancy between these two extreme positions,
the common-sense majority and the extremist individual, is a gap too
wide to be bridged.

Seymour's biggest problem is his inability to link cause and effect.
His helpless response to the chaos his daughter's bomb sets off in his
life manifests his inability to adjust his mind-set. In this, Levov's
repression has a metonymic quality, making him a literary incarnation
of a widespread reaction to the disrupting force of terror: avoidance
and repression. Merry, this pelican daughter who has fed on her par-

---

[11]   *Ibid.*, 89.
[12]   Derek Parker Royal, "Pastoral Dreams and National Identity in *American Pastoral* and *I Married a Communist*", in *Philip Roth: New Perspectives on an American
Author*, ed. Derek Parker Royal, New York: Praeger Frederick, 2005, 202.

ents' flesh like Regan and Goneril on Lear's, is too much to bear for Seymour Levov. And so he goes and resets to zero, divorces his estranged wife, marries again, has three sons and lives his shattered first life a second time, although (and this is the closing passage of the novel):

> ... the breach had been pounded in their fortification ... and now that it was opened it would not be closed again. They'll never recover. Everything is against them, everyone and everything that does not like their life. All the voices from without, condemning and rejecting their life! And what is wrong with their life? What on earth is less reprehensible than the life of the Levovs?[13]

Terror as fundamentalist religion

Mark Shechner, who interprets the novel as one about the Sixties that comes twenty years too late, places the role of terror in *American Pastoral* within the historical framework of the times: as only one possible form of protest among many in this protest-prone era, comparable to others such as demonstrations or drugs. To him, Merry is a "granola-terrorist" like most of the self-announced revolutionaries of pampered middle-class background, and he claims that "we don't need to know much about Merry Levov as the incarnation of Kathy Boudin et al. ... [because] we are revisiting for the nth time the theatre of rebellion and atonement that has been Roth's personal theatre ever since he started writing, since he found himself, or got himself, singled out as a literary terrorist."[14] Interpreted as such, the terror in *American Pastoral* is just a writer's literary means of disrupting a family and a social community convincingly; and, as the times are very liberal, the disruptive action has to be very radical. In this sense, literature and terror both stay in the picture simultaneously, and can share the same ground. Certainly, Roth's concern is not with terror itself, its motives and machinations, but with the shattering of identities and the repressive reactions it entails. Yet Shechner's view is too limited, because it does not do justice to the role of terror in the novel. Reducing terror to a literary means in *American Pastoral* is tantamount to exploring the deep structure of the text only half-heartedly. Terror, though not described graphically by depicting the actual terrorist act, is at the

---

13   Roth, *American Pastoral*, 423.
14   Shechner, *Up Society's Ass*, 163-64.

heart of the text, because it is the prism which bundles and diffuses the rays of human identity. Literature and terror, as represented in the text, cannot share the narrative realm. Instead, they are presented as mutually exclusive, the one supplants the other: terror (and its mass-attention) crowds out literature's basic concern, the individual. Insofar, Shechner's "literary terrorist" is hardly convincing, indeed an oxymoron.

Writers and narrators cannot but zoom in on the individual – focalization is their business. A bomb works the opposite way: it kills randomly, unfocused. This is why in societies aimed at individualization and the individual pursuit of happiness, nothing proves as disruptive and as irreconcilable with the sense of identity as the indiscriminate effects of terrorist acts. It is, modifying a title by Hanif Kureishi, either "the word or the bomb",[15] and, therefore, Merry is herself replaced by her bombing and its consequences and vanishes completely from the narrated world as a physical presence, only to return after she has forsworn violence by becoming a Jain. Moreover, it also makes sense, that in the very moments she prepares her final arguments to be placed (the bombs she builds), her speech impediment vanishes, because it is then that language and speech are no longer scrutinized, are unimportant. The bomb displaces the word.

In contrast to Shechner's merging of the terrorist's perspective with the writer's by dubbing Roth a "literary terrorist", I suggest that fundamentalist religion, or, more precisely, the relation between terror and fundamentalist religion, provides the key for interpreting the role of terrorism in *American Pastoral*. In Don DeLillo's *Mao II*, a father who is witnessing his daughter's marriage ceremony as one of thousands in a mass-wedding of the Moon-sect asks: "When the Old God leaves the world, what happens to all the unexpended faith?" And he proceeds to answer his own question:

> When the Old God goes, they pray to flies and bottletops. The terrible thing is they follow the man because he gives them what they need. He answers their yearning, unburdens them of free will and independent thought.[16]

---

[15] Hanif Kureishi, *The Word and the Bomb*, London: Faber and Faber, 2005.
[16] DeLillo, *Mao II*, 7.

The parallels to Levov's thoughts about his daughter are clear:

> Why must she always be enslaving herself to the handiest empty-
> headed idea? From the moment she had become old enough to think
> for herself she had been tyrannized instead by the thinking of crack-
> pots .... Why did a girl as smart as she was *strive* to let other people
> do her thinking for her?[17]

Both quotations point toward the overall framework that defines the
relationship between fundamentalist religion and terrorism today:
modernity and its prerequisites. Levov's despair over his daughter is
an echo of the philosophical assessment of modernity as ensuing from
enlightenment and independence of thought. Modern man, ever since
the Renaissance and after the French Revolution, is his own god. It is
modernity's core trait to find orientation not beyond its own scope,
time and place, that is, not in tradition, previous decades or transcendence but within itself.[18]

But as Habermas, referring to Hegel, points out, there is a price to
pay for this. In regaining the "treasures formerly squandered on hea-
ven",[19] as Hegel phrases it, modern man risks losing religion by dimi-
nishing it: "The Enlightenment's proud culture of reflection has
divided itself off from religion 'and ... established it *alongside* itself
or itself *alongside* it'."[20] Because of the incongruity of belief and
knowledge, one cannot compensate for the loss of the other. As little
as fundamentally religious, anti-modern societies can compensate for
the loss of modernity's central asset, the independence of mind and
thought, as hard pressed are thoroughly modernized and secular societies if they want to make up for the loss of transcendence, of something to believe in.

Modernity's main feature, therefore, is uncertainty and a constant
need to construct social accordance, to continuously negotiate meaning in an ongoing discourse of instability. Embedded in this discourse
is multiculturalism, which is "not a superficial exchange of festivals

---

[17] Roth, *American Pastoral*, 241.
[18] "Modernity can and will no longer borrow the criteria by which it takes its orientation from the models supplied by another epoch: *it has to create its normativity out
of itself*" (Jürgen Habermas, *The Philosophical Discourse of Modernity: Twelve Lec-
tures* [1985], trans. Frederick G. Lawrence, Cambridge, MA: MIT Press, 1990, 7).
[19] *Ibid.*, 7-8.
[20] *Ibid.*, 20.

and food, but a robust and committed exchange of ideas".[21] One possible source of mitigation for the difficulties created by this complex process is everything that promises certainty, and religion's, especially fundamentalist religion's, ultimate merit for a true believer is its capacity to provide such certainty. As a consequence, unrestricted thinking – which implicitly questions certainty – is set aside.

It is this very mechanism that pertains to Merry's attitude towards terror as well. In her absolute and extremist political stance she betrays the same disregard of rationality as religious fanatics do. Hers is a "certainty without enlightenment", instead of a "an enlightened certainty":[22] "she experienced not only her full freedom for the first time in her life but the exhilarating power of total self-certainty."[23] Casting aside the very critical thinking she claims as her prime concern (and the unique characteristic to set her apart from her parents), Merry becomes as dependent on pre-fabricated forms of certainty as any believer. Consequently, it is not surprising that religious terminology enters her discourse:

> "They're people with ideas, and some of them don't b-b-b-b-believe in the war. Most of them don't b-b-b-b-believe in the war."[24]

It is this striving for an ultimate certainty the terrorist submits to, just like the fundamentalist believer submits to God.

David Greenberg underpins the central role of this quasi-religious certainty in his review of a documentary film on the Weathermen by quoting Brian Flanagan, a former member. The conviction to know what was right is here revealed as an essentially anti-modern stance, which links the allegedly politically-leftist Weatherman to Islamic terrorists and even political terrorists from the other end of the spectrum, based on a common ideal of certainty:

---

[21] Kureishi, *The Word and the Bomb*, 100.
[22] Michael Meyer-Blank, "Aufgeklärte Gewissheit: Christliche, islamische und staatsbürgerliche Identität als schulische Bildungsaufgabe", in *Der 11 September 2001: Fragen, Folgen Hintergründe*, ed. Sabine Sielke, Frankfurt on Main: Peter Lang, 2002, 173.
[23] Roth, *American Pastoral*, 101.
[24] *Ibid.*, 104.

The only person in the film to invoke Sept. 11, Flanagan compares himself and his former comrades to Islamist terrorists and to Timothy McVeigh, suggesting that all shared the conviction that their own knowledge of what was right for society entitled them to break laws, to kill, to engage in terrorism. He is not particularly eloquent, especially compared to some of his more "glamorous" co-conspirators, but he stumbles onto the film's more profound utterances. "When you feel that you have right on your side," he says at one point, "you can do some pretty horrific things."[25]

The points of intersection between political and religious extremism are mirrored in *American Pastoral*'s rhetoric, which fuses elements of terrorist and religious discourse: an unabated search for "certitude", ideological positions that are characterized by "belief" and "conviction," the fight against "the evil system"[26] and the struggle towards a "self-transformation" aimed at "purity" and the complete subjection of the self to the chosen ideology, utterly defying the modesty of thinking and acting that characterizes the Swede. Compare the following quote from *American Pastoral*:

> There is something terrifyingly pure about their violence and the thirst for self-transformation. They renounce their roots to take as their models the revolutionaries whose conviction is enacted most ruthlessly.[27]

This link between religious and extremist political thinking and its linguistic manifestation in the merging of lexical elements from both discourses in *American Pastoral* is underpinned further when compared to statements on the political background of the Sixties and Seventies, for example regarding the Weathermen (by the essayist Peter Marin to journalist Gloria Emerson):

> The violence of the Weathermen is evidence of two things: first that they saw their nation and its *evils* clearly, and, secondly, that they had no adequate response to what they saw, and so were driven to ends which partook perhaps too much of the *evils* they discovered .... Nor

---

[25] David Greenberg, "Remembering the Weathermen Terrorists", *Slate Magazine*, 9 June 2003: http://97.74.65.51/readArticle.aspx?ARTID=17802 (accessed 13 March 2010).
[26] Roth, *American Pastoral*, 259.
[27] *Ibid.*, 254.

had they any religious or secular moral framework into which they could put the evil they saw, or which would dictate or suggest an adequate response. They were not, I think, essentially political, no matter how political their rhetoric got. They were *moral apocalyptists, violent Anabaptists of a kind, godless* in their response and yet driven by their discovery of *evil* as surely as those in the past for whom *God was* (I say this, remember, as a purely secular man) the only adequate force or *value to pit against evil* .... They had discovered the *moral void* at the heart of American life; they were shocked, astonished, *transformed*, but they had nowhere to go with their vision of the *void* but straight into it.[28]

Fundamentalist religion as terror: *Terrorist*

In John Updike's *Terrorist*, fundamentalist religion and terror amalgamate again in the focus on an individual mind, that of eighteen-year-old, "would-be jihadist"[29] Ahmad Mulloy. A seemingly plain and conventional youth about to graduate from his local high school, Ahmad is the son of an Egyptian exchange student who left his family when he was three, and Teresa Mulloy, a bohemian of Irish-American origin who works as a nurse's aid and paints abstract canvases in her spare time. Raising Ahmad as a single mother, she cannot afford any better than to live in a run-down neighborhood of the city of New Prospect, New Jersey, whose name is as ironical as Merry's is in *American Pastoral*. When the story begins, Ahmad has just changed to the vocational track of his school, despite excellent SAT scores. This brings him to a meeting with Jack Levy, the career counselor at Central High, who takes a liking to the strangely formal, somewhat stiff boy and repeatedly tries to convince Ahmad to go to college, even visiting him at home (which later leads to a short affair with his mother).

Ahmad's youth and teenage years have left him unsatisfied in his search for adult role models and something worth believing in. The continued absence of his father, his liberal and often indifferent mother, the sanctimonious members of Christian denominations around

---

[28]   Peter Marin, "The best thing ever written about the Weathermen: A letter written by Peter Marin to Gloria Emerson": http://www.markrudd.com/?/about-mark-rudd.html (accessed 15 March 2010); reprinted from *Harpers Magazine*, December 1987.

[29]   David Simpson, *9/11 – the Culture of Commemoration*, Chicago and London: The University of Chicago Press, 2006, 219.

him, or the non-observant Jew Jack Levy all disgust him. From this hollowness he finally turns to the mosque and finds a Yemeni imam, Sheikh Rashid, who teaches him the Qur'an in Arabic and becomes a surrogate father figure. It is this imam who offers Ahmad what he is searching for, but cannot find: transcendence and the certainty of fundamentalist Islamic[30] views, and thus a particularly close bond with tradition. This poses problems Ahmad experiences on a micro-level, but which on a macro-level – so the novel implies – tend to characterize Muslim societies around the world. Western capitalist societies, as portrayed by Updike, are materialist; they combine an abundance of choice not only with respect to material, but also immaterial issues. This often proves to be a threat to traditional but especially to fundamentalist Islam, as choice requires decision, selection, and reasoning, which do not sit well with the idea of a course pre-defined by the past.

Anthony Giddens states in his account of globalization's influence on family and tradition in *Runaway World*:

> What is distinctive about tradition is that it defines a kind of truth. For someone following a traditional practice, questions don't have to be asked about alternatives .... [But] under the influence of globalization not only public institutions but also everyday life are becoming

---

[30] Even though, as Malise Ruthven points out, "The words 'Islam' and 'Muslim' are disputed territory everywhere, a basic distinction appears to be widely accepted: Muslim is the broader term, referring to the wider cultural background, while Islam and Islamic refer to the specifically religious" (Malise Ruthven, *Islam: A Very Short Introduction*, Oxford: Oxford University Press, 1997, 4). Additionally, the term "Islamic" refers to moderate, mainstream versions of interpreting and practicing the respective faith (orthodoxy and orthopraxy), while the fundamentalist version is, for Ruthven, better described as "Islamism" since the suffix "ism" "expresses the relationship between pre-existing reality (in this case a religion) and its translation into a political ideology, just as communism ideologizes the reality of the commune, socialism the social" (*ibid.*, 19). Bernard Lewis takes this distinction even further by suggesting that the fundamentalist branches should rather be called radical Islamism, thereby implying that the linguistic "politicization" in itself (the "ism") is not necessarily radical or fundamentalist (Bernard Lewis, *The Crisis of Islam: Holy War and Unholy Terror*, New York, The Modern Library, 2003, 20) – a stance that is often not shared. This results in a synonymous use of the terms "Islamism, radical" or "fundamentalist Islamism" and "radical" or "fundamentalist Islamic" movements in much of the literature on this topic (see *Understanding September 11*, eds Craig Calhoun, Paul Price, and Ashley Timmer, New York: The New Press, 2002). My own usage in this article is based on the implication of extremism in the suffix "ism". Therefore I treat the terms "Islamic fundamentalism" and "Islamism" as synonymous, but reject "radical" or "fundamentalist Islamism" as tautological.

opened up from the hold of tradition ... and [societies] that remained more traditional are becoming detraditionalized.[31]

For Ahmad the extreme version of religious tradition, a fundamentalist Islamic position, holds the same promise of certainty Merry seeks in political extremism, a certainty that eschews the individual interpretation of the holy text in favor of guidance and prescribed exegesis, a *Straight Path* to a meaning that is not to be scrutinized: "In the fundamentalist scheme there is only one imaginer – God. The rest of us are his servants."[32]

In Ahmad's case, it is capitalist consumerism that symbolizes America's temptation to deviate from religion, the very same culture of material and immaterial choice making which constantly undermines religious tradition. Ahmad despises America for its consumerism. "I seek to walk the Straight Path", he admits:

> "In this country, it is not easy. There are too many paths, too much selling of many useless things. They brag of freedom, but freedom to no purpose becomes a kind of prison."[33]

Ahmad, before Islam "rendered him immune", used to experience trips to the Mall as some kind of attack: "the mother and son were besieged on all sides by attractive, ingenious things they didn't need and could not afford."[34] This culminates in Ahmad's tenet, the opening line of the novel: "Devils. These devils seek to take away my God."[35] This feeling of being besieged arguably reflects that of fundamentalist Islamic insurgents. Ahmad feels surrounded by people, even his own mother, whose sole concern is with themselves. What they lack from his point of view is a perspective beyond their petty personal and egoistic concerns. He longs for transcendence he cannot find in an environment aimed at consumerism, sex, and entertainment.

From Ahmad's point of view, the capitalist obsession with this abundance of choice carries an even deeper threat: that of having no identity at all. When Jack asks Ahmad: "Did the imam ever suggest

---

[31] Anthony Giddens, *Runaway World*, London and New York: Routledge, 2000, 41.
[32] Kureishi, *The Word and the Bomb*, 10.
[33] John Updike, *Terrorist*, New York: Alfred A. Knopf, 2006, 148.
[34] *Ibid.*, 151.
[35] *Ibid.*, 3.

that a bright boy like you, in a diverse and tolerant society like this one, needs to confront a variety of viewpoints?" Ahmad's answer is clear:

> "No" Ahmad says with surprising abruptness .... "Sheik Rashid did not suggest that, sir. He feels that such a relativistic approach trivializ- es religion, implying that it doesn't much matter. You believe this, I believe that, we all get along – that's the American way." "Right. And he doesn't like the American way?" "He hates it."[36]

According to Ahmad's perception, religion is being sucked into globa- lization's capitalist/materialist current typical of widely secularized societies like the American one and is therefore also relativized and marginalized in the process.[37] Instead of being an important public issue, it becomes a private one of little importance and influence, to Ahmad an insidious, menacing process that carries the ultimate risk of losing God. This deeply felt, constant threat to its protagonist within the novel is a manifestation of a widely perceived Islamic concern. Of all the accusations brought forward against the West, the one of seduc- ing Muslims to embrace economic development and risk losing con- nection to their religious ties weighs especially heavy and links *Ter- rorist* to a similar subtext as *American Pastoral* – the question of modernity and its compatibility with the quest for certainty.[38]

Like Merry in *American Pastoral*, Ahmad does not find satisfying answers to his basic concern that there must be more to life than what society offers. "Once you run out of steam, America doesn't give you much",[39] says Jack, and both terrorists-to-be, Merry and Ahmad, actively construct their own philosophy to fill that void.

As Thomas Simons remarks about the 9/11 jihadists:

> They were killers, to be sure. But they were also uncertain young men, torn from their roots, belonging nowhere, at home only in their small groups, frightened, exalted. To understand them we can do worse than

---

[36]   *Ibid.*, 39.
[37]   See Mark Juergensmeyer, "Religious Terror and Global War", in *Understanding September 11*, eds Craig Calhoun, Paul Price, and Ashley Timmer, New York: The New Press, 2002, 37.
[38]   *Ibid.*, 36.
[39]   Updike, *Terrorist*, 304.

reread Dostoyevsky, we can do worse than contemplate Raskolnikov in his tiny room, fingering his ax.

According to Simons, Dostoyevsky's fiction may offer an explanation as to why martyrdom often proves appealing to those who have advanced economically and socially:

> The young of both times and places – the Russian world after 1870 and the Arab world around 1970 – were seared by the frustration of always living second-rate lives in relation to those at the cutting edge of globalization. There are tremendous penalties for latecomers to the modernization sweepstakes. .... This reality is painful, and the pain often is felt most keenly not by the poorest, but by those who have progressed a little and are frustrated in their aspirations to go further.[40]

In *Terrorist*, the Sheik's cunning guidance senses Ahmad's void and purposefully leads him towards extremist circles. His advising the vocational track is part of the plan: Ahmad is supposed to train for a truck driving license, in order to blow up the Lincoln Tunnel in a suicide bombing. Part of the scheme is Ahmad's job at *Excellency Furnishings*, a Lebanese business where Charlie Chehab, the owner's son, drives with him and gradually brings up the topic of Jihad, testing Ahmad's willingness to die as a martyr.

Only late in the novel is Ahmad introduced fully to the actual plan, whose realization is finally averted by Jack. He catches Ahmad on his way to the tunnel, risking his life by riding with him and trying to talk him out of his plan. As they are sitting in a traffic jam in the tunnel, approaching the spot of maximal impact for the explosion, Ahmad suddenly frees himself from the imam's indoctrinations, realizing that God does not demand destruction. It is Jack's exhausted remark, "Do it .... I've been tired lately"[41] that prompts Ahmad's turn.

Even though Ahmad finally decides against executing his terrorist plot, fundamentalist religion and terror have become synonymous for him by way of submission. Referring to the twenty-fourth sura, "the

---

[40] Quoted from Michael J. Mazarr, "The Psychological Sources of Islamic Terrorism: Alienation and Identity in the Arab World", *Policy Review*, CXXV (June/July 2004): http://www.hoover.org/publications/policyreview/3438341.html (accessed 15 March 2010).

[41] Updike, *Terrorist*, 306.

Light", the Sheik contrasts the martyr's death to the hollowness of modern existence:

> "The enemy has only the mirage of selfishness, of many small selves and interests, to fight for: our side has a single sublime selflessness. We submit to God and become one with him, and with another."[42]

The fundamentalist religious terror Updike invokes shows certain parallels to the changes in Roth's character Merry: the communicative act is no longer carried by a verbal code, by an exchange through language, an exchange of ideas. It is instead "the continuation of the discourse by different means": "more a violent means of communication than a direct strike at militarily significant targets",[43] a "collision of symbols".[44] But it might be even more: a replacement to end all discourse. The bomb replaces the word, or in Jack Levy's resigned words: "O.K., if that's how you see it. You can't argue with an explosion."[45] In *Terrorist*, religious fundamentalism's contiguity to terror is the result of the subliminal links between the two, running along the lines of the unification of a religious group beyond any individuality, the submission to a core idea or God and the respective holy text, and the absolute certainty provided by sacrificing the incertitude of interpretation: "Fundamentalism implies the failure of our most significant attribute, our imagination."[46]

In order to overcome this deadlock, the secular or post-secular society according to Habermas needs to develop a language to be understood by both, its secularized as well as its religious citizens.[47]

---

[42] *Ibid.*, 235.

[43] Margaret Scanlan, *Plotting Terror: Novelists and Terrorists in Contemporary Fiction*, Charlottesville and London: University Press of Virginia, 2001, 5

[44] Alex Houen, *Terrorism and Modern Literature: From Joseph Conrad to Ciaran Carson*, Oxford and New York: Oxford University Press, 2002, 4.

[45] Updike, *Terrorist*, 305.

[46] Kureishi, *The Word and the Bomb*, 10.

[47] Habermas defines the post-secular society as one which combines modernity and religion; where religion, instead of eventually vanishing in a continuous process of secularization as in the secular society, remains part of society in a kind of cohabitation of modernity and religion, part of a secularized sphere that derives its moral and legal norms from the democratic, liberal, pluralistic and independent political foundations inherited from the Enlightenment (see Thomas M. Schmidt, "Gibt es eine moderne Religion? Jürgen Habermas und die Idee der 'postsäkularen Gesellschaft'", *Forschung Frankfurt* 2 [2009], 64, 67).

This constitutes an endeavor not easily achieved, as Ahmad, struggling with reining in his thoughts, painfully realizes. Time and again, the rationalist perspective of science enters his efforts to think along religiously pure, unsuspicious lines:

> He will not grow any taller, he thinks, in this life or the next. *If there is a next*, an inner devil murmurs. What evidence beyond the Prophet's blazing and divinely inspired words proves that there is a next? Who would forever stoke hell's boilers? .... What of the second law of thermodynamics?[48]

In both novels, the reasons for the protagonists' turn to terrorism seem to lie in a search for identity that goes astray. But Merry and Ahmad's motives can only partly fill the picture and explain their stories. When Seymour Levov inwardly cries out about his daughter: "Twisted! Crazed! By what? Thousands upon thousands of young people stuttered – they didn't all grow up to set off bombs!"[49] he voices the unanswered questions that still remain for the reader: "Why them?" with respect to the terrorists, "why us?" with respect to the victims. The indifference of terrorist attacks is what defines our reaction to them. Unlike natural catastrophes, they are intentional, especially in their indifference to the actual individuals they kill.

Many novels whose themes are based on terror eschew its actual depiction, as Robert Appelbaum and Alexis Paknadel show in their 2008 study of twenty-five novels ranging from 1970-2008.[50] Referring to 9/11, Birgit Däwes distinguishes five different modes of representing its terrorist act in literary texts, ranging from mimesis of the attacks (an example here is Frédéric Beigbeder's novel *Windows on the World*) to either omission of the terrorist violence altogether or its passing mention, functioning as a trigger for existential crises of loss, mourning, and individual adjustment.[51] David Simpson interprets this

---

[48] Updike, *Terrorist*, 5.
[49] Roth, *American Pastoral*, 92.
[50] Robert Appelbaum and Alexis Paknadel, "Terrorism and the Novel, 1970-2001", *Poetics Today*, XXIX/3 (Fall 2008), 387-436.
[51] See Birgit Däwes, "'The Obliging Imagination Set Free': Repräsentation der Krise/Krise der Repräsentation in der U.S.-amerikanischen *9/11 novel*", in *Nine Eleven: Ästhetische Verarbeitungen des 11. September 2001*, eds Ingo Irsigler and Christoph Jürgensen, Heidelberg: Winter, 2008, 67-87.

as avoidance. Such authors, he argues, "avoid the pornography of death by not describing death, but in doing so they raise questions about whether this decision is the result of a moral-aesthetic decorum or a critical testimony to the utter self-centredness of the people in their books".[52] I would suggest a further interpretation: the reason for avoiding the description of terrorist acts is the self-centeredness, or, expressed more positively, the individualized perspectives of the novels' readers.

What do we feel and think when we read about the terror, the bloodshed, the pain, the horror? The typical reaction to terror's effects are shock and disbelief: so why inflict such suffering? How is such hatred possible? These questions take us back to the last lines of *American Pastoral* quoted earlier, lines which, with respect to 9/11 and the fall of the towers, gain prophetic weight:

> … the breach had been pounded in their fortification … and now that it was opened it would not be closed again. They'll never recover. Everything is against them, everyone and everything that does not like their life. All the voices from without, condemning and rejecting their life! And what is wrong with their life? What on earth is less reprehensible than the life of the Levovs?[53]

Sheik Rashid and Ahmad could provide a long list of what is wrong, yet literature can go beyond that. By providing the various reasons for Merry's and Ahmad's terrorism, literature offers us new perspectives which take into account social, ethnic and geographic heterogeneousness. Beyond such rational approaches, it requires readers to engage with the characters' emotions and thereby offers an insight into "the other". Where, if not in literature, can we dwell inside other peoples' thoughts?

Terrorist, in its competency with regard to the religious, social, and political background of Islamic extremism, can at times be tiring. Updike is not on his home turf here, and critics have accused him of that. Yet by including suras in Arabic or focalizing Ahmad's being torn between scientific and religious modes of thinking, or on Jack's weariness of life's superficiality, he does succeed in creating new perspectives for the reader.

---

[52]   Simpson, *9/11*, 200.
[53]   Roth, *American Pastoral*, 423.

Merry and Ahmad's motives for plotting violence as woven into these novels only half explain them – neither her stuttering, liberal education, nor the abounding violence of the Sixties in Merry's case, nor the consumerist superficiality, the absence of a father or the implicit debasement of Muslim beliefs and practices surrounding him in Ahmad's case. Terror in these two novels is a means of laying bare the foundations of identity: what we believe in and what we are willing to fight for. In that sense, they might contribute to what Alfred Hornung, referring to Don DeLillo, calls "the grounding of literature in reality". Hornung describes the danger inherent to postmodern literature as "the abandonment of a factual world for a world of fiction". The inclination to separate the sign from its meaning turns literature into mere word games. Thus "forms of playful destructions of lives and cities celebrated in postmodern texts and thrillers" separate literature from reality.[54] Taking Tom Clancy's novel *Debt of Honor* (1994) as an example, Hornung argues that "human beings, their thoughts and emotions, are displaced by an all-out technological apparatus", just as, in postmodern theories of language, the signifier displaces the signified. In light of 9/11, he opts for a readjustment of our reality concepts:

> With the collapse of the buildings and the real deaths of people, postmodern assumptions and cherished ideas also collapsed and were grounded. A rethinking of our positions and a restoration of our reality concepts are urgently needed.[55]

Every novel is carried by a cultural undercurrent that feeds on its author's contemporary reality. In both *American Pastoral* and *Terrorist*, this foundation is our current phase of modernity: the globalized, post-industrial, secular western society. Moreover, in both novels terror as an extremist political ideology and religious fundamentalism reveal their mutual relationship, a kinship rooted in the promise of certainty: Terror takes on a religious function in Merry's case and religion becomes synonymous with terror in Ahmad's, as both are

---

[54] Alfred Hornung "Flying Planes Can Be Dangerous: Ground Zero Literature", in *Science, Technology, and the Humanities in Recent American Fiction*, eds Peter Freese and Charles B. Harris, Essen: Die blaue Eule, 2004, 400.
[55] *Ibid.*, 403.

applied by the protagonists as a means of finding and defining their identity.

For Merry, terror develops into a substitute religion, the final stage of an extremist political stance which gradually takes on the same basic, all-encompassing and defining function that religion has in fundamentalist contexts. Like religion in such cultural settings, Merry's political extremism serves as the defining core of identity, the decisive factor of every aspect of life: personal values, the social set, which career to choose. Consequently, after having been a political extremist for years, she finally becomes a Jain, a religious extremist. This extremism links her to fundamentalist characters like Updike's Ahmad or Slimane Benaissa's Raouf, an Islamist martyr in *The Last Night of a Damned Soul*.[56] The absoluteness that signifies the systematic realignment of their lives according to orthodox Muslim rules reveals a stony thoroughgoing quality similar to Merry's, a decisiveness which dumbfounds her father: "That's the only thing that gets anything done is to have strong ideas, Daddy."[57]

Literature reveals that the "strong ideas" of religious fundamentalism and terrorism have already developed a shared language, a common terminology of certainty and submission. "The unfinished project of modernity" (Habermas) in its mundane reality has yet to develop this mutual code, not in order to induce submission, but, on the contrary, to foster "an enlightened certainty".[58] The integration of religion and modernity requires a linguistic integration, a transfer of religious ideas into a philosophical discourse that does not risk or destroy the religious contents but becomes a "saving deconstruction" of them.[59] Although phenomena like the "The New Atheist novel"[60] point in a different direction, literature might be a prime source for such an integrated discourse: "The writer's fictions are committed to life and thus directed against the 'terror within our souls'."[61]

---

[56]   Slimane Benaissa, *The Last Night of a Damned Soul*, New York: Grove Press, 2003.
[57]   Roth, *American Pastoral*, 110.
[58]   See Meyer-Blank, "Aufgeklärte Gewissheit".
[59]   Schmidt, "Gibt es eine moderne Religion?", 67 (my translation).
[60]   Arthur Bradley and Andrew Tate, *The New Atheist Novel: Fiction, Philosophy and Polemic after 9/11*, London and New York: Continuum, 2010.
[61]   Heinz Ickstadt, "Bilder des Terrors und Terror der Bilder in den Romanen Don DeLillos", in *Der 11. September 2001*, 110 (my translation).

THE 9/11 NOVEL AND THE POLITICS OF NARCISSISM

ROY SCRANTON

In the time it takes to read this sentence, you could have at your fingertips a whole library of direct, first-person accounts of the terrorist attacks of September 11, 2001: planes flying into the towers, the towers' collapse, streets filled with smoke, all of it. Touch your fingers to plastic and you have government reports, personal accounts, conspiracy theories, audio, video, timelines, data and interpretation for pages. You can watch it happen again and again. You can watch a twenty-six-minute personal video on Youtube recorded from a hi-rise apartment east of the towers, edited to major events, first plane second plane, first fall second fall, boom, boom, boom, boom. You can watch people running from Trinity Church as WTC 2 collapses. You are enveloped in smoke and debris, ash and terror, you are there, it is happening all over again. Just like it did the first time: except for a small minority of people directly involved, this was exactly what it was. Observed. Mediated. Googled and CNNed. The attack happened on cable before it ever happened for real – it was a spectacle before it was an event. September 11 was almost instantly 9/11, the war cry of 9/11, the referent and touchstone of a whole new era, an historical event dehistoricized and become pure spectacle, "the telltale instant after which it is no longer the same … the 'When-it-all-changed'".[1]

How do you write a novel about this? September 11 presents a profound challenge to the art of fiction, because of its global scope, its wide social and political significance, its immense symbolic weight, and because it has left so little of the event itself to the imagination. A writer seeking to address the event through literature is confronted with exceedingly potent images and a dizzying profusion of narratives, so that the public event imposes a tyranny which the writer must

---

[1] Fredric Jameson, *Postmodernism, or, The Cultural Logic of Late Capitalism*, Durham, NC: Duke University Press, 1991, ix.

either submit to, undermine, or evade; the anxiety of influence becomes an anxiety of superfluence. How, the question arises, can a novel explore the impact of international events on individual lives, seriously look at the political and economic forces at work, and still perform the aesthetic, personal, and psychological insights and satisfactions we traditionally expect? Is it even possible for a novel to offer us, through the drama of 9/11, a picture of what Fredric Jameson calls "that enormous and threatening, yet only dimly perceivable, other reality of economic and social institutions"?[2] If it is true that the postmodern is "an attempt to think the present historically in an age that has forgotten to think historically in the first place", then September 11 erupts as a de-historicized historical event that perfectly embodies the challenge of this paradox, and provokes literature to achieve a respective sublimity that lifts us above the senselessness of the moment.[3]

I intend in this essay to consider how various novelists have attempted to meet the challenge of 9/11 and explore how they have succeeded or failed in personalizing the political and politicizing the personal, in creating a new signification out of the welter of history, and in thinking "the impossible totality of the contemporary world system"[4] in a way that seriously addresses the event's social and political significance. I will argue that the problem these novels run up against most explicitly is the political narcissism of contemporary American culture, which ignores the actual geopolitics of neoliberal global market expansion, resource dominance, and cultural conflict in favor of a self-absorbed narrative of wounding and loss. Whether the novels here examined address the problem of political narcissism or succumb to it will be the most important criterion of judgment.

Social narcissism: pax Americana

Claire Messud's *The Emperor's Children* (2007) and Jay McInerney's *The Good Life* (2006) present a glamorous view of upper-class New York society that always promises to, but never quite does, turn critical. Both Messud and McInerney show a deep indulgence for their

---

[2]   *Ibid.*, 38.
[3]   *Ibid.*, ix, 38. Perhaps a "conspiracy sublime" akin to Bruce Robbins' "workshop sublime" (Bruce Robbins, "The Sweatshop Sublime", *PMLA*, CXVII/1 [January 2002], 84-97).
[4]   Jameson, *Postmodernism*, 38.

characters that obstructs any serious critique of their milieu. This would not necessarily be a problem, except that 9/11 has a deeper impact than some business shake-ups and a change in lovers. For these writers, for their characters, as perhaps for much of their social set, 9/11 was a powerful, disturbing event that happened in New York, to New Yorkers, and had little wider significance. A disaster as random as an earthquake or an attack by King Kong, 9/11 in these works shakes up the scene, causing people to reconsider their decisions and think about their mortality.

Messud's book is by far the better novel and is more sophisticated, ironic, and critical than McInerney's, if flawed by the same narcissism. Too nice to be satire but too smart and closely observed to be pure fluff, Messud tries to write a real Jamesian or Flaubertian novel, but never manages to make her characters breathe. Her social narcissism does not come from blindness, but from a lack of scope and vision. *The Emperor's Children* tells the story of four young Americans and one Australian whose lives circle around the patriarchal Murray Thwaite, in a simmer of ambition, sexual desire, and social hypocrisy that is adeptly balanced by Messud, who brings a real attention and even love to her characters. Yet when Saudi Arabian terrorists fly planes into the towers of the World Trade Center, three-quarters of the way through the novel, all we are left with is a feeling of sympathetic shock. Our context never goes beyond the mirrored canyons of New York, the event's meaning never transcends that of a random disaster. We can see that the characters are trapped by their narcissistic response to a major historical event, yet by not providing any wider context than she does, Messud keeps us trapped there with them – which in the end suggests she is trapped there herself.

If for Messud 9/11 at least shakes up the lives of her characters, for Jay McInerney, in his novel *The Good Life*, 9/11 is a passing fad. Wholly absorbed with themselves, but in a cute, sort of good-natured way, the glitterati living "the good life" absorb 9/11 with hardly a blink: it adds new topics to the conversation, it makes it harder to get a cab in TriBeCa, it lets everyone take themselves a little more seriously, but in the end it is nothing more than this season's big event.

The Good Life tracks the lives and loves of Manhattan's upper-side sets, particularly two married couples, Russell and Corrine and Luke and Sasha, the bright-eyed denizens of the brightly-lit big city coming into middle-aged questions and disappointments. 9/11 gets the ball rolling by giving Luke and Corrine a chance to meet and begin an extramarital affair. The book is exhaustively concerned with the flags and markers of wealth and privilege, filled with dropped names, fancy cheeses, oenophilia, and gossip, with just the right leavening of literary allusion and earthy authenticity to make the whole thing seem totally fake. Not that we should doubt that McInerney knows and loves the good life he describes, but that very, and very obvious, self-satisfaction undermines any pretensions to either satire or seriousness.

Regarding 9/11, McInerney's novel offers little. His uptowners find fulfillment in a soup kitchen serving the brawny, heroic firefighters and National Guard soldiers working the rubble, "with their lusty appetites and small-town manners",[5] they find bomb-scares upsetting, they are moved and stricken by the missing-persons posters, and little more. His characters are so self-absorbed that 9/11 does not even register as a national event: The novel does not bother to mention the wounded, vengeful hysteria so prevalent at the time. Their narcissism is so complete that they cannot take 9/11 personally, or even seriously, because it hardly affects the easy gratification of their sensual and social desires. As Joyce Carol Oates points out in her review of the book: "at a time in our history when 'suicide bombers' – 'al-Qaeda' – 'Osama bin Laden' – 'Islam' – 'Saudi Arabia' – 'Palestine' – 'Israel' were commonplace words even among schoolchildren in the New York City region, the most overt political reference anyone in *The Good Life* makes is the complaint of a friend of Russell Calloway who feels that he will have to move his family to the suburbs."[6] Thinking about having to move to the suburbs seems to be the greatest sacrifice demanded of McInerney's characters, just like having to end an affair or shut down a business is all that is demanded of Messud's. We see here a profound political narcissism that refuses to give up the self's privileged centrality and cannot accept a complex historical event that threatens to undermine the giddiness of the consumer moment.

[5]   Jay McInerney, *The Good Life*, New York: Vintage, 2006, 141.
[6]   Joyce Carol Oates, "Dimming the Lights", *The New York Review of Books*, 6 April 2006: http://www.nybooks.com/articles/archives/2006/apr/06/dimming-the-lights/ (accessed 24 April 2008).

Literary narcissism: extreme and immense

For some, 9/11 was an opportunity to explore literary themes. For writers like this, reality ceases to be the subject and becomes merely matter, no longer a mystery to be plumbed but a trope to be shaped. In these novels, the terrorist attacks serve as a trauma that could have been any trauma, providing a colorful hook on which to hang personal conceits. Jonathan Safran Foer's *Extremely Loud and Incredibly Close* (2005) and Paul West's *The Immensity of the Here and Now* (2003) both exemplify this sort of literary narcissism.

Extremely Loud and Incredibly Close to my mind is a tedious, childish novel that brings to bear on 9/11 a whole arsenal of literary tricks, clever devices, and big thoughts, with all the subtlety of an attention-starved kindergartner. 9/11 for Foer is an occasion to bang his tambourine and show his depth and sensitivity, but the event exists outside history. It is the thing that took protagonist Oskar Schell's father from him, a stand-in for Death, and nothing more. History is subsumed into the novelist's artifice, and both suffer for it. As for politics, the most political Foer gets is to say that bad stuff is bad, and "Mohammed Atta was evil".[7]

Foer's novel tells the story of Oskar Schell, a nine-year-old boy whose father died in the attacks. Oskar is depressed because his dad is dead, and guilty because his father phoned that morning and left several messages on the answering machine, a fact that Oskar has since kept hidden from his grieving mother. Oskar likes to make up cute inventions, use figurative metaphors, and write letters to famous people. He also hurts himself and seems genuinely disturbed. This combination makes for an awful tone, a sort of tragedian's *Pollyanna* that comes across as inadvertently silly and earnestly distasteful. Oskar finds a key labeled "Black" in his father's closet, which starts the plot rolling on an epic quest across the five boroughs, Oskar wandering the city on his own looking for the door to his key. Adding to the whimsy of Oskar's adventures meeting the friendly, eccentric people of New York named Black, Foer brings in another narrative about Oskar's grandparents, German survivors of the firebombing of Dresden, a story of fabulist sentimentality created from scraps of nihilism and devastation, like Kafka by way of O. Henry.

---

[7]   Jonathan Safran Foer, *Extremely Loud and Incredibly Close*, New York: Houghton Mifflin, 2005, 159.

Extremely Loud and Incredibly Close wants to tell a simple tale: A young boy moves through suffering from innocence to experience. Loss, grief, and understanding are the points of the narrative arc he's drawing, but instead of working with that narrative, he works the narrative up into postmodern excess. And to what end? To manipulate the reader, certainly, but Foer's tricks do not seem to do anything else. The photos of doorknobs, intertextual insertions, typographical games, and idiosyncratic wordplay neither delight on their own nor open into deeper mysteries.

As with his ersatz experimentalism, Foer's politics are nothing more than a tool with which to work his designs on the reader. "At its heart", wrote Benjamin Markovits in his review of the book, "the novel has little to offer but the obvious and the sentimental. .... Yet ... however innocently, [it] may be complicit in worse feelings, too: the unmeasured hysteria of the American response to the attacks on its native soil."[8] This is related to what Keith Gessen wrote in his review: "the effect of the book as a whole is in fact precisely to pull the September 11 attacks out of history."[9] Pulled out of history, the attacks become a purely emotional signifier, used to manipulate viewers, voters, and readers. Foer uses history like propaganda, eliciting emotions for their own sake, failing to meet the challenge of events or of his art.

Paul West is a much more intelligent, experienced, and gifted writer than Foer, yet his novel *The Immensity of the Here and Now* falls into the same narcissistic trap as does *Extremely Loud and Incredibly Close*. Almost wholly interior, *The Immensity of the Here and Now* addresses itself to history but in a strictly literary and solipsistic intellectual way. As with Foer, West's concern with 9/11 is not with the particularities of the event itself but with what it might represent abstractly, in a narrative, as an idea – how it might be used to his own ends.

The Immensity of the Here and Now tells the story of Shrop, an academic philosopher who has suffered an attack of general amnesia somehow related to 9/11, and Quent, Shrop's analyst, a paraplegic former fighter pilot who lost his legs in the Vietnam War. Shrop visits Quent in the hopes of reconstructing his memory, a process stymied

[8] Benjamin Markovits, "The Horrors of History", *New Statesman*, 6 June 2005: http://www.newstatesman.com/200506060041 (accessed 24 April 2008).
[9] Keith Gessen, "Horror Tour", *The New York Review of Books*, 22 September 2005: http://www.nybooks.com/articles/18267 (accessed 24 April 2008).

by the fact that Quent feeds Shrop Wittgenstein's biography in place
of his own. The novel begins with alternating interior monologues
from the two characters, and we see quickly that they inhabit the sort
of dualistic, co-dependent, antagonistic relationship common to characters in the work of Samuel Beckett. Like Hamm and Clov, they
need each other and hate each other, they form caricatured mirrors of
each other, and their relationship is characterized by a constant struggle and negotiation somewhere between exasperation and ennui. Both
Shrop and Quent are fascinated by 9/11 and Ground Zero in particular,
and reflections on the event and the site run through their digressive,
allusive monologues. Poetic, philosophical, and sometimes quite moving, these reflections also tend to be somewhat abstract and even academic.

West's approach is to contrast the brute physicality of the event
against the airy, convoluted psychological responses attempting to
rationalize it. This contrast is embodied in the duality of the characters, which regularly shoves the material crudeness of Quent's physical disability up against the immaterial complexity of Shrop's psychological one, tending to privilege the authenticity, power, and inexplicable mystery of the former over what West seems to see as the impotence and self-indulgence of the latter. Although this privileging of the
material over the mental would seem to suggest that West would be
interested in the material causes of 9/11, his subject is finally the
mind-body split itself, that old Cartesian duality so deeply plumbed by
Beckett: 9/11 as pretext for philosophy.

West's 9/11 is a modern event, in a very comforting way: an irruption of the Absurd that tears apart the fabric of contemporary life. The
Historical Weight of the event is paramount in this sort of view, because it represents another failure of the Enlightenment, another failure of Civilization, another failure of Rationality to account for the
mysteries of the irrational animal man and his world:

> He has not compared enough, I think, with destruction in other cities
> such as London and Coventry, Warsaw, Dresden, Manila, and such a
> village as Lidice. That is not his way, he who fixes on the caliber and

configuration of the scab, attending like so many New Yorkers to the symbolic aspect of the twin towers' destruction.[10]

Here Quent asserts against Shrop's "symbolic aspect" the historical weight of devastated cities, leveling the full power of the Absurd against even Shrop's decidedly lame Rationality, seemingly unaware of the "symbolic aspect" of this interpretation itself. Perhaps West is being ironic, for there is no question he is a very intelligent and self-conscious novelist, yet at the same time it is hard not to feel that he is dressing 9/11 up in vintage gear because that is just how he sees it. It is a comforting way to see it, because we have over a hundred years of modernist response to modern absurdity, and it allows us to observe events with a certain sophisticated distance. Moreover, to couch 9/11 in terms of the old conflict between the body and mind both misses the point and abuses the notion of history. Why bother with 9/11 at all, really, except that it is a cultural identifier? Shrop's amnesia embodies our own narcissistic response to 9/11, but he is so subsumed into West's literary thematics that the event itself never escapes that narcissism. We have yet to escape into history.

Narcissism satirized: disorder and pathology
While *The Emperor's Children* and *The Good Life* gesture toward a satire of American culture and *The Immensity of the Here and Now* suggests the absurdity of our amnesiac state, none of the books I have considered as yet explicitly contextualizes the political narcissism of the American response to 9/11. I now turn to three books that, in my view, do precisely this. First I want to look at two satirical novels, Ken Kalfus' *A Disorder Peculiar to the Country* (2006) and Don DeLillo's *Falling Man* (2007), then in the final section turn to William Gibson's *Pattern Recognition* (2003).

Ken Kalfus' *A Disorder Peculiar to the Country* offers a strongly satirical critique of narcissistic politics. Beginning on the day of the attack itself, the book uses the failed marriage of Joyce and Marshall Harriman to reflect and parallel the political and cultural events that lead from 9/11 to the invasion of Iraq and beyond. Joyce and Marshall are young, married, generally successful New Yorkers with careers in Manhattan and an apartment in Brooklyn Heights. They have two

---

[10]   Paul West, *The Immensity of the Here and Now*, Rutherford, NJ: Voyant, 2003, 30.

children. They are also involved in a bitter divorce, which because of various complications forces them to continue to live together as they go through the legal proceedings, turning their lives into hellish battle-zones: "Feelings between Joyce and Marshall acquired the intensity of something historic, tribal, and ethnic, and when they watched news of wars on TV, reports from the Balkans or the West Bank, they would think, yes, yes, yes, that's how I feel about *you*."[11] This illustrates the main device of the novel: to contrast the intimate social and psycho-logical violence of the victimized New Yorkers with the wider, more abstract currents of geopolitics and the "War on Terror".

Kalfus' satire is rich, evocative, brilliantly apt, and often disturb-ing. He gives us a brief aside on the "Clash of Civilizations",[12] a wry look at Joyce's developing appreciation for Afghan jewelry, food, and culture,[13] clever resonances in the battles between the Harriman's children (including one squabble where the children come to violence over a "cheap plastic UN relief truck, some kind of Happy Meals prize"[14]), a sustained poke at US-Israeli politics,[15] and many other pointed scenes. The novel develops depth and strangeness as it builds from its original conceit, giving us, for example, a weirdly flat and unsettling account of Marshall's failed attempt to blow them all up with a suicide bomb, which ends with a puzzling moment of family togetherness:

> Joyce was still on her knees, trying to force the cap. Viola's hands were on her back, completing the circuit: Joyce touched Marshall at the hip, Marshall touched Victor, Victor's shoulders made contact at Viola's arm. Joyce worked to fasten the cap as if success would re-solve every single one of their problems. "You don't follow through with anything. That's what's wrong with you."[16]

---

[11] Ken Kalfus, *A Disorder Peculiar to the Country*, New York: Harper Perennial, 2006, 7.
[12] "[H]e was keenly aware that he was living in October 2001, under a wartime regime, traversing a battlefield terrain, in a city that bore the standard of one civilization under attack by another. *This* civilization comprised Barney, the *Times*, MetroCards, a raven-haired woman in tears standing on the street hailing a cab, yellow cabs, mojitos, divorce lawyers, and Derek Jeter" (*ibid.*, 47).
[13] *Ibid.*, 62.
[14] *Ibid.*, 66.
[15] *Ibid.*, 95-101.
[16] *Ibid.*, 191.

The novel's penultimate scene follows Marshall to a party where race, sex, and implicit violence come together in a disturbing scene of de-humanization and brutality, echoing the prisoner abuse scandals of Abu Ghraib: Marshall watches his children's preschool teacher per-form sex acts with a nervous young black male prostitute while being filmed and cheered on by a crowd of drunk and drugged party-goers. That the young man has had a paper bag put over his head, and that the preschool teacher is performing these acts in front of her boy-friend, only adds to the debauched, brutalized air of the scene, impli-cating American personal lives in American political torture. From there, the novel traces the last fall-out of the divorce between Joyce and Marshall, and ends with a surreal, jingoistic celebration of Ameri-can victory. After Saddam is caught, the US leaves Iraq a peaceful democracy, and a few months later the capture of Osama bin Laden provokes a mass, spontaneous street parade down to Ground Zero:

> All around him schoolchildren bumped each other with their back-packs, giggling. They sang and so did these suited businessmen and this gaggle of big-haired young women in heels and an old guy in a bomber jacket and another guy and another guy and an elderly woman who had come out with a walker. Marshall felt a huge emotion surg-ing within him: it was relief at bin Laden's capture, of course, but also sudden love for his country, at that moment an honest, unalloyed, un-compromised white-hot passion. He hadn't realized he knew so many words to so many patriotic songs. His face was wet, soaked.[17]

Kalfus' book is moving, funny, awful, and troubling, not least of which because of the explicit connection it makes between the petty, narcissistic brutality the characters show each other in their daily lives and wider political events, but what is perhaps most troubling is the way he suggests that our narcissism is so dehumanizing, so determi-nant in the way that other people become for us mere objects, mere reflectors of our own motives and desires, that there is no escape, ei-ther personally or politically. When the book opens, both Joyce and Marshall have trouble repressing their glee in response to the attacks – each of them thinks that the other has died. This easy cruelty is less malicious than it is symptomatic of their overwhelming self-absorption. Neither character ever manages to sustain any sort of reci-

---

[17] *Ibid.*, 236.

procal relationship with anyone else, not each other, not their kids, no one. They (and everyone else in the novel) are concerned wholly with what people are for them.

If we consider the bromide that "the personal is political" in terms of Kalfus' viewpoint, we are left with a view of American politics reflecting an American culture turned so far in on itself that it cannot even imagine what it is like to be someone else, much less begin to empathize. In an important scene, Marshall's lawyer pushes him again and again to say what Joyce "is like, really", but Marshall is incapable of forming an answer that sees her as a person with an existence beyond his own. For him, she either must relate to him some way or reflect him; she has no autonomy, as far as he is concerned. Joyce feels similarly about him, although for her he stands as the oppressor against whom she must war. Resentment and narcissism are the order of the day, and Kalfus' diagnosis suggests that they have so infected society that there is nothing worth saving. This is illustrated by Kalfus' "happy ending", which is blatantly false and hideously sentimental. The fantasy Kalfus offers us is nothing more than a reflection of our own infantile and bathetic desires.

The second novel I will consider here in terms of problematizing American political narcissism is Don DeLillo's *Falling Man*. This novel has been much reviewed and much treated, and the most common response seems to be a kind of disappointment. Called "The Man Who Invented 9/11" in *Esquire*'s review of the book, DeLillo was looked to for an explanation of the event because of his career-long treatment of themes of violence, spectacle, terrorism, and conspiracy. Books like *Mao II*, *Players*, *White Noise*, and *Libra* show DeLillo delving into the spirit of a paranoid, terrorized, postmodern world that seemed remarkably like the one we woke up to on September 12. DeLillo's book *Underworld*, a sweeping social history of the Cold War – with its now-eerie cover of a bird flying at the World Trade Center towers – seemed, for many reviewers, to set the form and standard of the novel that would have to be written, the novel DeLillo especially was expected to write, in response to 9/11. The book was a remarkable achievement, and it would make sense for Michiko Kakutani, for one, to say that "Given this achievement, the reader

approaches Mr. DeLillo's post-9/11 work with great anticipation."[18]
Yet what Kakutani fails to do in her review is to see "this achievement", and DeLillo's more recent works, in the context of his career.
Falling Man was critiqued for a variety of failings, but by and large
the reviewers seemed to miss what the book actually was: like DeLillo's earlier works, such as *Players*, *Great Jones Street*, and *Ameri-
cana*, *Falling Man* offers a cool satire of American life and American
narcissism. As Andrew O'Hagan points out, DeLillo "has become less
funny as he gets older",[19] but less funny does not mean less ironic. If
anything, in the unsettling books since *Underworld*, we see DeLillo's
early manic irony resurgent in an austere and heatless form, cold, un-
funny, with less and less desire to punchline the joke.

Falling Man is a novel in three parts, titled "Bill Lawton", "Ernst
Hechinger", and "David Janiak", all the names of people who appear
otherwise in the book, respectively, Osama bin Laden, Martin, and the
Falling Man. At this level, already, we are given a curious asymmetry
that suggests themes of mythology, spectacle, name, and alias: Bill
Lawton is what the main characters' son calls bin Laden with his
friends, Ernst Hechinger is possibly the real name of Martin, a European art dealer with a mysterious past, the lover of the mother of one
of the main characters, and David Janiak is the actual name of the
Falling Man, the performance artist who recreates a famous photo
from 9/11 of a man falling from the towers. Bin Laden is a terrorist,
Martin is an art dealer rumored to have once been a terrorist (but "one
of ours, which meant godless, Western, white"[20]), and Janiak is an
artist presenting himself as the victim of terror. All three names are
hidden, in the beginning, and must be uncovered one by one.

The two main characters in the novel are Keith Neudecker, a busi-
nessman who was working in the towers when they were attacked, and
his estranged wife Lianne. They come back together after the attacks,
with their son Justin, against the advice of Lianne's mother Nina, a
former professor and intellectual slowly letting herself go in her taste-
fully-done Manhattan apartment. The first two parts of the book trace

[18]   Michiko Kakutani, "A Man, a Woman and a Day of Terror", *New York Times*, 9
May 2007: http://www.nytimes.com/2007/05/09/books/09kaku.html (accessed 28
April 2008).
[19]   Andrew O'Hagan, "Racing Against Reality", *The New York Review of Books*,
28 June 2007: http://www.nybooks.com/articles/archives/2007/jun/28/racing-against-
reality/ (accessed 24 April 2008).
[20]   Don DeLillo, *Falling Man*, London: Picador, 2007, 195.

their reaction to the attacks: Keith's post-traumatic recovery and Lianne's efforts to cling to meaning, his affair with another survivor, her work with an Alzheimer's support group, each of them alternately lashing out and grasping for help. With the third part, however, we have jumped three years into the future, and things have slipped back to a kind of horrid normal, Keith playing poker in Vegas, Lianne casting about vaguely for God. In the last part, Nina is gone and Martin is disconnecting himself from America, claiming to be nauseated by the subject, claiming that "there's an empty space where America used to be".[21] Lianne has realized that Keith is motivated by a repressed desire for violence, that this "was at the heart of his restlessness", and realized in herself a need for higher authority, if not a father then a god; she realized "she wanted to be safe in the world and he did not".[22] This narrative, taking us from the morning of September 11, 2001 to a strange adjustment three years later, is crossed by the counter-narrative, beginning some time in the past, of Hammad, one of the hijackers, who dies when his plane crashes into Keith's tower. Hammad's story is more suggested than developed; the role it plays is not to bring us into the "mind of a terrorist", but rather to play left hand to the development of Keith and Lianne's story.

In typical fashion, DeLillo builds his novel from various symbols and images, tropes and allusions, assembling them like the objects in the Morandi still lifes on Nina's wall: poker games and language games, blitzed minutes of New York street and the hushed soulless-ness of Vegas hotels, obsessions with counting, supermarket check-outs, surgical masks and human shrapnel. The structure of the book suggests an effort to contextualize Keith and Lianne's narcissistic response to 9/11, giving us several vantages to view them (and the event) from. The three essential outside perspectives are the time jump three years forward, Martin the European, and Hammad the Terrorist. It is clear from what we see that Keith and Lianne's responses, how-ever human, are inadequate to the event and its fallout. Like Kalfus, DeLillo is giving us our response, turning the mirror back on America. He frames that mirror with the time jump, Martin, Hammad, and even the Falling Man. If we do not like what we see, if we find Keith ado-lescent and weak, if we find Lianne somewhat pathetic, if we find the

---

[21] *Ibid.*, 193.
[22] *Ibid.*, 215, 216.

literal, in-your-face crudeness of the Falling Man's act to be both sterile and irritating, then perhaps, thus suggests DeLillo through his framing perspectives, we have not risen to the event. The political narcissism embodied in Keith Neudecker's nihilistic trajectory is our own. *Falling Man* may not have risen above that narcissism, but at least DeLillo critiques it, and just because some critics missed the punchline does not mean that there is no joke.

Welcome to the future: goodbye twentieth century

Beyond satirizing American narcissism, a fuller literary response to 9/11 would rise to explain it, or contextualize it, or help us understand its role in our world. William Gibson's *Pattern Recognition* (2003) works to do just this. It is interesting and not a little ironic that what may be the most intelligent, visionary, and meaningful literary response to 9/11 comes from a science fiction writer.

William Gibson has been famous ever since his 1984 novel *Neuromancer*, in which he coined the word "cyberspace" and inaugurated the "cyberpunk" genre. This science fiction genre is characterized by a dystopian, near-future milieu, vast corporate governance, intricate plots, heavy reliance on information technologies, especially computers, the internet, and mass media, and marginal anti-hero protagonists. Drawing heavily on noir narrative traditions, cyberpunk reconfigures the "mean street" past into a darkly visionary future. Fredric Jameson calls cyberpunk "fully as much an expression of transnational corporate realities as it is of global paranoia itself", singling out Gibson for his "representational innovations".[23] What is interesting is that Gibson has always been aware that his future was just a mask for the present: "Predicting the future, [he] has always maintained, is mostly a matter of managing not to blink as you witness the present."[24] With *Pattern Recognition* and his more recent work *Spook Country*, Gibson's darkly fantastic tomorrow has merged seamlessly with a darkly fantastic present. Though the novel is not explicitly about 9/11, the attack overshadows the work and works through it in a profound way.

Cayce Pollard, the novel's protagonist, is a trendspotter (Gibson calls her a "coolhunter") who makes a fair amount of money vetting ad work for major corporations. She had been in SoHo the morning of

---

[23] Jameson, *Postmodernism*, 38.
[24] Lisa Zeidner, "Netscape", *The New York Times*, 19 January 2003: http://www.nytimes.com/2003/01/19/books/netscape.html (accessed 28 April 2008).

the attacks, on her way to a meeting, looking into the window of an antique shop. She hears a boom somewhere, "one of those unexplained events in the sonic backdrop of lower Manhattan", just before or just after she watched a single petal fall from a dead rose in the shop display.[25] Unknown to her at the time, her father, Win Pollard, was in a taxi headed downtown, likely to visit old company friends in WTC 7. Win had been in the spy business, a fact which adds mysterious resonance to his disappearance that day, as if into thin air. His presence haunts Cayce throughout *Pattern Recognition*.

The old patriarch, the Cold Warrior lost in a cloud of smoke, has been replaced by a new father figure, the cunning and rapacious Hubertus Bigend, who is described as looking like "Tom Cruise with too many teeth".[26] Bigend is something like a traditional puppet-master villain, but not so much evil as amoral and not so much villainous as simply predatory. He represents, through his secret, super-successful company Blue Ant, the globalized, post-industrial, neoliberal corporate world: everything is fungible, everything is commodified, everything is marketable. For Bigend and his ilk, there are no values but market values. Cayce is hired by Bigend to find the creators of a mysterious series of films that have been released onto the internet, which have attracted a cult-like following, in part because they have remained uncommodified. The footage serves as the MacGuffin to take us from London to Tokyo to Moscow, yet it also serves to open up questions of art and commerce, creation and meaning: The films are short, unidentifiable segments that seem to come from somewhere or anywhere in the twentieth century. The films turn out to be made and distributed by a pair of Russian sisters, twins named Stella and Nora (referring explicitly to Tennessee Williams and James Joyce). Their uncle, Volkov, one of the new Russian oligarchs, indulges them by placing at their disposal the resources of a small Hollywood production studio. Nora, who actually makes the footage, suffered brain damage from a Claymore mine when their high-placed parents were assassinated. Stella works with Russian programmers to distribute it through the web. Cayce manages to track them down, with the nearly unlimited resources of Blue Ant behind her, a bit of luck, and a turn back to the Cold War spy world of her father.

---

[25]   William Gibson, *Pattern Recognition*, New York: Berkeley Books, 2003, 139.
[26]   *Ibid.*, 59.

The plot follows Cayce Pollard in her job as a "coolhunter". As she describes herself at one point, what she does "is pattern recognition. I try to recognize a pattern before anyone else does". Her interlocutor asks, "And then?" "I point a commodifier at it",[27] she says.

On the one hand, then, we have a question of "recognizing patterns":

> These passages also suggest a deep resonance between Cayce's activity and the work of the novelist: if the present has been rendered so fluid and unstable as to make the classical vocation of the realist novel impossible – any picture of the present being hopelessly obsolete long before the work saw the light of day – the novelist's task shifts to one of pattern recognition, a mapping of broader trends and directions in which our global situation tends.[28]

On the other hand we have the question of commodification. There is an over-arching pattern at work here, a metanarrative of predatory capitalist expansion and marketization: As soon as something new is recognized, the Bigends sweep in and snap it up, repackage it, sell it back. Whatever the Cayce Pollards of the world might be seeking to do, suggests Gibson's narrative, they are little more than cats' paws in a global capitalist system.

But the plot is only one aspect of the novel's efforts to comprehend the contemporary world. In its language, images, cultural and social commentary, the interpersonal relationships between the characters, and even Cayce's own psychology, Gibson works to pin down a moment as clearly and specifically as possible. From email etiquette to simulacral fashion, from Russian politics to Starbucks to Pilates, from neologisms like "Bladerunnered" and "Zaprudered" to a bar called "Charlie Don't Surf", Gibson's pitch-perfect rendering glows with a seductive hi-gloss shine, reflecting back to us our logoed, consumer-driven narcissistic spectacle. Cayce herself represents something of an embodied critique, performing a visceral *No Logo*: She is physically repelled by famous logos, especially the Michelin Man and Tommy Hilfiger, which induce in her nausea, confusion, and panic. As well, Cayce's peregrinations and meetings with the rich and dangerous give

---

[27] *Ibid.*, 88.
[28] Phillip E. Wegner, "Recognizing the Patterns", *New Literary History*, XXXVIII/1 (Winter 2007), 183-200.

Gibson the chance to wax theoretical: "For us, of course", says Bigend, "things change so abruptly, so violently, so profoundly, that futures like our grandparents' have insufficient 'now' to stand on. We have no future because our present is too volatile."[29] Some have even gone so far as to say that Gibson's work "successfully occupies a middle ground between literature and social theory which in itself makes a significant contribution to modes of perceiving and under-standing our emergent post-modern world".[30]

What does this all have to do with 9/11? Nothing and everything. What *Pattern Recognition* portrays is the epochal change in the world around Cayce Pollard. She totters perilously between eras: the nostal-gic Cold War of her real father, and the threatening global market-place of her new foster-father, Hubertus Bigend. *Pattern Recognition* works like Cayce does, trying to envision an imminent, immanent fu-ture already present. 9/11, the planes crashing into the towers as a rose petal drops in the window of an unnamed Soho shop, is the hinge of a turning world.

In the final pages of the book, after Cayce has found the sisters and all the subplots have been either dropped or tied up, our hero goes to visit her friend Damien, a filmmaker, at his documentary shoot. He is filming the amateur unearthing of an archeological site: Russians dig-ging up World War II trenches around St Petersburg. At one point, Damien emailed her, they found a whole Stuka. Cayce finds herself,

> … out of some need she hadn't understood, down in one of the trenches, furiously shoveling gray muck and bones, her face streaked with tears. Neither Peter nor Damien had asked her why, but she thinks now that if they had she might have told them she was weeping for her century, though whether the one past or the one present she doesn't know.[31]

It is facile to say that 9/11 represents the end of something, the end of the twentieth century; it is an easy statement and we all know it is true. William Gibson's remarkable achievement is to dramatize this,

---

29   Gibson, *Pattern Recognition*, 59.
30   Richard Skeates, "A Melancholy Future Poetic", *CITY*, VIII/1 (April 2004), 140.
31   Gibson, *Pattern Recognition*, 367.

to juxtapose two eras in conflict and suggest a way to see them, to his-
toricize the personal and personalize the historical.

There is a disturbing sense of time in most of these 9/11 novels, an
"immensity of the here and now" that drowns out the very possibility
of context. Whether this is a hallmark of the postmodern or a symptom of cultural narcissism, it suggests an unwillingness to grapple
with actual events, political powers, and historical trends. What this
means for America, for the future, or for the novel, is not for me to
say. I cannot bring up these points without recalling that *Ulysses* was
written during World War I and that Beckett wrote his trilogy hiding
from the Nazis in the south of France. Literature springs from the relationship between the individual and society, and no doubt sometimes
narcissism is the best defense for the fragile ego in an unstable, atom-
ized world.

Yet there is something profoundly unsettling about seeing political
events interpreted through a deeply narcissistic filter, something
powerfully troubling about seeing skilled, talented writers take up a
subject of serious historical and political importance as an object in
frivolous dramas. 9/11 has not changed the way the individual relates
to society, or the way we relate to history or the future, but it stands in
some sense as the metaphor and symbol of such changes. The question
is what the novel can or should do in terms of portraying, dramatizing,
and problematizing both these changes and the role of 9/11 in marking
or symbolizing them. If the novel is to do serious cultural work today,
should not we expect some effort devoted to understanding the complex global systems of capital and communication that shape our
world? Perhaps what DeLillo's Bill Gray said in *Mao II* was correct,
and the novelist has ceded cultural power to the terrorist, and perhaps
composer Karlheinz Stockhausen was correct when he called 9/11
"the greatest possible work of art in the entire cosmos".[32] Or perhaps,
more pointedly, we stand in need of a deep and wide rethinking of
what "art", "the novel", and "cultural power" mean in a world shaped
by mass media information technologies – we must drag Walter Benjamin onto Youtube. What is eminently clear, in the end, is that grap-
pling with 9/11 remains a serious challenge to the art of fiction and the
role of literature.

---

[32] Quoted in "Höllensturz", *Frankfurter Allgemeine Zeitung*, 19 September 2001:
http://fazarchiv.faz.net/FAZ.ein (accessed 5 November 2010; my translation).

AFTER THE APOCALYPSE:
NOVELISTS AND TERRORISTS SINCE 9/11

MARGARET SCANLAN

When we think about terrorism in literature, we usually begin with questions of representation. It seems reasonable to ask whether Heinrich Böll's *The Lost Honor of Katharina Blum* accurately represents the way German newspapers covered the Baader-Meinhof Group, or whether, along with indicting the IRA for killing civilians, a popular thriller writer like Gerald Seymour or Jack Higgins also finds himself perpetuating unfair stereotypes about the working-class Irish Catholics from whom that organization recruits its members. Even if we have little faith that poets remain "the unacknowledged legislators of mankind", we find ourselves looking for the real-world implications of fictional terrorism. Can a writer, for example, represent the horrors of being trapped on the top story of the World Trade Center without encouraging popular American revenge fantasies, which continue to have real-world military consequences? Then, too, because every discussion of terrorism at least implicitly addresses the terrorist's claim to wreak violence in the name of some nationalist or religious ideal, questions of representation quickly acquire an ethical edge.

At a recent workshop on terrorism and literature, I was struck by the claim of a bright young scholar that we were "ethically obliged" to represent state terror whenever we spoke of insurgent terrorism. One sees her point almost instinctively, though had the novel of manners been at issue, we would have been startled to hear a Bloomsbury novelist whose subject was an unfaithful wife criticized for failing to bring to mind all the male adulterers circulating in his milieu. Most of us share Joseph Conrad's concern that a novel may offer up other people's suffering as entertainment, or leave us detached, prey to that "saving callousness" in even sensitive readers that responds to a violent history told by a great writer with a "purely aesthetic admiration of its rendering".[1] And finally, the unanswerable question raised by trauma theory and Holocaust studies emerges: does anyone who is not a survivor have a right to represent such unrepresentable experiences? And after all, is it not the nature of trauma to be unrepresentable even for the victim, whose inability to integrate the narrative of violence into his/her waking experience leads to involuntary flashbacks and terrifying nightmares?

These are all questions with which scholars of literature and terrorism, to say nothing of novelists, have long been familiar. They become particularly discouraging when one contemplates the attacks of September 11, 2001, in part because current events, such as the recent Swiss referendum on minarets, or the speed with which the right-wing media connected the White House gate-crashing Tareq Salahi to "terrorism apologist Rashid Khalidi", suggest that Islam and even Arabic names seem threatening to many Europeans and Americans.[2] One might speculate that the post-9/11 novel of terrorism so frequently evades the main events, as well as the hijackers and their immediate victims, out of an understandable desire to avoid some of the pitfalls of direct representation we have just noted. Almost a decade later, we still lack a traditionally realistic novel that represents the perpetrators at some length, attempting to account for their motives, perhaps interlacing their story with an account of the doomed airline passengers and the military and government officials charged with responding to the catastrophe. Don DeLillo's *Falling Man* (2007), with its brief glimpses into a hijacker's mind and its two or three page description of survivors making their way down the stairs in the World Trade Center, comes closer than most to such a model. Yet even DeLillo focuses almost exclusively on the survivor's numbness and evasions. Many other writers have produced a genre we

---

[1]   Joseph Conrad, "Autocracy and War" (1905), in *Notes on Life and Letters*, Garden City, NJ: Doubleday, 1924, 83.
[2]   Cathryn Friar, "White House Gatecrashers Michaele and Tareq Salahi Have Ties to Terrorism Sympathizer", *Right Pundits.com*, 30 November 2009: http://www.right pundits.com/?p=5087 (accessed 10 December 2009). The left-leaning *Huffington Post* published a story headlined "Tareq Salahi Bio: Was on American Task Force on Palestine", noting that his biography was removed from the organization's website after the incident. This association also received a great deal of play in the right-wing blogosphere, with the clear implication that it was sinister. See http://www. huffingtonpost.com/2009/12/01/tareq-salahi-bio-was-on-a_n_375745.html (accessed 10 December 2009).

might characterize as the 9/11 novel of manners, in which the World Trade Center's collapse emerges only at the margins of a narrative focused on the relationships, love affairs and rivalries, of affluent New Yorkers. One thinks of Jay McInerney's *The Good Life* (2006), Claire Messud's *The Emperor's Children* (2006), of Wendy Wasserstein's *Elements of Style* (2006), or even Joseph O'Neill's *Netherland* (2008).

It is possible, however, for a writer to engage with the events of 9/11 in a novel freer of the conventions of literary realism, raising issues that outstrip our usual concern with representation and its ethical discontents. Cormac McCarthy's *The Road*, which James Wood somewhat testily characterizes as a "9/11 novel pretending not to be one",[3] offers an excellent case in point. While it never mentions the World Trade Center or Pentagon, *The Road* confronts issues September 11 and the subsequent War on Terror prompt. McCarthy's grim post-Apocalyptic America evokes the desperation felt by many on the political left as the Bush administration, virtually unopposed by liberal institutions such as the Democratic Party and the *New York Times*, rushed to war in Afghanistan and Iraq and repressed civil liberties at home. The novel offers a fresh perspective on traditional religious language and belief, which both the fundamentalist Islamic rhetoric of the attackers and the evangelical Christian rhetoric of US political conservatives had arrogated to themselves. If it does not represent political terrorism, *The Road* dwells long on barbarity and violence as behaviors that preceded and might well outlast the modern state. Even more importantly, its portrayal of American violence, long a McCarthy theme, defuses the conception of a well-meaning democracy besieged by fiendish outsiders on which the War on Terror depends.

McCarthy's novel offers a literary variation on the post-nuclear apocalypse, a popular genre in both North American fiction and film – examples include Walter Miller's *A Canticle for Leibowitz* (1959) and Margaret Atwood's *The Handmaid's Tale* (1986). McCarthy, however, avoids any direct reference to nuclear weapons or radiation sickness and leaves no clues to any public, political history that triggered the "long sheer of light and … series of low concussions" that stopped

---

[3]   James Wood, "Getting to the End", *The New Republic*, CCXXXVI/16 (21 May 2007), 44.

the clocks at 1:17 a.m. in some unspecified year.[4] *The Road* is set perhaps a decade after the first firestorms, in a world where plants and
animals can no longer grow; the earth is covered in ashes, and sooty
clouds create something close to a nuclear winter. The few remaining
human beings survive either by salvaging canned food or eating each
other. Lacking dates and political allusions, the novel observes few of
the realistic conventions for representing time:

> He thought the month was October, but he wasn't sure. He hadn't kept
> a calendar for years. (4)

We are in mythic, visionary time, the time of plague in Thebes, or the
time of history as experienced by Walter Benjamin's angel, whose
face is turned toward the past: "where a chain of events appears before
us, he sees one single catastrophe."[5]

The central figures in this wasteland – for the novel is so literary as
to seem constructed of salvaged remnants of Western literature – are a
nameless father struggling to save his equally nameless son. If September 11 is never mentioned, the "bitter ashes" (219) that cover the
novel's landscape and form a thick fog behind which "the banished
sun circles the earth like a grieving mother with a lamp" (32) recall
those early photographs of ghostly New Yorkers emerging from the
darkened streets leading away from the World Center, their clothing
and features a uniform thick gray. So do the father's memories of the
first victims of the firestorms, "sitting on the sidewalk … half immo-
late and smoking in their clothes. Like failed sectarian suicides" (32).
September 11, too, provides the first grisly connotations of the "box-
cutter" he finds in an abandoned garage and carefully fits with a new
blade, hoping to shave scavenged Colt .45 cartridges to fit his own
pistol (120, 149).

---

[4]   Cormac McCarthy, *The Road*, New York: Random-Vintage, 2006, 52 (unless
specified otherwise, all subsequent references to this edition are indicated by page
numbers in the text).
[5]   Walter Benjamin, "On the Concept of History" (1940), in *Selected Writings*, trans.
Edmund Jephcott *et al.*, eds Howard Eiland and Michael Jennings, Cambridge, MA:
Harvard University Press, 2003, IV, 392 (emphases in original). Also, as Thomas
Schaub perceptively argues, citing Bakhtin's "Forms of Time and the Chronotope in
the Novel", the metaphor of the road is "a key chronotope, for in the image '[t]ime, as
it were, fuses together with space and flows in it'" (Thomas Schaub, "Secular Scripture and Cormac McCarthy's *The Road*", *Renascence*, LXI/3 [Spring 2009], 244).

At a time when the Bush administration and much of the US main-stream press focused on violence generated by an alien Axis of Evil, McCarthy focused on the violence of the West, particularly American violence. Though the narrator once describes the boy as "looking like something out of a death camp", allusions to World War II usually evoke damage inflicted by Americans, rather than Germans or Japanese (117). Firestorms like those in Tokyo and Dresden have left the dead "mummified ... their faces split and shrunken on their skulls" (191), their "incinerate corpses shrunk to the size of a child" (273). The deeper American past offers no consolations; walking south, father and son find an old plantation house; crossing its porch, the father recalls that "chattel slaves had once trod those boards bringing food and drink on silver trays" (106). Huddled in its basement they find naked and starving people apparently held captive by four men and two women whose approach sends father and son fleeing. The word "terror" occurs twice in this episode and is repeated only once, when the son falls ill and his father believes he is dying (111, 113, 247).

While the father has memories of natural beauty in America, he never idealizes its past. The narrator's characterization of man and boy "thin and filthy as street addicts" reminds us that America was no utopia before the firestorms (127). A description of post-catastrophe cities in which "blackened looters ... crawled from the rubble white of tooth and eye carrying charred and anonymous tins of food in nylon nets like shoppers in the commissaries of hell" seems to deconstruct President Bush's famous advice soon after 9/11 that Americans go shopping to defy the terrorists.[6] Finally, when the father reflects on the cruel futility of people attacking the "image" of "evil ... as they conceived it to be" because they have no actual "remedy", his mind goes back to a domestic incident. As a child he saw "rough men" pour gasoline on a nest of snakes and stand watching as they "twisted horribly and ... crawled burning across the floor ... to illuminate its darker recesses" (188, 189). The barbarians who terrify this father and son are natives seen riding in wagons drawn by harnessed slaves, their foot soldiers armed with lengths of pipe and spears beaten out of old truck

---

[6] George W. Bush, "President Bush Addresses the Nation", *The Washington Post*, 20 September 2001: http://www.washingtonpost.com/wpsrv/nation/specials/attacked/transcripts/bushaddress_092001.html (accessed 10 December 2009).

springs. It is white heterosexual American males who have fitted a "consort of catamites ... in dog collars and yoked each to each" (92). The same men are responsible for the pregnancies of the women who march alongside them, their offspring apparently slated to share the fate of the "charred human infant headless and gutted and blackening on the spit" father and son find by the road (198).

The Road, then, instantiates the vision of terror we find in theorists like Jean Baudrillard and Slavoj Žižek, who argue that a "war on terror" can never be won because "the external threat the community is fighting is its own inherent essence".[7] Although in October 2001 many Americans took offense at Baudrillard's remark about the World Trade Center and Pentagon bombings, that is, that al-Qaeda "*did* it, but we *wished for* it",[8] his point was never that making an apocalyptic film like *Mars Attacks!* was the moral equivalent of flying a jetliner into an office building. Rather, he argued that all human beings have an "allergy to any definitive order" that creates a "will to destroy it" that increases as "the power of power" does.[9] "Terrorism, like viruses, is everywhere", he observes, "and is at the very heart of this culture which combats it, and the visible fracture that pits the exploited and the underdeveloped ... against the Western world secretly connects with the fracture internal to the dominant system".[10] If an Islamist caliphate were as powerful as America, it too would fuel destructive outrage. According to Baudrillard, then, terrorism needs to be conceived "beyond Islam and America, as the emergence of a radical antagonism at the very heart of ... globalization".[11] Certainly, McCarthy's virtual excision of Islam suggests a desire to imagine what terrorism looks like without an external enemy. Perhaps that is why the novel never comes closer to Islam than a stray reference to a thief whose fingers have been cut off by cult members, or the proclamation by an old man met on the road that "There is no God and we are his prophets" (255, 170).

Baudrillard assures us that we do not need a theory of the death drive to understand terrorism.[12] Slavoj Žižek would disagree to the

---

[7]   Slavoy Žižek, *Violence: Six Side-Ways Reflections*, New York: Picador, 2008, 27.
[8]   Jean Baudrillard, *The Spirit of Terrorism* (2002), trans. Chris Turner, 2nd edn, London: Verso, 2003, 5.
[9]   *Ibid.*, 6, 7.
[10] *Ibid.*, 10.
[11] *Ibid.*, 57.
[12] See *ibid.*, 6.

extent that he finds an element of barbarism in human nature. Žižek
says that "every clash of civilizations is really a clash of underlying
barbarisms"; all too often, human beings "falsify clues so that a catastrophe which is a 'suicide' (the result of immanent antagonisms) appears as the work of a criminal agent".[13] If people in McCarthy's
post-apocalyptic world once sought a scapegoat, that time has passed.
Recalling a night shortly before his son's birth when he and his wife
had sat at their window, "and watched distant cities burn", McCarthy's protagonist can only conclude that they inhabited "a creation
perfectly evolved to meet its own end" (59). Žižek, moreover, considers the relationship between subjective and systemic violence so "intricate" that he posits that "violence is not a direct property of some
acts, but is distributed between acts and their contexts, between activi-
ty and inactivity"; "sometimes doing nothing is the most violent thing
to do".[14] Certainly the extreme conditions of the post-apocalyptic
world support that conclusion. When the boy's father explains that "he
wasn't going to kill" a starving thief they left on the road, his son's
reply is irrefutable: "But we did kill him" (260).

With his characters required to put all of their energy into the Dar-
winian struggle of their dystopian existence, McCarthy creates a world
in which even the memory of modern life is lost: his hero never recalls
professional sports or films, gives no hint about what he did for a living. True, the scavengers occasionally find some relic of the old life,
like a telephone in an abandoned gas station; watching his father dial
his grandfather's number, the boy asks "What are you doing?" (4).
But more than the contents of an electronic consumer culture have
gone missing. America is beginning to resemble medieval and even
pre-historic Europe, with "cairns … signs in gypsy language, lost pat-
terans"[15] (180); at a crossroads the ground is "set with dolmen stones
where the spoken bones of oracles moldered" (261). Once there is
even a sign of pre-Columbian history, a "white quartz arrowhead, per-

---

[13]   Žižek, *Violence*, 212.
[14]   *Ibid.*, 213, 217.
[15]   The *OED* cites the following 1857 definition of the now obsolete word "patteran":
"the gypsy trail, the handful of grass which the gypsies strew in the roads as they
travel, to give information to any of their companions who may be behind, as to the
route they have taken" (*Oxford English Dictionary*, Third Edition, June 2005; online
version September 2011: http://www.oed.com/view/Entry/260831 [accessed 29 September 2011]).

fect as the day it was made" (203). The spirit of a distant past is reviving in the Yeatsian manner along with its artifacts, "Phantoms not heard from in a thousand years rousing slowly from their sleep" (116).

Of course the modern literary system, with its dependence on presses and computers, is as extinct as major league baseball or the United States Congress. Actual books are seldom encountered and never read. In an abandoned house the father picks up a "soggy" volume, opens it, and then puts it back (130); on a wrecked ship he finds "books in spanish [*sic*] strewn … swollen and shapeless" (226). Years earlier he had stood "in the charred ruins of a library where blackened books lay in pools of water". Then there were signs of vandalism: "Shelves tipped over. Some rage at the lies arranged in their thousands row on row." The father, not sharing this rage, discovers to his surprise that books "were predicated on a time to come", that even the space they continue to occupy "was itself an expectation" (187). Clearly, the romantic vision of art creating a better world has failed, but the allusiveness of *The Road* suggests that a classic view of literature telling essential truths about unchanging realities bears up as long as people do. From the "dark in the woods" to which the man awakes in the novel's first line of the novel to the footprint in the sand that alerts him to the presence of a thief near its end, the novel is woven of strands of pre-Romantic literature (3, 253).

Writing, too, seems to be disappearing; though the boy can write the alphabet, father and son no longer "work on his lessons" (245). Twice they consider the impulse to write down a "letter to the good guys" or simply record "that a living man spoke these lines", but they desist (245, 261). Though *The Road* tends to affirm rather than debunk classic literature, it also shows how the impulse to tell stories might follow print and writing into oblivion. Early on, the father tells his son "old stories of courage and justice as he remembered them", and the boy takes them to heart, repeatedly referring to "bad guys" and his belief that he and his father are the "good guys"; "this is what the good guys do", his father assures him, "they keep trying" (41, 137). Confident that they are "carrying the fire", the boy appears to believe his father's assurance that "nothing bad is going to happen to us" (83). But such reassurances ring hollow as the father's health deteriorates; toward the end, when he asks his son if he wants a story, the boy refuses. Stories, he says, are "not like real life"; when the father proposes that "a lot of bad things have happened but we're still here" is a story both truthful and valuable, the boy seems unpersuaded (269). A deeper problem is that as the referents of stories – crows and cowboys and bears – disappear, so does language, "the names of things slowly following those things into oblivion" (88). With them perish the words that name the "things one believed to be true ... the sacred idiom shorn of its referents and so of its reality" (89).

Yet those values, and some form of religious belief, do survive to the novel's end. Although knowledge of currency systems or computers have become irrelevant, the oldest motifs and impulses of the human condition match what reality remains, for example, Job's frequently evoked lament that we are born into trouble as "the sparks fly upward" (31, 96, 137, 169, 237). Fire and famine and fear remain as real as ever; the advice of Job's wife, "curse God and die", still offers a realistic and emotionally resonant possibility (114). After the boy's father dies, a small family, perhaps a community, finds him, identifying themselves as "good guys" who are "carrying the fire" (283). The last scene shows the boy keeping his promise to talk to his dead father, as a kind woman encourages him to believe "that the breath of God was his breath though it pass from man to man through all of time" (286). Possibly she, like the boy's father, believes in "a thing that even death cannot undo" (210). The novel's last paragraph is entirely ambiguous, evoking the lost trout of vanished streams whose backs bore "vermiculate patterns that were maps of the world in its becoming ... a thing ... that could not be made right again". Yet in the deep place they inhabited, "all things were older than man and they hummed with mystery" (287). As the boy's father wondered if giant squid in the depths of the ocean might have survived the catastrophe, a reader might wonder if life is renewing itself in distant invisible places.

Read through the lens of *Plotting Terror*, then, *The Road* takes us about as far toward the end of literature and revolution, the romantic vision of human beings making a better world, as we can imagine. Everything is in ruins and cannot be made right. From this perspective, the novel's allusions to Genesis and Job, its metaphor of carrying light in a dark time, are reminders of Morse Peck's old insight that "romanticism is spilt religion", or that the salvific vision of art in High Modernists like Joyce and Proust echoes the transcendent claims of Christianity. The possibility that the last paragraph contains a Christ image generations of college students have been taught to find in the

Quentin section of *The Sound and the Fury* is, again from this perspective, excessive if not embarrassing. But 9/11 also forces us to recognize a further relationship, between religion and terror. From a point of view widely articulated since 2001 by, among others, Christopher Hitchens, al-Qaeda's atrocities only confirm a truth abundantly illustrated in the Children's Crusade and the Spanish Inquisition: religion breeds messianic violence. For the native English, to whom it must sometimes seem that the only religious people are aliens, this perspective offers some solace.

Such solace is unavailable to Americans who acknowledge that religious literalism and enthusiasm can lead to barbarous actions. Many natives, particularly of the south and west where McCarthy sets his novels, embrace varieties of evangelical and fundamentalist Christianity as inhospitable to contemporary secular society as Wahhabism. That the two popular evangelists who took to the air waves on September 13, 2001 to blame "abortionists, feminists, gays and lesbians" for the attacks sounded much like the Islamic extremists who planned them was an irony almost too obvious to discuss.[3] All the same, the tie between religion and terror may be more interesting than a simplistic model of cause and effect suggests. Terry Eagleton argues that "terror begins as a religious idea ... and religion is all about deeply ambivalent powers which both enrapture and annihilate".[16] Following the encounter of the rational ruler Pentheus with Dionysus in Euripides' *Bacchae*, Pentheus is destroyed because, Eagleton argues, he "cannot see that reason, to be effective, must be rooted in forces which are not reasonable in themselves .... No ... rule of reason can flourish which does not pay its respects to the elements of unreason which lie at its heart."[17]

---

[3]   Jerry Falwell made the comment, to which Pat Robertson replied "I totally concur" on the 13 September 2001 telecast of the Christian Broadcasting Network's *Seven Hundred Club* (http://www.actupny.org/YELL/falwell.html [accessed 10 December 2009]). On the following day, Falwell told CNN that he "would never blame any human being except the terrorists" and apologized if he had given that impression. In his apology, however, he reiterated that the ACLU and other organizations "which have attempted to secularize America have removed our nation from its relationship with Christ on which it was founded" (http://archives.cnn.com/2001/US/09/14/Falwell.apology/ [accessed 10 December 2009]).

[16]   Terry Eagleton, *Reason, Faith, and Revolution: Reflections on the God Debate*, New Haven, CT: Yale University Press, 2009, 2.

[17]   *Ibid.*, 8.

In arguing that reason must acknowledge the "elements of unreason" that lie at its heart, Eagleton echoes Baudrillard and Žižek's argument that no war that frames terror as wholly alien to us can ever be won. Like Žižek, Eagleton looks for models of how human beings might realistically acknowledge their own irrationality and violence without conceding public life to the barbarians. Greek tragedy provides an important model for Eagleton, since it allows audiences to experience their own self-destructive impulses and sadism vicariously. Identification with the hero forces us to "act out a symbolic openness to our own mortality, yet because it is he, not us, who dies, this humility is laced with a triumphant sense of immortality".[18] Eagleton also agrees with Žižek that religion has become "one of the … places from which one can deploy critical doubts about today's society", even as "one of the sites of resistance".[19] Like tragedy, Christianity "touches on a certain ineluctability in things … which is scandalous to those contemporary thinkers who are in love with the contingent, the random, the perpetually protean". Because it shares tragedy's insight that "at the core of the self lies a power which makes it which it is, yet which is unutterably foreign to it", Christianity permits believers to acknowledge their own violence rather than project its image on the alien Other, "some hideous, misshapen creature which must be banished from [the] gates".[20]

The Road evokes the end times of an America where all the barbarians are native and where sending an army halfway around the world to extinguish terror is no longer feasible. Ever a protective father, its central character uses his last bullet to kill a cannibal who holds a knife to his child's throat, but also recognizes his affinity to that desperate stranger: "My brother at last" (75). He is a model of constancy and love who all the same marvels at his son's generosity in feeding another stranger encountered on the same road. When the recipient speculates that the boy believes in God and will "get over it", the father responds that he does not know what the boy believes, but knows "he won't" get over it (174). Neither, apparently, will the good people who welcome him into their family out of a disinterested generosity that matches his own.

---

[18]   *Ibid.*, 27
[19]   Žižek, *Violence*, 82.
[20]   Eagleton, *Reason, Faith, and Revolution*, 25, 140.

It is a fable, a myth, and not a political story, and an audience convinced that a selfless human being is as much of a fantasy as a talking rabbit will remain unconvinced. Yet this myth has work to do. It creates out of recognizably American materials – home-canned peaches and abandoned cars, T.S. Eliot's "Waste Land" and William Faulkner's haunted South, the ashes of September 11 and the shame and revulsion of Abu Ghraib – a world that bears little resemblance to the clashing ideological Americas proposed by, say, George Bush and Osama bin Laden.

For all its horrors, then, McCarthy's fictional America is not quite the Evil Satan of its worst enemies or the depthless Disneyland of its own satirists. It is a place where people remain recognizably human, their generosity as well as their violence more visible as the bounties of nature vanish with the consumer economy. These Americans have no illusions about their innocence or their invincibility; nonetheless among them are people who find plausible and useful some idea of a transcendent spirit that, for all their flaws, animates human beings and encourages them to find life sacred. McCarthy has imagined a world without terrorism only by projecting a world without politics, deconstructing the twenty-first century until its origins in barbarism are laid bare. Perhaps, muses his central character, "in the world's destruction it would be possible at last to see how it was made" (274). What Terry Eagleton says of Sophocles' plague-ridden Thebes may be equally true for McCarthy's dystopian America: that it is a place stripped bare so we can see what we must acknowledge about human nature before we can build a just and humane world.

Naturally many reviews of *The Road* and its film version express dismay at the story's bleakness, which such critics read as despair or hopelessness. A partisan of the novel is tempted to dismiss this response out of hand on the grounds that it runs too close to the familiar undergraduate complaint that any serious work of literature, whether *Oedipus Rex* or *Hamlet* or *Wuthering Heights*, is "too depressing". Yet even if we acknowledge that at least two of the novel's recurrent themes, violence and starvation, are current realities to which no easy solution offers itself, we may share the naive reader's desire for literature to affirm our capacity to create a better world, even as it underscores the evils of our own. For some readers, the apparent rescue of the nameless little boy at the end of *The Road* and the symbolism of the mysteriously vital trout will always seem to come too late, to be unearned, at odds with the novel's own logic of decline and loss. But we might consider reading the novel's ending through the eyes of a critic intimately acquainted with the apocalyptic imagination who adjures us to "brush history against the grain".

Walter Benjamin argued that "the tradition of the oppressed teaches us that the 'state of emergency' in which we live is not the exception but the rule", and that we must "attain to a conception of history that accords with this insight". Benjamin dismisses conventional "amazement" that the brutalities of the twentieth century are "'still' possible" as "*not* philosophical".[21] The destruction of the World Trade Center, like the adoption of the Nuremberg Laws or the torture of prisoners in Guantanamo Bay, seems like a vestige of the primitive past to middle-class people whose comfortable lives shelter them from the hunger, violence, and racism that are the daily experience of millions. Such a fundamentally Romantic conception of history assigns barbarism to the past because it identifies with the past's victors, whose spoils are our cultural history. But Benjamin's alternative conception of history recognizes that a true picture of the past is speeding by: to capture it one must seize "a memory as it flashes up in a moment of danger".[22]

Benjamin's famous image for such a history was Klee's "Angelus Novus", who, as we noted earlier, sees history as one long catastrophe. The angel "would like to … awaken the dead and … make whole what has been smashed", but "a storm … blowing from Paradise … has got caught up in his wings" and "drives him irresistibly into the future" as the rubble-heap before him grows sky-high. For Benjamin, "what we call progress is *this* storm".[23] Within a few months of writing these words, Benjamin committed suicide in a Spanish border town, apparently convinced that he was about to be handed back to the Vichy authorities. Yet his text implies a fragile possibility, not realized in his own life, that the notion of history as a single catastrophe carries a prospect of hope. As he notes in an addendum to "On the Concept of History", an alternative vision of history "establishes a

---

[21] Benjamin, "On the Concept of History", 392 (emphasis in original).
[22] *Ibid.*, 391.
[23] *Ibid.*, 392 (emphasis in original).

concept of the present as now-time shot through with splinters of messianic time".[24]

Benjamin's conception of "now-time" is easier to understand in an
aesthetic context than in a metaphysical one. *The Road* does not pre-
tend to document an actual history, but to create a fictional dystopia to
which the reader's actual present is a prelude. The reader is not
coaxed into believing that this story tells us, in Benjamin's phrase,
"how it really was".[25] Rather the reader's experience of history is
altered, disrupted, and must inhabit an imaginary world where a little
boy can drink what is apparently the last Coke in North America even
as he acknowledges that the refrigerator, or at least the local supermarket, is overflowing with Coca-Cola. When the novel's last paragraph evokes the superb trout on whose "backs were vermiculate
patterns that were maps of the world in its becoming", it takes us out
of the story's time, into an undated past that we belatedly acknowledge as our own present. But it also evokes "an even more ancient
time",[26] the mythic time of creation. From this perspective the beautiful image offers the reassurance we have all experienced, however
briefly, on waking up from a nightmare. The story we have just read,
however credible, makes no truth claims about politics, but it does
make one about the trout, whose breed still swim in the cold waters of
Montana, that they are more marvelous than we can understand and
imaginatively transport us to a world perpetually fresh and mysterious.
This is perhaps a vision of what it means for history to be "shot
through with splinters of messianic time", a time belonging neither to
the past or present but to a continuous reality. It is certainly part of
what it means for a novel to respond to terrorism, or to a war on
terrorism, without representing its key events or reproducing the rhetoric in which it is publicly debated. Perhaps it is also a model for how
the novel can confront terrorism without giving in to the all too plausible despair it often engenders.

---

24 *Ibid.*, 397.
25 *Ibid.*, 391.
26 Schaub, "Secular Scripture and Cormac McCarthy's *The Road*", 158.

LITERARY ACCOUNTS OF TERRORISM IN RECENT GERMAN LITERATURE: AN ATTEMPT AT MARGINALIZATION?

MICHAEL KÖNIG

Ten years after the attacks of September 11, 2001, the impact of the events still determines current German political and cultural debates. This can be seen in the repeated discussions about security and defense in the German public sphere, in controversies about problems of multiculturalism and the origins of home-grown terrorism, or in the heated debate about the extension of the mandate for the German *Bundeswehr* as part of the International Security Assistance Force (ISAF) in Afghanistan and the ensuing legal conflicts in international law. On a national level, the impact of the attacks become apparent in recurrent broadcasts on the "war on terrorism" in German public television, as well as in the death notes of German soldiers killed during their service abroad.

Against this historical backdrop, the present essay will outline recent developments in German literature pertaining specifically to the events of September 11. Whereas fiction written in the immediate aftermath of 9/11 and explicitly addressing the attacks tends to consider the latter as an aesthetic and poetic caesura, more recent texts move beyond 9/11, thus opening the door for broader discussions about the social and cultural implications of terrorism – such as the increasing surveillance of the public sphere or the possibilities of a counterculture established by a violent revolt against state control. The following discussion will attempt to explore the causes behind this shift (or widening of perspectives), arguing that the aesthetic sphere of literature strongly correlates with politics in this regard. The main questions to be addressed are: first, how does recent German literature respond to the cultural disorder of terrorism? And second, which aesthetic approaches are implicated in this response? As I shall demonstrate, the texts differ not only with respect to literary genre (there are post-9/11 short stories, novels, fictional reports, or weblog texts, to name but a few possibilities), but also in their respective narrative structures, that is, in how they address the events and to what extent they functionalize them within the narration. Moreover, they differ with respect to the impact that they ascribe to the attacks in relation to their characters as well as, most crucially, in the moral issues that they raise – issues that have implications outside of the aesthetic sphere.

The first wave of German post-9/11 fiction
A number of German writers reacted to the events of September 11 with contributions beginning on the day of the attacks and continuing until 2008. The texts published shortly after the attacks reflect a deep and disruptive lack of perception, which is related to the unfathomable dimensions of the events themselves as well as to their subsequent representations in the media. Such texts document a dominant personal crisis. They address the lack of comprehension, lost sense of reality, and direct impact of the tragic deaths of 3,000 innocent victims in both towers of the World Trade Center. Most authors respond to the disruption with diary-like fictions that adhere to strictly chronological narrative patterns. Furthermore, they withdraw from the situation with the help of self-referentiality and inwardness in order to deal with grief and trauma. As a general trend, the events inspire reflections about the overlap between ethics and poetics in the period following 9/11. Authors like Ulrich Peltzer or Kathrin Röggla and Else Buschheuer (the latter two both young female German writers who lived and worked in Manhattan during September 2001) understand the tragic attacks mainly as a biographical and aesthetic caesura.

Ulrich Peltzer interprets the collapse of the World Trade Center as a split or cut, as is reflected in the narrative structure of his novel *Bryant Park*. The first section of the novel deals with the young German historian Stefan Matenaar who is in the USA to conduct genealogical research, but instead wastes his time on the terrace of the New York Public Library. Suddenly, in the middle of that plot, a completely new narrative sets in, indicated by a capital letter.[1] We are introduced to a person called "ulrich" (*sic*),[2] an apparently different narrator (and probably the author of the novel) who tells us about himself during the late afternoon of September 11. Then, in almost the same

---

[1] See Ulrich Peltzer, *Bryant Park* (2002), Berlin: Berliner Taschenbuch Verlag, 2004, 134.
[2] *Ibid.*, 139.

manner, the novel abruptly switches back to the previous story about the German historian in New York. What first seems like an unmotivated demolition of the story – a judgment pronounced in various reviews[3] – upon closer inspection turns out to be a carefully devised and coherent way of handling the terrorist attacks in literary form. This is suggested by the novel itself, which at a certain point emphasizes the effects of split screens, visual and audio cuts, scratches and movie-interruptions. The whole text consists of several nonlinear narratives that are marked as memories which the protagonist recalls while sitting in New York's Bryant Park during his breaks. Among them is a visit to his friend Nils, a drug dealer, in the projection room of a shabby cinema. Stefan Matenaar meticulously remembers every detail of the screening technology and every single one of his friend's gestures when loading and changing the film roles in order to deliver a trouble-free illusion to the audience:

> I, wriggling myself between the equipment, came to Nils, who was standing at the film table, observing how a film segment ran screechingly from its plastic nucleus upon a role with wire-like spoke crossings, on which he held his right hand to stop it, whenever one of the strips of white tape that mark the beginning or the end became visible. …. Hardly recognizable due to the momentum of the film reel, these white marks on the edge of the film between individual scenes, end or beginning, foot or head, were edges that needed to be glued together very precisely in order to avoid interruptions, cropped images and audio glitches, those not planned as artistic gestures during the presentation, split screens and similar effects. A white dot flashed, and Nil's palm lowered itself onto the slick edge of the film role, slowed it, while he took care not to land his fingers under the spokes. As if he had noticed me between the projectors, or as if he had not expected someone else, he welcomed me saying my name without even raising his head. I would be his last guest for today.[4]

---

[3]   See, for example, Stephan Krass, "Der Zipfel der Wahrheit", *Neue Zürcher Zeitung*, 21 March 2002, 35; Volker Weidermann, "Die Wörter sind unter uns. Die Bücher zum 11. September sind da: Lauter Katastrophen – bis auf Ulrich Peltzer", *Frankfurter Allgemeine Sonntagszeitung*, 17 February 2002, 27.

[4]   Peltzer, *Bryant Park*, 58, 61-62 (my translation).

Obviously, the text's emphasis on the intricacies of screening film so as to create a seamless illusion reflects not only on the technical but also on the aesthetic manner of depicting the attacks, and thus implicitly on the poetic requirements for providing an undisturbed aesthetic appearance. With this scene, the text self-referentially reflects its own poetic procedure of narrative interruption: the author interprets the events as a moment of disruption and implements this interpretation poetically as a cut in his own text. A completely new and different story flashes into the first narrative taking place at Bryant Park.

Like *Bryant Park*, several texts published shortly after the attacks integrate the persona of the author into the fiction; in some cases, the narrative is identified as the product of its own fictional setting (in the fashion of a *mise en abyme*). These texts ask whether or not writing after the attacks is still possible from an aesthetic and, more importantly, from an ethical point of view. Their very subjectivity and introspection seem to legitimize the inability of the texts to deal with the lack of poetic resources caused by the gravity of the events. The literary descriptions of the disaster serve predominantly to recover the integrity of both characters and authors alike.

The desire of protagonists and authors for veracity and documentation is a significant attribute of these writings. Similarly, the texts enact a substitution, replacing the symbolic gap caused by the terrorist attacks in various ways. While early 9/11 texts, as mentioned above, follow a strong chronological order, they are not able to re-establish integrity or sovereignty – for example, the power of interpretation – and remain within a fragmentary narrative style. Yet they are highly reflective. Kathrin Röggla's journalistic report *really ground zero* (2004), a text which mixes documentation and narration, tells us about the days after the attacks. A short title precedes every single entry of Röggla's diary-like fiction, but there is no notable continuity or formal structure to the text. The urgent depiction – the narrator takes part in a peace demonstration and memorial party, interviews pedestrians on the streets, and takes photos of missing-persons posters in lower Manhattan – lacks any sort of concept. The narrator is the only authority who keeps the various entries together. While she is always characterized by her narrative agency, she constantly calls herself and common ways of talking about the events into question. Thus, she distinguishes between the real space of the attacks and their representations in the media. The "real events" or, in the words of her title, "really ground zero", cannot be told or described in a literary text:

> ... the mixture of death-zone, nuclear fallout area and lunarscape cannot be illustrated. It seems over-exposed, weird and two-dimensional, because the brownish white swallows every contrast and negates spatial depth. It cements the picture into black and white.[5]

What therefore emerge as striking qualities of early German 9/11 literature are mediality, reflectivity, and an awareness of the poetic "program", that is, programmatic ideas of how to write about the events. Moreover, these early texts explore the ethical implications of the writing process, raising the question of whether one may write about the attacks and the collapsed buildings, as well as the jumpers and the murdered, while standing on the sidelines. Early texts ask how writing is possible from a spatial and cultural distance.

The fact that German literature about September 11 was always bound by generally asserted claims in the media, and was therefore caught between the will for free expression and strong statements in literary and cultural supplements, reviews, articles, and radio shows, leads to additional moral considerations. No wonder that Bodo Kirchhoff, a German author, immediately declared "Now it takes you and your book"[6] after he had learned about the attacks while sitting in a train to his next reading show, and a woman in the same compartment had suddenly started crying. Kirchhoff's fear, which he describes in an article citing the reactions of different German writers, is easy to explain. He was afraid that 9/11 could influence the perception of both his recently published texts and those on which he was currently working. On closer examination, Kirchhoff's considerations strike the heart of the entire German debate. How to react to 9/11 was not merely decided by the authors themselves, but was also strongly determined by the media and public discourse. Nevertheless, authors do not write about September 11 in a unified manner – instead, they react to the terrorist attacks in very different ways. They assert, to a greater or

---

[5]   Kathrin Röggla, *really ground zero: 11. september und folgendes*, Frankfurt on Main: S. Fischer, 2004, 9 (my translation).

[6]   Bodo Kirchhoff, *Der Spiegel*, 8 October 2001, 228 (my translation). Kirchhoff's statements are part of the article "Literatur: Vorbeben der Angst" by Volker Hage.

lesser extent, their claim to express their own feelings and thoughts, or even subvert verdicts raised in the media. The diary as literary genre – in Buschheuer's case, her internet-diary *www.else-buschheuer.de* – legitimizes their deep and sometimes non-reflective feelings.

The problematic setting of strong moral standards on the one hand, and the likewise strong will for free literary expression on the other, led for instance to the assumption that the German author Max Goldt deliberately eschewed public judgments. The humorous author, who addresses the events in various entries of his diary fiction *Wenn man einen weißen Anzug anhat* (*When One Wears a White Suit*, 2002), only briefly refers to the days before and after the attacks. At first sight, he cynically rejects public gestures of consternation. The fictitious narrator holds the minute of silence, as he says, simply because "in the first place, there is no one I could talk to".[7] The ubiquitously repeated sentence: "Nothing will ever be the same again" only leads him to reflect on the fact that the word "between-seasons jacket"[8] has now a very different meaning. The narrator's remarks seem absurd and petty. However, upon a closer look, Goldt offers highly reflected thoughts on literary commentary in times of deep mourning. With the comparison between Paul Celan's poem "Todesfuge" ("Death Fugue"), written between 1944 and 1945,[9] and the humoristic poem "Die Made" ("The Maggot") by the German comedian Heinz Erhardt, who was mainly famous in the late 1950s, in one of his odd and anecdotal columns, the narrator explores the question of whether aesthetic pleasure is permissible when its object has emerged from experiences of vast sorrow.

The point is significant in light of the fact that Celan's poem addresses the Jewish author's horrible impressions from Rumanian labor camps during the Nazi dictatorship.[10] Ruminating on Celan's poem in connection with the attendant question of its possible enjoy-

---

[7] Max Goldt, *Wenn man einen weißen Anzug anhat*, Reinbek: Rowohlt, 2002, 26 (my translation).
[8] *Ibid.*, 22 (my translation).
[9] Paul Celan, "Todesfuge" (1948), in *Ausgewählte Gedichte*, Frankfurt on Main: Suhrkamp, 1970, 18-19.
[10] See Volker Mergenthaler's important statement on this issue: "Celan wieder(ge)holt: Zur poetischen Produktivmachung kultureller Tradition in Max Goldts 'Tagebuch-Buch' *Wenn man einen weißen Anzug anhat*", *Trans: Internet-Zeitschrift für* Kulturwissenschaften, XVI, n.p.: http://www.inst.at/trans/16Nr/02_1/ mergenthaler16.htm (accessed 2 June 2010).

ment, the narrator in Goldt's diary fiction refers to what is known as the debate about lyric poetry after Auschwitz, particularly to Theodor W. Adorno's dictum that writing after Auschwitz shall remain reserved only for the direct victims. Transferred to the statements about the recent terrorist attacks in Manhattan, this reference constitutes an implicit interdiction for the non-participant narrator to issue his statement in light of the deaths of nearly 3,000 innocent people. Consequently, the narrator indirectly decides to abstain. This act puts another complexion on the following passage: "I do not read newspapers today", comments the narrator on the day after:

> You can easily imagine what is written in them. The level of knowledge from TV yesterday evening, garnished with several comments from writers and actors, who always put their pre-formulated notes next to the phone after such events, hoping that they will be called by the media.[11]

The primarily superficial and defiant approach in Goldt's diary fiction is therefore, upon closer inspection, a conscious and deliberate abstention or decent silence.

The second wave
A second wave of texts appeared between the middle of 2005 and the end of 2006. In these more recent texts, which were published with a greater temporal distance to the attacks, the events of September 11, 2001 are still an important and integral part of the narration: while the attacks persist as a functional biographical turning point or plot trigger, 9/11 is just one part of a larger narrative construction and no longer its principal thematic focus. The notable deep rupture found in earlier works is replaced by an attempt to functionalize the events within the narrative.

These more recent German 9/11 novels share various features. For instance, several of them take place in foreign countries or cities (such as London and New York), whose alien topographies trigger different kinds of identity crises. Through representations of hybrid situations of temporarily exiled characters, the texts provide different views on either American or German culture.

---

[11]   Goldt, *Wenn man einen weißen Anzug anhat*, 23 (my translation).

The title character of Pia Frankenberg's *Nora*[12] is a German woman who left Germany in the late 1970s after her mother had denounced her for being a member of the Red Army Faction (RAF), a radical terrorist group. Now living in New York, Nora watches television on the morning of the attacks. Among the New Yorkers present at the scene, she notices a crying woman, the young mother Amy, who lost her husband in one of the towers. Nora begins to stalk Amy after she has met her again by chance in a supermarket. The novel ends with a political discussion about American foreign policy and state action in times of unknown terrorist threats. It links various discourses about the American present with the German past, especially the German history of terrorism, while it also traces Nora's process of identity formation.

The same applies to Susanne Riedel's *Eine Frau aus Amerika* (*A Woman from America*).[13] The male protagonist Hannes left Germany almost thirty years ago. He remembers his hometown of Berlin as grey, rainy, cold, and full of unfriendly inhabitants. His wife Sharon becomes a direct eyewitness of the attacks on September 11, and returns home traumatized. Hannes cannot help her. Their relationship gets increasingly complicated until Sharon finally dies from asystole (cardiac arrest) after a fierce quarrel. Hannes thereafter flies to Berlin, where he finds out that Sharon originally was an adopted German-Jewish orphan who grew up in the United States, though she never told him about her Jewish origins. Hannes falls into deep mourning. The events of 9/11 have alienated him from his wife. While 9/11 serves as a trigger for the subsequent fateful and partly unreliable plot, the text's implicit concern seems to be to provide evidence for the lasting harm that has been done to the Jewish people by the Germans. The novel consists of different diary entries written by Hannes and reveals all kinds of German prejudices against Americans in general and allegedly typical American behavior in particular.

In Katharina Hacker's *Die Habenichtse* (*The Have-nots*),[14] a German couple meets on September 11 after they had lost sight of each other for almost ten years. They move to London because a colleague of the protagonist, Jakob, died in the World Trade Center and Jakob takes his job. In this novel, 9/11 functions as the most crucial part of

---

[12]   Pia Frankenberg, *Nora*, Berlin: Rowohlt, 2006.
[13]   Susanne Riedel, *Eine Frau aus Amerika*, Berlin: Berlin Verlag, 2003.
[14]   Katharina Hacker, *Die Habenichtse*, Frankfurt on Main: Suhrkamp, 2006.

the narrative, since the whole love story would not have been possible without the terrorist attacks. The date of the attacks symbolically represents the foundation of their relationship, since the couple has met again after ten years on September 11. The death of Jakob's colleague makes it possible for them to move to the British capital. Because the text starts *in medias res* and is told through varying narratives, from different points of view, it is 9/11 which lends the multi-layered novel its basic narrative structure. Moreover, the war preparations for the Third Gulf War in Iraq and the fear of a terrorist attack in the British capital produce a permanent background noise. However, even though Jakob and Isabelle's whole relationship is based on the tragic and symbolic date, neither of them can fill the date with their own meaning. They remain the "have-nots" mentioned in the title. Their "adamant aimlessness",[15] highlighted by a literary critic, is very significant.

In Thomas Hettche's *Woraus wir gemacht sind (That Which We Are Made of)*,[16] once again a German couple, the young writer Niklas Kalf and his pregnant wife Liz, flies to Manhattan one year after September 11. On the morning of the Memorial Day, Liz vanishes without a trace. An odyssey starts across the country, from East to West coast, and finally leads Niklas from the small city of Marfa, Texas, to the Pacific Palisades of Los Angeles. During this journey, Niklas suffers an identity crisis, feeling lost in the middle of the Texan desert. The alien topography dominates the narration, which undertakes an analysis and comparison of cultural identities. Like Hettche's novel and several other German 9/11-texts published in recent years, *Woraus wir gemacht sind* addresses issues like nationality and foreignness, historical memory – for instance, about America's role in the Second World War – and current American foreign policies.

Moreover, recent texts bring into focus the vulnerable corporality of their protagonists. In Marlene Streeruwitz's novel *Entfernung. (sic) (Distance.)*,[17] the attacks on the London tube on July 7, 2005 rather than the attacks on the World Trade Center are part of a latent scena-

---

[15] Meike Fessmann, "Unerbittliche Ziellosigkeit", *Süddeutsche Zeitung*, 5 April 2006, 16 (my translation).

[16] Thomas Hettche, *Woraus wir gemacht sind*, Cologne: Kiepenheuer und Witsch, 2006.

[17] Marlene Streeruwitz, *Entfernung.*, Frankfurt on Main: S. Fischer, 2006.

rio of constant terrorist threat. Selma Brechthold, the forty-nine-year-old protagonist, is plagued by a deep existential and biographical crisis. She had worked as a cultural manager until she was dismissed because of a younger and probably more attractive female assistant. Her longstanding partner left her after he had admitted his paternity of a young child from a secret relationship with another woman. Selma travels to London, in order to meet an old friend and to take a last chance for a job. Realizing quickly that her plan is totally desperate, she leaves the disappointing meeting. On the next morning, she becomes a victim of the bomb attack. Selma survives wounded, refuses medical care, and strays traumatized through the inscrutable urban spheres of the huge British capital. The story ends as Selma continues walking confused and disoriented around the city. The novel depicts a history of suffering and the permanent presence of terror, especially in Selma's thoughts as she fearfully notices several CCTV cameras, or in her drastic visions of 9/11. Among other things, she imagines inhaling dead bodies as grey dust and thus preserving the dead that were killed in the rubble of the collapsed Twin Towers.

Although the terrorist act has a deep impact both on Selma's body and thoughts and the imagination of 9/11 is depressing, the text itself seems unaffected in poetic or aesthetic terms. 9/11 is no longer the central subject of the novel, and neither are the terrorist attacks on the London underground. The terrorist threat is only one of the corporal dangers that Selma suffers over the course of the narrative. That the narrative setting connects a foreign topography with the protagonist's identity crisis is one of the thematic similarities between Streeruwitz's novel and other 9/11 texts. The novel depicts its protagonist's vulnerability without identifying 9/11 as its sole cause. 9/11 is juxtaposed with other forms of mental and physical violence. The novel furthermore makes clear that the original meaning of the terrorist attacks as a poetically endangering impact has changed. Former aspects that were attributed to September 11, such as a crisis of perception and writerly expression and an aesthetic and poetic caesura, are hardly recognizable here any longer.

Accordingly, in Thomas Pletzinger's novel *Bestattung eines Hundes* (*Burial of a Dog*),[18] the attacks of September 11 are just mentioned in a few sentences, and it is hard to explain why they are re-

---

[18]	Thomas Pletzinger, *Bestattung eines Hundes*, Cologne: Kiepenheuer und Witsch, 2008.

ferred to at all. It is remarkable that not a single text depicts the attacks themselves. Not a single text presents immediate victims (Amy's husband in Frankenberg's novel truly is an exception), and not a single character directly bears physical consequences of the collapses. Nor does any text offer an action-packed and thrilling plot, which seems reserved for the more commercial section of crime fiction and literature about espionage. The texts seem to refuse direct fictionalization and the depiction of the tragedy as predominantly "American". Not a single author asserts his or her own aesthetic autonomy against the heteronomy of the events, or in other words, sets his or her poetic will against the independence of the real. There is neither pure fiction nor pure factuality. Early German post-9/11 fiction offers a more factographical approach. While it unfolds fictional parts, it still contains identifiable historical facts. This leads me to the conclusion that early 9/11 fiction is thoroughly marked by a deep narrative crisis. The authors react to the tragic events in a paradoxical way: They cope with the narrative crisis through their own act of writing, in which they, in turn, address their writing problems.

No wonder that "having-to-write, not-being-able-to-sleep, having-to-stay" ("Schreibenmüssen, Nichtschlafenkönnen, Bleibenmüssen") is the motto of one of the entries in Buschheuer's internet diary shortly after September 11, 2001.[19] She seems to manage the trauma through her own dialogic writing. Although some protagonists in German post-9/11 fiction seemingly communicate deep sorrow, there is no antagonistic return to emotional forms of literary expression. At the same time, the trauma does not appear to yield experimental literary forms. Each analyzed text responds to the terrorist attacks in its very own way; the body of German post-9/11 fiction lacks a single unified narrative of the tragic events. And that finally leads me to recent texts about terrorism and politically motivated violence.

The most recent German terrorism fiction
Aside from German literary publications that directly engage with the tragic events of 9/11, recent texts reveal a broader scope concerning the phenomenon of international terrorism. Where 9/11 texts range, as we have seen, from strategies of withdrawal and fragmentation to

---

[19] Else Buschheuer, *www.else-buschheuer.de: Das New York Tagebuch*, Cologne: Kiepenheuer und Witsch, 2002, 205.

strategies of normalization and aestheticization, I would like to focus now on texts that take into consideration historical and political perspectives, the impact of terrorism on social behavior in connection with influences from the state or the media, and the depiction of perpetrators and terrorist acts themselves. Although German literature about September 11 shows a wide variety of approaches, many recent literary fictions fail to examine the phenomenon of terrorism, or to take a close look at the perpetrators and their social backgrounds. Authors who undertake this endeavor include Sherko Fatah, Ulrich Peltzer and Christoph Peters. By moving beyond 9/11, these texts open the door for broader discussion about the social and cultural implications of terrorist disruptions.

Preliminary analyses show that there are mainly four groups of themes and procedures that can be found in recent German literature about terrorism. First, there is what I call "literary paranoia". Quite a few texts link terrorism to different aspects of public surveillance and control of space. They play with the disorder of the system through terrorism, the increasing paranoia and the need for preventive security measures. And they discuss a possible revolt against these measures. In Ulrich Peltzer's *Teil der Lösung* (*Part of the Solution*),[20] Christian, a middle-aged and indebted free journalist, is engrossed in the story of the Red Brigades, an Italian terrorist group that committed several attacks between 1970 and 1988. Peltzer's text addresses controversial issues in recent debates about the political and social implications of the terrorist threat, such as CCTV, surveillance, and the increasing control of the public sphere. In this novel, it is not the terrorist acts that are dangerous because of their unpredictable and random nature – the danger rather seems to arise from government methods of surveillance and observation. The state can be anywhere, anytime.

It is not a coincidence that the text has recourse to the dark and defeatist movie *Escape from New York* (1981, dir. John Carpenter), which creates a terrifying, dystopian vision of the future. In 1997, the whole city of New York has become the most dangerous place on earth. Manhattan is surrounded by a "containment wall" and is used as a prison. Convicts are imprisoned for life, and escape has been made impossible. The main character Snake Plissken (played by Kurt Russell) is on a tough mission. He needs to rescue the President, whose

[20] Ulrich Peltzer, *Teil der Lösung*, Zurich: Ammann, 2007.

plane has crashed between the waste buildings on the Big Apple, and he has little time to do so. The references to this movie suggest that Peltzer's text participates in the recent security debate. At one point in the novel, an agent of the German state security questions the range of governmental control when he asks:

> "Where is the threat to our society, and where shall we concentrate our means? How do we define national security and police protection after the events of September 11?"[21]

The text itself imitates the effects of permanent monitoring as well as fragmentary police investigations. Through the mounting paranoia and desire for security measures, the public perception of the terrorist threat, even in the aesthetic sphere of literature, marks a shift from "disciplinary society" to "control society".[22]

And that leads to the second aspect, which I call the "myth of a counterculture". *Teil der Lösung* directly connects the depiction of politically motivated violence with the idea of an anarchistic protest movement. Like other texts, it issues a fundamental critique of the system and the impact of globalization, and it imagines ways of rallying against these forces. Recent "terror" texts examine the currency of violent resistance against institutional paternalism or the idea of violent revolution as the beginning of a social utopia.

These texts show that, thirdly, recent German literature about terrorism is characterized by a strong movement toward re-politicization. It engages with German history and politics and hence with the terrorism of the Red Army Faction in the Seventies and Eighties. Discussions about German terrorism have become more urgent in the last few years, first when Brigitte Mohnhaupt and Eva Haule, both former terrorist of the RAF, were released from custody in 2007; again, when the former German Federal President had to decide on the reprieve of detained German RAF terrorists Christian Klar and Birgit Hogefeld; and most recently, when Verena Becker, also a former RAF-member, who had already been reprieved in 1989, was again suspected, as the

---

[21] *Ibid.*, 351 (my translation).
[22] See *Bild – Raum – Kontrolle: Videoüberwachung als Zeichen gesellschaftlichen Wandels*, eds Jörg Metelmann and Leon Hempel, Frankfurt on Main: Suhrkamp, 2005.

result of DNA analysis, of murdering the Federal Public Prosecutor Siegfried Buback in 1977.

Fourth, some recent "terror" texts pursue analyses of foreign perpetrators and their ideological and religious frames of mind. Sherko Fatah's novel *Das dunkle Schiff* (*The Dark Ship*)[23] emphasizes the cultural differences between Western liberal and Muslim culture, as he places an Alevite as a stowaway in a dark ship from Asia to Europe. It is remarkable that the male protagonist, Kerim, does not become a fundamentalist until he arrives in Europe, although his hatred derives from horrible events years before. In the poignant introductory scene, the then young protagonist becomes a witness to one of the seemingly common repressions of the Alevite minority in Iraq. A helicopter lands close to peasant women collecting herbs in the surrounding hills, loads them and takes off, only to soon throw them out again. In *Ein Zimmer im Haus des Krieges* (*A Room in the House of War*),[24] Christoph Peters writes about the German convert Jochen "Abdallah" Sawatzky, who becomes a member of an Egyptian terrorist group that plans a massacre on tourists. The attack fails and Sawatzky is arrested. During subsequent talks with the German ambassador in Egypt, Sawatzky betrays that he is still trapped in his religious and misanthropic thoughts. Both authors try to understand terrorist mindsets and aesthetically capitalize upon these foreign cultural spheres, yet their attempts turn out to be short sighted.

While Fatah provides an impressive portrait of a foreign fundamentalist and Peters depicts the personal background of a miserably failed, middle-aged drug-dealer, the reasons for their respective hatred remain mysterious. Still Fatah's and Peters' novels seem to be exceptions since most authors do not endeavor to understand the intricacies of foreign terrorist mindsets, motivations, and fascinations. Instead, their perspectives are unsatisfyingly confined to the European cultural sphere. They do not want, as Frauke Meyer-Gosau observes, "to enter the enemy's mind".[25] But why is that?

---

[23] Sherko Fatah, *Das dunkle Schiff*, Salzburg: Jung und Jung, 2008.
[24] Christoph Peters, *Ein Zimmer im Haus des Krieges*, Munich: btb, 2007.
[25] Frauke Meyer-Gosau, "Versuch, den Kopf des Feindes zu entern", *Literaturen*, 9 (2006), 54-61.

Conclusion: the culture of fear

Literature seems to correlate with politics in this respect. Preliminary findings suggest that we live in a culture of fear. Terrorism creates fear – that much seems obvious. What seems equally obvious is that rhetorical strategies of talking about the phenomenon reinforce that fear and that they are, in turn, productive of terror. It is therefore important to ask whether there is a direct link between the Western culture of fear and acts of symbolic terrorism aimed directly at the heart of Western societies. Changes in how we deal with the terrorist threat are immediately apparent in current discussions. Whereas former debates concentrated on questions such as whether the violent means to achieve political and social goals is acceptable or not, today we only wonder what kind of security measures can prevent terrorist attacks and how to secure the public sphere. Discussions have shifted from a broader focus, taking into account ideological issues, to a much narrower perspective that seems all too defeatist. The only issues placed on political agendas today are how to shelter the citizenry from alleged attacks and how to justify comprehensive security measures.

In public discourse, there are scarcely any attempts to understand the reasons for terrorism on a political level (for example, by questioning the emergence of Islamism out of nationalism in Muslim countries) or from a cultural standpoint (for example, by questioning the origins of a feeling of Western cultural dominance). Instead, the terrorist threat is referred to not only as a physical threat, but also as a potentially ideological danger with an infective potential, or as a kind of psychological virus. Due to its unpredictable and random character, it gets assigned a kind of almightiness that does not really correspond to its actual political dimensions. "In recent years, resilience has emerged as a key concept among emergency planners",[26] states the British sociologist Frank Furedi. Indeed, it seems that fear has become the crucial element of political discourse, and that a concept of resilience that encourages the image of vulnerability (of highly developed Western economies) has caused a fatalistic dread of terrorism. Out of the struggle against terrorism, politics attempts to achieve self-confidence and to generate social cohesion.

---

[26] Frank Furedi, *Invitation to Terror: The Expanding Empire of the Unknown*, London and New York: Continuum, 2007, 18.

No wonder, then, that the EU defines itself mainly in terms of a high-security society and a victim society (which could be noticed after the attacks in London and in Madrid). Commenting on statements to the effect that a terrorist attack may occur anywhere, anytime, Furedi observes:

> These are statements that constitute a public acknowledgement of confusion and fear. They represent an invitation to be terrorized.[27]

It really seems, as Furedi states, that Western cultures contain an inability to provide a meaningful account of the issues at stake.[28] The intellectual, scientific and moral heritage of Western culture seems to arouse more and more suspicion about itself. This feeling partly originates in the shock about the attacks of September 11, as Werner Jung described it shortly after the tragic events:

> The sense of security is gone, formerly known certainties and everyday life have to be placed under question or have disappeared altogether. The experience of risk in our society has forced its way into the foreground.[29]

Recent German literature about terrorism reflects on these common self-doubts. It offers different, sometimes extreme modes of cultural criticism – not in the least in the form of radicalization. This leads me back to Ulrich Peltzer's novel *Teil der Lösung*, where a German security officer considers the motives of the young urban guerilla in the German capital of Berlin:

> If you were young and unsatisfied about the condition of the world, disgusted by poverty and hunger, by increasing unemployment, and it dawned upon you that you do not have any legal opportunities to change anything. No mass movement, no political party that you could join. Instead the fiddle of politicians, who you thought were responsible, and bankers, who earn as much money as one million Africans during one year. That radicalizes one automatically.[30]

---

[27] *Ibid.*, 11.
[28] *Ibid.*, 19.
[29] Werner Jung, "Bombenstimmung", *Neues Deutschland*, VII/VIII (September 2002), 18 (my translation).
[30] Peltzer, *Teil der Lösung*, 349-50 (my translation).

Despite Europe's ongoing political confrontation with the phenomenon of terrorism the impact of the attacks on the World Trade Center has been fading within the sphere of literature. In 2008, the editorial team of one of the most popular German literary histories suggested that the process of literarizing 9/11 has come to a close.[31] Later that same year, the German weekly review *Die Zeit* even announced "The End of 9/11", arguing that the "intellectual enjoyment of the state of emergency" appears to be over and that "a return to a normal liberal position" (owing to judicial decisions by the German Federal Constitutional Court) can be noticed.[32]

Against the background of these developments, it is important to investigate how literature relates to political discourse, and how it aesthetically and poetically handles the rhetorical construction of vulnerability and resilience. With regard to literature about terrorism, the quoted headline – "The End of 9/11" – has to be called into question. It would perhaps be too much to demand a politically engaged literature, but in this context literature has become contentious again. Complex events require equally complex aesthetic and poetic approaches and call for a complex and deep analysis. Scholars should analyze the connection between social responses to certain events and their reflections in literature. Moreover, the social impact of technological developments such as CCTV, the use of radio-frequency identification, or government data-mining needs to be explored: how do these innovations correlate with new modes of social behavior, such as the careless use of social networking services? How does literature, in an assumed liaison between text and cultural context, take part in social and political changes? How could literature possibly change our perception of the terrorist threat? Are there texts that convey the possibility of cultural intermediation?

Literature reveals much about a nation's self-conception. Most recent German "terror" texts do not deal with non-Western cultures; they neither seek to understand the differences between "us" and "them" nor do they ask for the reasons for the increasing number of terrorist attacks. In my view, such inquiries are missing as much from

---

[31] See *Deutsche Literaturgeschichte: Von den Anfängen bis zur Gegenwart*, eds Wolfgang Beutin *et al.*, Stuttgart and Weimar: Metzler, 2008, 717.

[32] Heinrich Wefing, "Das Ende von 9/11", in *Die Zeit*, 20 November 2008, 1 (my translation).

recent German literature as they are from politics. The texts rather evoke our own cultural mindset and explore our own cultural dissatisfaction in times of political and, lately, economic crises. In this respect they appear highly introspective, even navel-gazing. Where early 9/11 texts had to deal with the impossible depiction of the unbelievable events of September 11 and the ensuing trauma, recent "terror" texts broaden the scope, but at the same time still remain caught within their own cultural sphere and therefore disregard the complexity of the terrorist threat as a cross-cultural problem – and that truly is an attempt at marginalization.

Narrativizations of Terror:
Media and Modes, Plot and Form

DOUBLE-MEDIATED TERRORISM: GERHARD RICHTER AND DON DELILLO'S "BAADER-MEINHOF"

ULRICH MEURER

Almost everyone is familiar with Jacques-Louis David's classicist painting of the dead Jean Paul Marat in his bathtub. In terms of public awareness, it is closely followed by the engraving that depicts the assassination of Abraham Lincoln, published 1865 by the New York printmaking firm Currier and Ives. Even more pivotal "icons of terror", deeply embedded in our cultural consciousness, are provided by the Zapruder amateur film shot on Dallas' Dealey Plaza – so formative that even reenactments of the event for the cinema or TV tend to imitate its grainy home movie aesthetics and unsteady *mise-en-scène*.[1] Then there are the press photos and film stills of police officials in tracksuits on the roof of the athletes' accommodations in Munich; a Lufthansa-airplane waiting on the landing runway in Mogadishu;[2] the odd honeycomb-like structure of the Alfred P. Murrah federal building in Oklahoma City stripped of its façade; a bulky white cloud hovering over Manhattan Island; the glaucous frontal view of the Moscow musical theater's stage and a handful of blurred masked figures.

Certainly, these images differ in terms of their political function. With growing historical distance, they can bear witness to a collective past and, just like David's famous painting, become agents of national pride. Don DeLillo in "The Power of History" refers to photographs

---

[1]   See, for example, Gordon Davidson and David Green's two-part ABC television film *The Trial of Lee Harvey Oswald* (1977) that restages the assassination on location in Dallas.

[2]   The image takes a prominent place in Johan Grimonprez's video-essay *Dial H-I-S-T-O-R-Y* (1998). The film explores the media's obsession with airplane hijackings from the 1960s to '90s by compiling TV coverage and voiceovers from Don DeLillo's novels *White Noise* and *Mao II*.

by Mathew Brady which might well show Civil War carnage, but nevertheless evoke an undamaged relationship to an exalted and heroic era.[3] By contrast, videotapes or TV images of violence create an entirely different kind of social bond. They add to a proliferate consumerism by fusing isolated private and collective experience: "On the one hand, a past is imagined in which shared meaning attaches to resonant, nationally significant events; on the other, a present is conceived in which occasions of symbolic contiguity are achieved only through the mass-mediated news of violence, atrocity, and disaster."[4]

However, this historical difference does not affect the basic mechanism that underlies the iconic status of both pre-modern and contemporary images. Their notoriety is obtained firstly through excessive repetition and secondly – and more importantly – by operating as synecdoche. Re-emerging again and again, they invariably show only a fraction of the event, omit its core and thus demand to be complemented or completed by the viewer's recollection and imagination. The high frequency of their media recurrence as well as their challenging void concerning a real reference have triggered the notion of the image answering to the event's desaturation. With respect to the WTC attacks, Jean Baudrillard, in his essay on the "Spirit of Terrorism", reflates his well-known posit that the "disaster movie" from Manhattan consumes and neutralizes the event. While at first (and with a certain feeling of relief) one meant to detect the return of the violent real, reality had in fact jealously absorbed all the energy of fiction and merged terrorism's black magic with the white magic of cinema.[5] However, if one does not subscribe to the loss of the real, surrounded and in the end substituted by simulacra, the void displayed by the icon of terror may just as well suggest that the event does not disintegrate. It simply seems to take place somewhere else or – to be more precise – it has taken place, it will take place just outside the frame (this also applies to the images that, on the face of it, show

---

[3]   Don DeLillo, "The Power of History", *New York Times Magazine*, 7 September 1997, 63.
[4]   Jeremy Green, "Disaster Footage: Spectacles of Violence in DeLillo's Fiction", *Modern Fiction Studies*, XLV/3 (Autumn 1999), 574.
[5]   Jean Baudrillard, *The Spirit of Terrorism* (2002), trans. Chris Turner, London and New York: Verso, 2003, 29-30.

everything; in their blunt evidence they, too, appear strangely insufficient).

Accordingly, it is not so much Baudrillard as it is Roland Barthes' concept of "anterior future" which informs the present argument and is fittingly educed in Barthes' *Camera Lucida* from a picture that could well be called an "icon of terror". The photograph by Alexander Gardner shows Lewis Payne, who attempted unsuccessfully to assassinate Secretary of State William H. Seward on the same evening that Booth shot Abraham Lincoln and who is now waiting for his executioner. Leaning against the cell's scarred and riveted metal wall and enchained with handcuffs, the irritatingly beautiful young man looks directly into the camera. His face wears an expression of withdrawn earnestness (he has long eluded our intrusive gaze); in contrast to his plain and dark clothing, Payne's illuminated features seem to attain an almost angelic glow. At large, the photograph draws its fascination from a distinctive mixture of sharply focused physicality and otherworldly aloofness.

Apart from its visual qualities, the picture greatly owes its famousness to Roland Barthes, who defines its *punctum* as the appearance of completed imminence:

> I read at the same time *This will be* and *this has been*; I observe with horror an anterior future of which death is the stake. By giving me the absolute past of the pose (aorist), the photograph tells me death in the future.[6]

Thus, by inscribing time into the image, it becomes legible. However, one might well ask whether this legibility does not arise from a fundamental invisibility. The photo is infused with a concept of death, but at the same time it shows its own inability to make death visible. It tells, as Barthes says, it does not show, for death lies somewhere between the moment when Gardner takes the picture in the delinquent's cell and the moment when we acknowledge Payne's death as a past event. When Barthes (this time referring to the portrait of his mother) declares that he shudders, like Donald Winnicott's psychotic patient, over a catastrophe which has already occurred, he implicitly

---

[6]   Roland Barthes, *Camera Lucida: Reflections on Photography* (1980), trans. Richard Howard, New York: Farrar, Straus and Giroux, 1981, 96 (emphases in original).

designates the gap between anticipation and recollection in which death and terror become invisible.[7]

This could lead to the conclusion that icons of terror draw their fascination precisely from closing in on the event from both sides, from its announcement and retrospection, and simultaneously from denying it. In the same manner, one sifts through the collection of more than two dozen photographs documenting the assassination of Archduke Franz Ferdinand of Austria-Este at the Museum of Military History in Vienna with a sense of a constant convergence of time lines that never meet. One of the pictures shows the heir to the throne and his wife, the Duchess Sophie von Hohenberg, as they get into their vehicle. Another one depicts the motorcade driving through Sarajevo. And what we see next is the arrest of the anarchist Gavrilo Princip surrounded by Bosnian townsmen, officials and police constables. What we never get to see is the throwing of the grenade (hitting the car, then bouncing from the rear part of the auto body) or the instant when Princip finally approaches the royal couple and fires his shots, puncturing Franz Ferdinand's right cervical artery.

One may argue that during the nineteenth and early twentieth centuries visual media had not yet developed the necessary speed or interfused quotidian life and cultural practice that they have today. Consequently, every quick and transient fit of violence had to escape the slow and inert camera's gaze. One may also argue that this is the reason for other, non-optical methods of representation filling the informational gap in order to at least provide an *ex-post*-image of the incidence.

The very second that William Prince of Orange is shot by the Jesuit assassin Balthasar Gerards in 1584 (incidentally the first murder of a world leader by a handgun), the precise moment when Abraham Lincoln is hit by the bullet, the instant that Princip pulls the trigger are now subject to medial reconstruction (see Plate 1). But still, the image does not capture the event – it can only imitate or simulate its pres-

---

[7]   Don DeLillo's *Mao II* seems to allude directly to Barthes' concept of a photograph's "anterior future": the novel's protagonist Bill Gray likens his own photo session to embalming and remarks in perfect accordance with Barthes' *Camera Lucida* that "these pictures are the announcement of my dying" (Don DeLillo, *Mao II*, New York: Scribner, 1991, 43); see also Laura Barrett, "'Here but also There': Subjectivity and Postmodern Space in *Mao II*", *Modern Fiction Studies*, XLV/3 (Fall 1999), 796.

ence. All three pictures, the engravings as well as the contemporary Austrian drawing, expose their ostensible instantaneousness by emphasizing the cloud of smoke discharged by the pistol – a mere graphic index of the non-expanded momentary, of the single point where anticipation and recollection meet. In view of these images' marked but palpably missed actuality the question arises: do they show the assassination, do they transport the terror? What is more, doubt cannot be fully explained away by referring to the deficient and always delayed media. The viewer's disappointment and unease do not so much arise from the fact that he or she is dealing with dated and inappropriate techniques of representation while 150 years later one is accustomed to ever present, fast, high-resolution images which can capture the point of time and thus, perhaps, the essence of terror. Rather, it is the uncanny certainty that right in the center of the fastest image there is a blind spot, that something should be visible which even in a photograph, a film, or a live stream video on the internet is constantly lost.

Plate 1: The assassinations of (from left to right) William Prince of Orange,[8] Abraham Lincoln,[9] Archduke Franz Ferdinand.[10]

This is why to this day the Zapruder film is so closely scrutinized, for again – as in Barthes' famous photo – the important detail and "deci-

---

[8] Open source document; source: http://commons.wikimedia.org/wiki/File: Moordwillemzwijger2.jpg (accessed 30 June 2011).
[9] Open source document; source: http://en.wikipedia.org/wiki/File: The_ Assassination_of_President_Lincoln_-_Currier_and_Ives_2.png (accessed 30 June 2011).
[10] Open source document; source: http://members.fortunecity.com/mikaelxii/ sarajevo.jpg (accessed 30 June 2011).

sive moment" which could unveil the secret is intermediate. It is always located between the single images, between one frame and the next: Kennedy will be shot, Kennedy has been shot.[11] Likewise, the impossible position of the event might explain why for days on end every news channel could not refrain from obsessively repeating the footage of American Airlines Flight 11 and United Airlines Flight 175 crashing into World Trade Center's north and south tower, which in turn is said to have caused post traumatic stress disorder in US television audiences.[12] It seems that this reaction can less be ascribed to seeing too much than, on the contrary, to seeing not enough. Remarkably, a central symptom of PTSD is not only the recurring memory but also the incessant mental or actual re-staging of the traumatic incident, its ongoing active repetition independent of its medial catalyst. Both the material's provider and its recipient get caught in an infinite loop, trying to extricate the meaning of "terrorism" and being thrown back on a sequence of insignificant time segments.

Painting (photographs of) terror

Terrorism's hysterical and always tenuous presence/absence in the media makes up one of the main topics of Gerhard Richter's series of paintings entitled *October 18, 1977*. In winter 2000/2001, Don DeLillo visited the New York Museum of Modern Art where Richter's

[11] This specific hiatus becomes paradoxically "visible" in Bruce Conner's 1967 avant-garde film *Report*. To a large extent, the movie's first part assembles found footage dealing with Kennedy's death. But the crucial traumatic moment of the assassination "is 'illustrated' by the flickering alternation of black-and-white frames, creating what is commonly known as a 'flicker film'. Conner 'represents' this failure of comprehension as a trauma to the film itself, a breaking down of conventional and straightforwardly illustrative representation. This section has been discussed as an attempt to simulate the fluctuating consciousness of the dying Kennedy, but its affect is actually more primal than this and acts to communicate the limits of representation (particularly in relation to death)" (Adrian Danks, "Shooting the President: Bruce Conner's *Report*", *Senses of Cinema*, 50 [2009], n.p.: http://archive.sensesofcinema. com/contents/cteq/09/50/report.html [accessed 26 May 2010]). Moreover, when the film's soundtrack (taken from radio broadcasts of the day) mentions the word "death", the gap appears on the material level of the celluloid itself: invisible for the audience during projection, three of the film's white frames are punctured as if shot through by bullets.

[12] See Florian Rötzer, "Propaganda der Tat: Gewaltinszenierung in der Echtzeitmedienwelt", *Du: Die Zeitschrift der Kultur*, 736 (May 2003), 76.

works were shown as part of a larger exhibition called *Open Ends* and drew on them as thematic basis for his short story "Baader-Meinhof". In contrast to a press photo or newspaper report, these highly reflexive works of art consciously deal with the representational gap in which the incident is lost. What is more, both paintings and text exhibit a new quality and position of the gap. They invent a different kind of interstice and thereby succeed in regaining at least an altered version of the "real".

When we take stock of what Gerhard Richter worked on between March and November 1988 and leave out the paintings he himself did not include in the cycle when it was exhibited,[13] the list of the remaining fifteen canvases reads as follows: a youthful portrait of Ulrike Meinhof, sentimental in a bourgeois way; twice the arrest of Holger Meins, forced to surrender to the clenched power of the State (all we see is the bare back wall of a Frankfurt apartment building and the shadowy lump of an armored car); three times Gudrun Ensslin, neutral (almost like a pop star), when she is presented to press photographers after her arrest; once Ensslin hanged in her Stammheim prison cell; then another cell dominated by a bookcase and a black overcoat; Andreas Baader's silent, gray record player in which his suicide gun was said to have been hidden; twice Baader shot; three times the head of the dead Meinhof after she has been cut down, the strangulation mark clearly visible on her neck; and finally a big, unspecific burial, the funeral of Baader, Ensslin and Meinhof at the Dornhalden cemetery in Stuttgart. While the paintings vary greatly in size,[14] they are all kept in dull shades of gray and appear rather blurred or diffuse.

Without exception, the different components of the cycle are based on photographic or filmic samples. Richter's *Atlas*, a scrapbook-like collection of templates for his paintings and at the same time an autonomous work of archival art, contains 100 Baader-Meinhof photos; his work-album holds 102 additional reproductions of wanted posters, images from illustrated magazines or television stills, police photo-

---

[13] The whole cycle includes nineteen paintings. See *Gerhard Richter: October 18, 1977*, ed. Robert Storr, New York: The Museum of Modern Art, 2000, 95.

[14] The smallest canvas, *Dead III*, measures 35 x 40 cm, the largest, *Funeral*, is 200 x 320 cm in size.

graphs and even pictures that belonged to former terrorists.[15] Richter's practice of copying these photographic templates obviously refers to their symptomatic emptiness. By choosing images which hold the said iconic status, Richter formulates a critique aimed at the widely known originals' lack of expressiveness. At the same time, reducing the cycle of paintings to this critical stance must seem trivial, for their author is subtly insisting on the telltale differences in genres – studio portrait, photo-journalism, forensic shot – that belie any homogenizing rejection of mass media and their restricted informative value. Moreover, he is reliant on these images to measure out the distance between photography and painting in order to find that impossible *lieu* in the media no-man's-land where the essential event's anticipation and recollection can finally converge. Accordingly, the exhibition catalogue states that "we are confronted with a continuum of representations stretched taut between the abstract concepts of photography and painting, each of which by asserting its own conventional reality implicitly questions the conventions and the truth of the other."[16]

Thus, while at first sight the paintings do not directly refer to terrorism but to several intermediary representational systems, an interspace is created which allows for transcending the deficiencies of these modes of representation and makes something visible that was concealed by the mere technical reproduction. Richter implements a paradox: whereas for instance the portrait of Lewis Payne as pure photography points to the hiatus between a prospective event and its past completion, the paintings of *October 18, 1977* constitute a gap in themselves and thereby develop the potency to accommodate the event. A consistent, singular, and monologic medium produces a void (even though Barthes declares this void to be the photo's *punctum*); yet a composite, plural and dialogic representation is able to at least evoke a singularity. And this singularity could perhaps be called "death". When asked by an interviewer whether he had been sure that the subject of terrorism could be dealt with, Gerhard Richter replied that "the wish was there that it might be – had to be – paintable":

---

[15]   See *Gerhard Richter*, 99, and also Catharina Manchanda's "Note on Richter's photographic models for *October 18, 1977*" in *ibid.*, 149.
[16]   *Ibid.*, 106.

The [images] that weren't paintable were the ones I did paint. The dead. To start with, I wanted more to paint the whole business, the world as it then was, the living reality – I was thinking in terms of something big and comprehensive. But then it all evolved quite differently, in the direction of death. And that's really not all that unpaintable.[17]

This is the point where Baudrillard's argument collapses. While he postulates the breakdown of the semiotic connection between the "picture" and the "pictured", resulting in a fundamental ambiguity, a mirage of possibilities that eliminate truth, Richter's cycle of paintings renounces such elegant *trompe-l'œil*. Instead, his work accounts for the necessary urge to understand terrorism as well as death in general, to collect fragmentary evidence and to re-implant it into its historical context. While Baudrillard stops doubting, Richter deliberately creates a space for doubt by constantly questioning the cultural meaning of his material.

Writing (about paintings of photographs of) terror
It is this quality in Richter's paintings that permits one to align them with Don DeLillo's literary work. DeLillo's preoccupation with terrorism and mediatization begins no later than with the short story "The Uniforms", published in 1970, and certainly does not end with his novel *Falling Man*. In between, *The Players*, *The Names*, *Libra*, *Mao II*, *Underworld*, and *Cosmopolis* as well as non-fiction pieces such as "American Blood", "Silhouette City: Hitler", "Manson and the Millennium", "In the Ruins of the Future", or "Assassination Aura" all discuss diverse occurrences of political violence and their visual or verbal representability. In the process, DeLillo more than once pursues a strategy of layering or linking various media; he resorts to photography, film, television, home video, and the internet, producing

---

[17] Richter quoted in *ibid.*, 101. The question whether Richter's subject is "paintable" or not recurs in his artistic occupation with 9/11: does the event itself forbid its rendering which tends to aestheticize or fall short of the referent? Accordingly, working on the single, small format painting *September* proves to be difficult. Richter more than once almost destroys the canvas and needs more than two years to finish it. See Hubertus Butin, "Der Tag, an dem die Welt unscharf wurde", *Frankfurter Allgemeine Zeitung*, 4 June 2008, 31. I thank Michael König for calling my attention to Butin's article on Richter's *September*.

textual strata which add up to a seemingly closed referential system
with its connection to reality drastically thinning out.

In this manner, "The Uniforms" foregrounds its complex mediation
process by drawing upon Jean-Luc Godard's movie *Weekend*,[18] whose
protagonists happen to be kidnapped by a band of anti-bourgeois and
ultra-violent Hippie-terrorists. DeLillo adopts the film's random atrocities, main motifs, reserved narrative attitude, and fragmented mon-
tage style, and thereby points to the text's secondary or derivational
status.[19] Moreover, the opening section of his novel *The Players*, titled
"The Movie", raises this procedure to yet another intermedial level.
On board an airplane a film is shown in which terrorists massacre a
group of wealthy golfers – a scene that, in turn, is clearly taken from
"The Uniforms": from Godard's movie to DeLillo's short story to
another movie in a DeLillo novel.

Similarly, Don DeLillo's story "Baader-Meinhof" deals with terrorism as a phenomenon filtered by visual media and then "meta-
mediated" by literature. Its first part describes how a nameless young
woman and a man meet at a gallery in New York City where Gerhard
Richter's RAF cycle is on exhibition. Their hesitant, guarded, and
sometimes cautiously ironic conversation about the pictures' possible
content and meaning is then continued in the gallery's snack bar. We
learn that while she is visiting the gallery for the third day in a row, he
merely kills time before his next job interview. Abruptly, the setting
changes to the woman's smallish apartment, where, after the stranger
gradually has earned her trust, he begins to pressure her with barely
disguised erotic innuendo. She manages to elude his importunities and
physical advances, locks herself in the bathroom and listens to him

---

[18]   See Don DeLillo, "The Uniforms", *Carolina Quarterly*, XII/1 (Winter 1970), 4-
11.
[19]   In fact, "The Uniforms" underlines the rhetorical and ideological historicity of
mediating terrorism. While Mark Osteen describes Godard's movies as "terrorist acts"
or a "series of guerrilla raids" which turn their "theoretical rifle" against capitalism,
bourgeois culture and the conventions of classic cinema (Mark Osteen, "Children of
Godard and Coca-Cola: Cinema and Consumerism in Don DeLillo's Early Fiction,"
Contemporary Literature, XXXVII/3 [Fall 1996], 46), DeLillo's "rifle" aims at
Godard himself. His short story hyperbolizes the formal characteristics of *Weekend* in
such a way that the movie is shown to transform terrorism – or any political action –
into pure aestheticism: Godard's somewhat dated "terrorist act" has ironically become
a canonized and easily consumable artifact.

masturbating on her bed (at least this is what his concentrated nasal breathing seems to indicate). Then, after desperately asking the woman's forgiveness, he leaves the apartment and the following day waits for her in the gallery.

To begin with, the story's overall stylistic flatness and calculated ambiguity approximate Richter's works and DeLillo's text. By referring to the paintings, the author seems to devise an analogy between their non-distinctive way of depiction and his own literary mode. Avoiding the detailed clarity of classical ekphrasis, "Baader-Meinhof" confines itself to hinting at the pictures' illegibility and their rather vague effect on the observer:

> "Why do you think he did it this way?"
> She did not turn to look at him.
> "So shadowy. No colour."
> She said, "I don't know", and went to the next set of images, called "Man Shot Down."[20]

The dead Ulrike Meinhof appears "in nuances of obscurity and pall", another triptych shows Gudrun Ensslin "maybe smiling, smiling, and probably not smiling". The woman in the gallery concentrates on an "unknown object at the edge of the frame, the disparity or uncertainty". In the painting of the burial she does not realize at first "that the three whitish objects near the centre of the picture were coffins".

All this not only invokes Richter's obfuscating technique of painting or the protagonists' indistinct gaze and emotional condition, it also reflects DeLillo's strategy of communicating this condition. The meticulous observation of psychological as well as physical reactions that, nevertheless, refuses to reveal any deeper truth – DeLillo's way of locating every secret on the surface of the perceived – can well be called a dominant of his literary texts. Accordingly, the quasi "empathetic" rendering of Richter's blurred paintings and a correspondent approach to the ill-defined characters result in a likewise "accurately

---

[20] This and all subsequent quotations are from the online version of the text, which does not give page numbers: Don DeLillo, "Looking at Meinhof", *The Guardian*, 17 August 2002: http://www.guardian.co.uk/books/2002/aug/17/fiction.originalwriting (accessed 27 May 2010). (First publ. in *New Yorker*, 1 April 2002, 78-82.)

blurred" storyline and style: the minute observation of diffuse objects generates sharply defined out-of-focus images.

This leads to the possible location of the gap that may become the *lieu* of the invisible. Blanks and vacancies of any sort determine the text's plot and structure. They may assume the form of a temporal hiatus, as the unemployed male protagonist explains to his new acquaintance in the gallery: "I'm frankly here to pass the time. That's what I do between job interviews." With regard to the story's character constellation, another gap opens up between him and her, a clearance in which a potential relation or even relationship can crystallize. While she hesitates to bridge the divide and shuns "an inflection of mutual sympathy, a comradeship", he insists on their similarity. Likewise, as DeLillo cuts out the joint between the story's two main sections, the very structure of the text centers on the interstice between the encounter-scene in the gallery and the separation-scene in the apartment, located precisely in the middle of the text and harboring an undisclosed moment of decision (growing trust, or lust, or both). And finally, the gap appears as a peculiar cognitive distance between her apartment as she knows it and the same apartment after the irritating intrusion:

> She saw everything twice now. She was where she wanted to be, and alone, but nothing was the same. Bastard. Nearly everything in the room had a double effect – what it was and the association it carried in her mind. She went out walking, and when she came back the connection was still there, at the coffee table, on the bed, in the bathroom.[21]

---

[21] This doubled perception germinates in Don DeLillo's *Falling Man.* According to David Brauner, "double vision" as a response to trauma becomes something of a leitmotif in the novel; it "insistently explores how the 'ordinary run of hours' that constitutes daily life after 9/11 both differs radically from, and at the same time closely resembles, the quotidian structure that preceded it" (David Brauner, "'The Days After' and 'The Ordinary Run of Hours': Counternarratives and Double Vision in Don DeLillo's *Falling Man*", *Review of International American Studies*, III/3-IV/1 [Winter 2008/Spring 2009], 73, 74). Thus, just like the unnamed protagonist of "Baader-Meinhof", Keith Neudecker begins to see things differently in the temporal gap between the falling of the first and second tower, and returning briefly to his apartment after the attacks, the place seems changed into a strange and impersonal movie set (see Don DeLillo, *Falling Man*, New York: Scribner, 2007, 5, 26).

Aside from these narrative and formal gaps that account for the distinctly twofold structure of "Baader-Meinhof", it is the mentioned blind spot, lingering in media representations, that informs the story's argument. Just like Gardner's photo of Lewis Payne conveys an "anterior future of which death is the stake", the triptych of Gudrun Ensslin or Richter's portrait of the young Ulrike Meinhof highlight the "absolute past of the pose" and at the same time communicate "death in the future". Hence, it is not only some inexplicit grief for the portrayed individuals which makes the gallery-visitor feel "that she was sitting as a person does in a mortuary chapel, keeping watch over the body of a relative or friend". Rather, she seems half knowingly to associate her feeling of loss with the act of seeing. Looking at the pictures resembles attending the laying-out of a body, and "[this] was sometimes called the viewing, she believed": both experiences pertain to the visual and tell about death, but they are equally characterized by a temporal displacement and specific exclusion of the dying moment. Meanwhile, "Baader-Meinhof", with a view to this absence inside the visual, is highly conscious of that other gap between image and text. Echoing Gerhard Richter's paintings, the story marks the distance between media in order to find a place where the essential event, where political or personal terrorism can finally surface. Only this time the recipient is confronted with a continuum of representations not stretched between the concepts of photography and painting but between painting and text, each of which questions the conventions and the truth of the other.[22]

Provided that DeLillo's usage of extrinsic media serves the same function as Richter's technique and actually tries to create an inter-

---

[22] In this context, it may be permitted to ignore the systematic difference between an image-image-relation in the first case and an image-text-relation in the second, the more so as W.J.T. Mitchell, in his attempt to differentiate between the "unimaginable" and the "unspeakable" of terrorism and its representations, resorts to the well-known Saussurean image of the *signifiant* and the *signifié* being two sides of the same coin. Mitchell envisages one face of the coin with eyes and a gag in its mouth, the other with a mouth and blindfolded eyes, to demonstrate that in the face of terrorism, blindness and muteness, the failure of the visual and the verbal are inseparable. The constellation states a difference and at the same makes the two concepts interchangeable. See William J.T. Mitchell, "Das Unaussprechliche und das Unvorstellbare: Wort und Bild in einer Zeit des Terrors", in *Bild und Einbildungskraft*, eds Bernd Hüppauf and Christoph Wulf, Munich: Fink, 2006, 333.

space for the emergence of the unrepresentable, it seems rather odd that "Baader-Meinhof" deals with the RAF. Albeit medialized by contemporary art and thus gaining some topicality, the "Deutscher Herbst" barely affects the condition in post-9/11 Manhattan or reflects the acuteness of terror. In fact, DeLillo's protagonist admits: "It was 25 years ago. I don't know what it was like then, in Germany, with bombings and kidnappings." This creates the impression that the story refers to *October 18, 1977* not so much to display the otherwise inexpressible core of terrorist and state violence, but to install a simple metaphor for the failure of interpersonal communication. Apparently, DeLillo fabricates an equivalence between excessive political and quotidian emotional "terrorism", and in both cases the event or the moment of death (with or without quotation marks) remains unutterable and defies representation. A first content-related argument to refute this charge would be that neither the paintings nor the text deal exclusively with terrorism and death.

Plate 2: Gerhard Richter, "Beerdigung"/"Funeral" (1988), oil on canvas, The Museum of Modern Art, New York.[23]

---

[23] *Gerhard Richter*, 23. © Gerhard Richter 2011. Reproduced by kind permission of the artist.

Although the MoMA catalogue states: *"October 18, 1977* bombards us with death from every side",[24] the same text speculates about a single tree near the upper edge of the painting titled *Funeral* (Plate 2), a simple vertical with lateral branches that does not appear on the original photograph, and might, after all, not be a tree but a cross:

> Richter has since made a sculptural multiple of a similarly proportioned cross and he has painted his wife Sabina with their son as a kind of Madonna and child. In light of this, it is hard not to acknowledge the deliberateness of what Richter has done and recognize his addition to *Funeral* as a discrete benediction at the end of a modern-day passion play.[25]

Likewise, the female protagonist in Don DeLillo's short story knows that the paintings are based on photographs but has not seen them and therefore cannot ascertain whether "there was a bare tree, a dead tree beyond the cemetery, in one of the photos, that consisted of a spindly trunk with … two branches forming a transverse piece near the top of the trunk". Nevertheless, she responds to her urge to furnish the cool and withdrawn painting with a consoling deeper meaning and begins to see more than just a tree:

> It was a cross. She saw it as a cross, and it made her feel, right or wrong, that there was an element of forgiveness in the picture, that the two men and the woman, terrorists, and Ulrike before them, terrorist, were not beyond forgiveness.

Indeed, the human ability to forgive soon becomes the story's center of focus when the male protagonist leans against the door of the bathroom where the woman has sought shelter from his obtrusion. She hears his barely audible voice saying: "Forgive me …. I'm so sorry. Please. I don't know what to say." Against this background, the text's ending opens up to the possibility of reconciliation; she returns to the museum the next day, he sits alone on a bench, his back to the entrance, looking at that same painting called *Funeral*. The closing image thus seems to indicate that, while death and suffering – as

---

[24] *Ibid.*, 105.
[25] *Ibid.*, 110.

Gerhard Richter points out – have in fact always been the artistic themes and therefore are not in the least unrepresentable, it is forgiveness which demands special artistic handling. Much more fragile, exigent, and able to move the thematic core from the blunt fact of dying to a moral quality, it might be forgiveness, not death, that has to be made visible in the media's interspace.

Another argument against the apparent equation of actual and private terrorism in "Baader-Meinhof" would be that it is precisely their linkage which provides the central theme of DeLillo's literary work. Once we realize that acts of politically motivated violence are a form of communication, a manipulation of symbols interfering with the collective inventory of images and affecting every single person, the difference between terrorism and the individual's mental or emotional disposition becomes meaningless. Including terrorism into the sign systems of Western culture explains its dependency on mediatization,[26] its tactics of deliberately staging assaults for media consumption and also the general effort of images to translate[27] the respective violent act. But this concept also implants terrorism in everyday life and thereby nullifies the charge of mere analogy. Accordingly, Glen Scott Allen states that "if terrorists have become nearly ubiquitous players in the contemporary social narrative, then, whatever the intent of their 'expressive' acts, they contribute as much to the formation of *our* identity as to their own, and their acts of seemingly random and 'meaningless' violence have become an integral component of what being a modern individual *means*".

---

[26] W.J.T. Mitchell states that the terrorist's production of words and images, of symbolic forms of violence, is much more significant than his concrete physical acts. He describes terrorism as a war of signs transmitted by the mass media, a form of psychological warfare that realizes the combination of violence and symbol through spectacle. See Mitchell, "Das Unaussprechliche und das Unvorstellbare", 335.

[27] Glen Scott Allen, "Raids on the Conscious: Pynchon's Legacy of Paranoia and the Terrorism of Uncertainty in Don DeLillo's *Ratner's Star*", *Postmodern Culture*, IV/2 (January 1994), n.p.: http://muse.uq.edu.au/journals/postmodern_culture/v004/4.2 allen.html (accessed 27 May 2010). Allen describes terrorism as a language that does not belong to the sphere of possible enunciations and is constantly dismissed as incomprehensible and "insane" by society's discourse: "It is, in terms of cultural linguistics, essentially impossible for most 'First World' Western civilians to 'read' the terrorist text" (*ibid.*). Therefore, terrorism constantly has to be translated, interpreted and mediated in order to become audible/visible.

If the postmodern mindset is generally characterized by a pervasive sense of anxiety and vulnerability, this conception is paralleled and reinforced by terrorism's chief objective to convey exactly this widespread sense of vulnerability "which produces consequent paranoia and guilt in the civilian".[28] It is thus no longer possible to conceive of terrorism as merely correspondent to the individual's quotidian actions. Rather, it is directly responsible for the insight, formulated by "Baader-Meinhof", that we cannot control our environments and destinies. Political terrorism is not like emotional cruelty or isolation, it effects (and is effected by) mental states such as these. Moreover, the close and causal association of private and public trauma inside a single sign-structure provides the only basis for an artistic approach to terrorism. While metaphor or analogy would shut off one sphere from the other, a circuit between them allows for counter-narratives such as DeLillo's own text. In his reading of "In the Ruins of the Future", David Brauner states that "the best – perhaps the only – way of responding to the 'massive spectacle' that was 9/11 is microcosmically, by constructing a counternarrative out of small objects and marginal stories, rather then focusing on the towers themselves".[29] Apparently, this other perspective could well be the elliptical story of two unemployed New Yorkers meeting at an exhibition of Richter's Baader-Meinhof cycle ten months before the attack.

It seems that, because the short story was written in the aftermath of 9/11 without mentioning the World Trade Center, because it resorts to German terrorism of the 1970s, the deep impression of political violence on the collective imaginary becomes all the more tangible. Reciprocally, Jean-Christophe Amman, director of the Frankfurt *Museum für Moderne Kunst*, had strongly protested against Gerhard Richter's decision to sell his paintings to New York, and had stated that their relocation to America would render them "ineffective". The *Tageszeitung*, asserting a lack of knowledge concerning the RAF in America, had questioned the public's ability to grasp the meaning of the images.[30] Meanwhile, it was Richter himself who thought of the United States as a hospitable environment for his work: "Due to their distance to the RAF, maybe the Americans can see the overall aspect of

---

[28] *Ibid.*
[29] Brauner, "'The Days After' and 'The Ordinary Run of Hours'", 74.
[30] See *Gerhard Richter*, 35.

the subject that affects almost every modern or even non-modern country: the general danger of belief in ideology or fanaticism or madness."[31] This seems also a quite accurate description of Don De-Lillo's literary intentions. Evading any romantic generalization, "Baader-Meinhof" displaces terrorism from its narrow historical confines and relocates it in an overstrained cultural mind and memory. Thus, it is not only the gap between painting and literature that offers a paradoxical space for the representation of terrorism and at the same time initiates the reflection on various strategies of visualization. It is also the gap between the historical matrix and its artistic abstraction that is predestined to expose terrorism's unrepresentable *chora*.

The ethics of medialization
DeLillo's strategy of approaching cultural phenomena by displacing them from their immediate context and dissecting their numerous layers of representation is more than an attempt to lay open the operations of reality. Certainly, the author is often referred to as a keen and clear-sighted observer of postmodern high-tech occidental civilization. His work is conceived as an "act of cultural criticism" or a kind of "anatomy, an effort to represent [our] culture in its totality".[32] This notion doubtlessly springs from the traditional mimetic ideal of novels reproducing a precedent world. The fact that the characteristics of DeLillo's fiction also extend to his factual or essayistic texts adds to his reputation as diagnostician of his times: albeit aesthetically condensed, both genres truthfully document the postmodern condition. Even if the world had supposedly perished in a multitude of images, the basic equation *novel* = *reality* still seems intact.

However, "Baader-Meinhof" does not depict the reality of terrorism, nor does it merely capture its medial manifestations. It is a literary text medializing a set of visual artworks that, in turn, build on technically reproduced medializations of historical events. This un-

---

[31] Richter quoted in *ibid.*, 36. For the same reason, one hesitates to concur with Hubertus Butin's opinion that the most appropriate place for Gerhard Richter's *September*, dealing with the WTC attacks, would be a museum in New York City (see Butin, "Der Tag", 31).
[32] Frank Lentricchia, "The American Writer as Bad Citizen", in *Introducing Don DeLillo*, ed. Frank Lentricchia, Durham, NC and London: Duke University Press, 1991, 2.

usual quantity of representational components finally leads to a qualitative reversion: it establishes a utopian space which is not so much concerned with reproducing the entanglements of reality and the media, but formulates an artistic alternative, an unthought-of sphere beyond replication, perhaps suggested by the story's open ending. The text appears less like an analysis than it is an intervention, reflecting on art's potential to implement its cathartic vision as a cultural antidote. This is why Richter blurs the outlines of his subject, not to depict it more clearly (a cliché of art criticism), but to make room for a thought which neither reality nor its images can provide and which does not exist outside or without the painting. Likewise, Don DeLillo's "Baader-Meinhof" transcends terrorism, its representations, and its effect on the postmodern individual. In the gaps between those instances, and by denying narrow psychological or cultural realism, the story tries to invent a literary as well as ethical mode to counteract the possibility of terrorism itself.

In this respect, one might detect traits of the Greek tragedy's moral claim to expel violence through its depiction in order to allow for the utopia of the *polis*. And, apart from his recourse to civil reason, one may even think of Kant's equally idealistic concept of the dynamic sublime, the abhorrent, terrorizing spectacle reminding the individual of his or her insuperable spiritual powers.[33] Admittedly, DeLillo's aesthetic practice veers away from these antecessors inasmuch as it double- or triple-mediates the formerly immediate shock, a possible reason being the constant repetition of terrorist images that, at best, induces a queasy numbness in the recipient. Therefore, an indirect gaze promises a better image – not of the real object, but of its cultural halo and utopian reverse: "To look at a star by glances – to view it in a

---

[33] See Immanuel Kant, *Critique of Judgement* (1790), New York: Cosimo Classics, 2007, 75. The connection between DeLillo's fiction and the concept of sublimity has by now become a critical topos. See, for example, Joseph Tabbi, "From the Sublime to the Beautiful to the Poltitical: Don DeLillo at Midcareer", *Postmodern Sublime: Technology and American Writing from Mailer to Cyberpunk*, Ithaca and London: Cornell University Press, 1995, 169-207, or Stephen Bernstein, "*Libra* and the Historical Sublime", *Postmodern Culture*, IV/2 (January 1994), n.p.: http://muse.jhu.edu/journals/postmodern_culture/v004/4.2bernstein.html (accessed 27 May 2010).

side-long way, by turning toward it the exterior portions of the *retina*
… – is to have the best appreciation of its luster."[34]

---

[34]   Edgar Allan Poe, "The Murders in the Rue Morgue" (1841), in *The Complete Tales and Poems*, New York: Vintage, 1975, 153.

A Fantastic Tale of Terror: Argentina's "Disappeared" and Their Narrative Representation in Julio Cortázar's "Second Time Round"

Kirsten Mahlke

Terror between aesthetics and politics

It is rather uncanny that terror denominates at the same time an aesthetic effect and an act of real violence. What if they collapse, by historical coincidences, into one phenomenon? In the following, I will contextualize a historical particularity of Argentine state terror and analyze its representation in one of the first short stories to depict the "Disappeared", the social group known since the 1970s throughout the world as the "Desaparecidos". These people, who are neither declared dead nor alive, belong to a conceptual register that is beyond conventional categories of space-time and can therefore be understood as a fantastic dimension of social discourse – a dimension that could even tentatively be termed "fantastic reality" as it undermines historical and social common sense. The euphemism of disappearances was used by the military Junta to confound the real operational sequence of abduction, torture, murder, and secret disposal of the corpses, a method well known to induce the highest effect of terror among the population.

Any effort to reintegrate the "Disappeared" into realistic modes of representation is tinged with the uncanny, an effect described by Sigmund Freud in his etymological-psychoanalytical analysis of "Das Unheimliche": "an uncanny effect is often and easily produced when the distinction between imagination and reality is effaced, as when something that we have hitherto regarded as imaginary appears before us in reality, or when a symbol takes over the full functions of the thing it symbolizes, and so on."[1] This uncanny effect is the prerequi-

---

[1]   Sigmund Freud, "The Uncanny" (1919), in *The Standard Edition of the Complete Psychological Works of Sigmund Freud*, trans. under the general editorship of James

site on which the following observations about state terror in Argentina build. Terror is an aesthetic and political phenomenon, which means that it is effective as anxiety increased to a high degree, and that it is actively produced by certain methods that are particularly effective in state terror.[2] Going beyond the difficulties of defining who is a terrorist and what is terrorism, I would like to approach the phenomenon of terror at precisely the intersection of aesthetics and politics.

It is no coincidence that Freud chose a fantastic tale by E.T.A Hoffmann for his analysis of the uncanny as an ambivalent form of anxiety. Literary fiction can, according to Freud, under certain circumstances produce feelings of anxiety resembling those caused by real lived occurrences:

> The situation is altered as soon as the writer pretends to move in the world of common reality. In this case he accepts as well all the conditions operating to produce uncanny feelings in real life; and everything that would have an uncanny effect in reality has it in his story.[3]

The criterion of ordinariness for the effect of the uncanny underlies most basic definitions of the fantastic: the fictive world must be represented in a manner as everyday and familiar as possible in order for the effect of the fantastical to emerge all the more emphatically.

At this point, I have to explain which theoretical models I use when referring to the fantastic. Since at least Tzvetan Todorov, there have been numerous attempts to define the term, which in the end represent an impossible classification venture, similar to attempts to define realism. Thus, I rely on components of various models that are relevant for my set of questions. One is the Two-Worlds-Model, according to which:

Strachey in collaboration with Anna Freud, London: The Hogarth Press and the Institute of Psychoanalysis, 1955, XXVII, 244.

[2]   One of the biggest differences between state-terror and the terrorism addressed by most of the contributors to the present volume is that state-terror is executed by those in political power. This means that state terror benefits from institutions of the government which then establish terror as a legal means or even as a political goal in itself. Another important difference between state and global terrorism is that the military dictators execute state-terror in the state of impunity, knowing that they will not be punished. Thus terror is produced by power in a legal situation, but it is evident that jurisdiction has not been followed in Argentina, as we will see later on.

[3]   Freud, "The Uncanny", 244.

> In a world which is indeed our world, the one we know, there occurs
> an event which cannot be explained by the laws of this same familiar
> world. The person who experiences the event must opt for one of two
> possible solutions: either he is the victim of an illusion of the senses,
> of a product of the imagination – and the laws of the world then
> remain what they are; or else the event has indeed taken place, it is an
> integral part of reality – but then this reality is controlled by laws un-
> known to us.[4]

In a critique of Todorov that accounts for cases of the fantastic which
do not allow for a division into two opposed frames of explanation but
from start to finish remain trapped within the everyday, Jaime Alazraki has defined such cases of the "neo-fantastic" as containing three
features: a) it abandons the moment of "hesitation" which disturbs the
reader due to the fact that the uncanny fact inserts itself into the everyday from the first line on; b) the exceptional is accepted because the
frame is realistic, which distinguishes it from the category of the
"marvelous" (for example, fairy tales); and c) the fantastic fact generates a metaphor which can only explain itself, given that in light of
this metaphor every interpretation must be reconsidered at the end
and, thus, this polysemy, the impossibility of an unequivocal exit, an-
nihilates the others.[5]

Because Freud's essay on the uncanny remarkably anticipates and
heuristically predates in the ways described above the definition of
the fantastic that Todorov's *Introduction à la littérature fantastique*
develops, I would like to cast Freud's uncanny as both an aesthetic
effect and simultaneous precondition of terror. The fantastic would
then constitute the field between the real and the fictive that is marked
by the effect of the uncanny.

It is impossible to draw a line between fiction and reality under
conditions of terror, because terror lives on fiction as a category of the
real. In this problem Hannah Arendt saw precisely the greatest misunderstanding on the part of observers of totalitarian states: that common

---

[4]   Tzvetan Todorov, *The Fantastic: A Structural Approach to a Literary Genre*
(1970), trans. Richard Howard, Cleveland, OH: Case Western Reserve University
Press, 1973, 25.

[5]   Jaime Alazraki, *En busca del unicornio: Los cuentos de Julio Cortázar. Elemen-
tos para una poética de los neofantástico*, Madrid: Editorial Gredos, 1983, 10 (my
translation).

sense and natural laws could not take insane movements such as National Socialism or Stalinism seriously, because their goals contradicted common sense.[6] Neighboring states could not believe that dictatorial fiction could become reality. They were in a condition of what Todorov calls *"hésitation"*, a condition that he ascribes to the "fantastic".

Alongside the banality of the reality depicted, a further criterion of the uncanny applies to the level of characters: "Many people experience the feeling in the highest degree in relation to death and dead bodies, to the return of the dead, and to spirits and ghosts."[7] The deceased in and of themselves are not uncanny, but the possibility of their return to or presence among the living is. Inversely, uncanny is also the possibility of dying in an inexplicable way in the midst of everyday life. The threshold between life and death is the site of the uncanny, which structures the fantastic within a narrative.

The "Disappeared"
An ungraspable anxiety of death as an omnipresent threat, which however was caused by neither the observation of murder nor the discovery of corpses and hence produced an especially profound uncertainty, terrorized Argentine society between 1976 and 1983. State terror methodically generated a social group that resists traditional analytic categories used by history and the social sciences: the "Disappeared". By now it seems probable – and indeed in many cases has been proven – that the many thousand "Disappeared" were all systematically disposed of or murdered by order of the state. This method, which is a faithful copy of Hitler's "night and fog" operations, was perfected during the dictatorship and resulted in 30,000 missing people or "Desaparecidos". It targeted an ever growing group of persons who were perceived as "subversive" for liberal capitalism or a Junta dedicated to "Western Christian values", although it became increasingly unclear who was actually designated by the term. Already in 1976, the militant members of the Peronist party were practically immobilized. Most of the "terrorists" had already been killed or were in prison. Thus, the "war against terrorism" became a form of state terrorism after 1976, which, in the absence of real opponents, had to

[6]   See Hannah Arendt, *The Origins of Totalitarianism* (1951/1968), new edn with added prefaces, San Diego, New York, and London: Harcourt, Inc., 1973.
[7]   Freud, "The Uncanny", 242.

find or invent them. The definition of "the terrorists" was quickly adapted to the goal of aiming state terror at innocent persons as well.

One of the three highest-ranking generals of the military dictatorship, General Rafael Videla, defined in a public speech in 1978 all that could be considered a terrorist, even when such suspects do not set off bombs: "A terrorist is not just someone with a gun or a bomb but also someone who spreads ideas which are contrary to Western and Christian civilization." Furthermore, Ibérico Saint Jean, the governor of the province of Buenos Aires detailed the order of those to be killed: "First we will kill the subversives, then their collaborators, then their sympathizers, afterwards the indifferent, and finally the lukewarm."[8] Both concepts, terrorists and "Disappeared", whose referents partly coincide, are constitutive (that is, opposing) elements of a dictatorial fiction, which can be summarized in the three keywords "Nation", "Family", and the "Catholic Church". Together they comprise the homogeneous "Western values". People who stand in the way of the project to clean up the nation must disappear. That the national fiction was to be taken literally turned out to be more than true.

The criminal sequence "kidnap-torture-kill-dispose of" subsumed under the euphemism of "disappearance" was one of the most effective subterranean forms of collective psychological terror. Terror is understood here in the sense of executed violence and the paralyzing, extreme anxiety producing and silencing effect among the populace.[9]

The notion that people simply disappeared suggests acts of magic by those responsible. The trick to this repressive method, which was the main terrorist strategy employed by the Argentine military, consists in abducting, torturing, and killing people, without ever informing the relatives about the place of captivity, and then to remove the corpse without leaving a trace. The Atlantic Ocean and the River Plate were used as a dumpsite for many of them. Following Jean Baudril-

---

[8] Quoted in Eduardo Galeano, *Memoria del Fuego: El Siglo del Viento*, 11th edn, Madrid: Siglo, 2007, 282 (my translation).

[9] This very early definition of "terror" was given to the French "terreur" as early as in the fourteenth century. See Gerd van den Heuvel, "Terreur, Terroriste, Terrorisme", in *Handbuch politisch-sozialer Grundbegriffe in Frankreich 1680-1820*, vol III: *Philosophe, Philosophie; Terreur, Terroriste, Terrorisme*, eds Rolf Reichardt and Eberhard Schmitt, Munich: R. Oldenbourg, 1985, 90-91.

lard, who called a murder of corpses the "perfect crime",[10] this strategy is tantamount to the calculated logical consequence – no body, no
killer, no provable crime, no judgment; and finally – no corpse, no
funeral, and no grief.

Their actual death apparently changes nothing about the fact that
they are labeled as "Disappeared", that they are accorded the paradoxical status of being present-absent. The adherence to a category originally introduced by the military, which can be understood rhetorically
as euphemism, politically as disinformation, and morally as dishones-
ty, reveals a perpetuation of effects of the terror beyond the end of the
dictatorship and the consolidation of democracy. The impact of this
redoubled deficiency of social life or, and this is of interest in this
essay, its effect on storytelling, is enormous.

The "Disappeared" is, I argue, a designation that is uncanny in the
Freudian sense and whose narrative representation bears fantastical
traits, a phenomenon whose effect on language is described by the
sociologist Gabriel Gatti: "Language recoils, and then the words that
we use in order to speak about things; the procedures by which we
represent them start to hedge as soon as they come into contact with
these entities and their surroundings and begin to stutter because it is
impossible to comfortably cope with them."[11] If a realistic representation of the "Disappeared" draws on features of the fantastic, then a
fantastic narrative must conversely become realistic through the representation of the disappearance of a person.

The "Disappeared" are discursively present in family biographies,
social activities, as well as in art and politics. Their impact exceeds
that which is evoked by the memory of dead victims of state terror.
This particular effect arises from the fact that the "Disappeared" are
aesthetically uncanny figures. While they certainly embody the presence of death, the act of speaking about them by definition renders
them not properly dead; they assume a space – limbo – between life
and death that stands outside of the time and space of history. The
"Disappeared" inhabit a space and time that are not historically conclusive, and thereby explode the structural conditions of realistic narrative. A special quality of disappearing and having disappeared is

---

[10] See Jean Baudrillard, *The Perfect Crime* (1995), trans. Chris Turner, London and
New York: Verso, 1996.
[11] Gabriel Gatti, *El Detenido-Desaparecido: Narrativas posibles para una catástro-
fe de la identidad*, Montevideo: Ediciones Trilce, 2008, 12 (my translation).

conditioned by the verb's nominalization in the perfect tense in perpetuity, which defies all responsibility through the intransitive and subject-related verb form itself (one can only disappear on one's own, for external influences suggest immediately a realm of magic or crime: "let something/someone disappear" and "make one disappear", but no reference at all to alternatives of political actions). The concept of "disappearance" consolidates the executor's state of impunity. The allegation that people disappeared can only be affirmed because the cases were hardly ever investigated and brought to court. It is manifestly opposed to laws of nature and common sense, and this point is exactly why I want to associate the phenomenon of the "Disappeared" with the structure of fantastic stories. The superimposition of magical or criminal connotations onto a missing cause or responsibility in the figure of the "Disappeared" also forms the centerpiece of Julio Cortázar's fantastical short story "Second Time Round".

The fantastic as a narrative mode of terror
Cortázar's narrative fell victim to the censor of the Argentine military in 1977 because it addresses the theme of "forced disappearance". It is, however, free of characteristics of a political reportage, for neither places, nor persons, nor time are named. By including this narrative in a collection of short stories with the explicit subtitle *Fantastic Stories*,[12] the genre is clearly defined through its paratext. The question is: what happens to the definition of the fantastic when it is very clearly mimetic, and to be sure, not only with respect to the representation of the properly common sense world of bureaucracy that is depicted here, but also with respect to the irruption of inexplicable events? Does the literary fiction represent the experience of terror?

The analysis of these questions is predicated on three assumptions that urgently have to be tested: first, the fantastic is a narrative mode of spreading terror; second, terror constitutes itself on the basis of the fantastic; third, the fantastic is a suitable form of representation, that is, it can best represent terror.

It is not a question of which fantastic stories can best represent which forms of terrorist violence. Rather, the problem runs in both directions: in addition to raw violence, terrorism itself requires a

[12] The short story appeared in 1977 in Cortázar's collection *Alguien que anda por ahí* (Madrid: Alfaguara) and was banned in the same year in Argentina by censor.

certain form of narrative that enables it to proliferate among the people. And secondly, the results of the criminal acts are transformed into figures of fantastic tales.

My analysis will show that the Argentine self-description of state terror does not lead in the direction of excesses committed by hot-blooded and exotic banana republic despots, but rather stands in more immediate proximity to dry bureaucratic annihilation known in Germany and best described (or better, prescribed) in Kafka's *The Trial*. Cortázar's "Second Time Round" narratologically condenses Kafka's hypotext in a textual relationship that can be described as symbiotic: narrative perspective, atmosphere, representation of space, and aesthetic construction of the uncanny are almost congruent in both texts. Death stands invisible and meaningless in the room. And yet there is an essential difference in referentiality and thus in reception: whereas Kafka describes a possible world, Cortázar imitates a real one. The leap from Kafka's foreshadowing of human destruction by bureaucratic acts of power to Cortázar's fictionalization of a horizon of experience that was real at the time of its publication takes place through a complex displacement on two levels: through an intertextual relation on the level of text and through a transgression of the border between fiction and historical documentation on the level of reference.

This categorial displacement cannot be explained by an analysis of the intertextual relationship between both texts alone. Therefore, one inevitably needs to look at both the aesthetic and political-historical effects. In *The Trial*,[13] Kafka's protagonist K. over the course of a year repeatedly encounters the fatuous low-level civil servants and executors of an unassailable power assigned to the jurisdiction of the law. He believes that he is innocent, yet this belief later becomes increasingly irrelevant, because it does not seem to be a question of innocence or guilt at all, but instead a matter of a fully arbitrary and preposterous act of bureaucracy. Neither the verdict nor the reason for his detainment are ever remotely mentioned, a circumstance which from the start can be described as uncanny. In numerous visits to the officials, he attempts to clarify the seeming misunderstanding, yet

---

[13]   The novel *Der Process* was first published in 1925 by Verlag die Schmiede, Berlin, and translated several times into English. I use David Wyllie's translation from *Project Gutenberg*: Franz Kafka, *The Trial* (1925), trans. David Wyllie, *Project Gutenberg*, 2003: http://www.gutenberg.org/dirs/etext05/ktrial11.txt (accessed 13 May 2011).

given the lack of explanations ("the main question is: Who is issuing the indictment? What office is conducting this affair? Are you officials?"), rational argument and semantic conventions ("'I see you've misunderstood me', said the supervisor who was already at the door. 'It's true that you're under arrest, but that shouldn't stop you from carrying out your job. And there shouldn't be anything to stop you carrying on with your usual life.'") contradictory reactions of low-level officials, allies, and spectators ("Across the street, the people were still there at the window, and it was only now that K. had gone up to his window that they seemed to become uneasy about quietly watching what was going on."), he finally loses the strength to resist.

Despite boldly defending his logical train of thought until the end, a lucidly arguing K. cannot defend himself against the cumulative absurdity mounting around him. Thus, the never uttered death sentence is practically executed with his compliance. Aside from both executioners and K. himself, nobody but the reader is a witness to the last breath of K. and the surviving shame. In "Second Time Round", Cortázar splices the narrative voice that in *The Trial* narrates in close proximity to K. into two separate voices:[14] at the beginning and end, one hears the lower officials in their simple office from the perspective of the first-person plural. Their fatuous character is perceptible in their colloquial speech, their homogeneous interests (drinking coffee, betting on horses, reading the newspaper) and their standardized self-description as merely executing orders within a hierarchical system. People are casually summoned into the office where they apparently perform everyday bureaucratic tasks such as filling out paperwork. Those responsible sit "up there", have no name and do not give clear instructions, except that the subpoenas should proceed without fuss.

The second narrative voice approximates or almost melds with the figure of María Elena, a *Doppelgänger* of K. who obediently follows the orders of the official yellow letter to appear at a particular time at a particular place, although she does not seem to know either the summoning agency or the purpose of her summons. Her emotional reaction of shame (she turns red as she enters the waiting room and ascribes this to her shyness before unfamiliar people; she turns red a

---

[14] I refer to the following English translation of the narrative: Julio Cortázar, "Second Time Around", trans. Gregory Rabass, *Books Abroad*, L/3 (Summer 1976), 517-52.

second time as she holds back her question to the others waiting as to why there is a second summons), of astonishment (the agency is outfitted with neither a flag nor an elevator and is located in a part of town where no one would expect to find it), and of fear correspond to Kafka's protagonists, in particular to K. His surprise, his quizzical, almost arrogant disbelief regarding his arrest which culminates in a shame that survives his death, designates the spectrum of the uncanny in the affects of the innocent victim in the face of a bureaucratic terror that Cortázar's protagonist also undergoes.

For an unknown reason, the young girl is summoned to a ministry located on a certain street in Buenos Aires for questioning. The girl, who is depicted as a very pensive and logically arguing character (like K.), knows that this summons concerns a bureaucratic matter, and so she goes, arrives at the office at the indicated time, and enters a long narrow hall filled with cigarette smoke (like all the halls K. is summoned to) where she sees a second door and a group of people waiting, an old woman, a young man, and a few others. Behind the second door is the office. She has to sit down to wait her turn, for there are many others scheduled to enter before she does. As usually happens in such instances, she begins talking with the people around her. Among them is a young man, Carlos, who quickly tells her that this is already his second time around because there is a first summons during which one must fill out papers and answer questions, and then there is a second call. As they talk about these matters, the others in succession continue to go in. These people remain in the office five or ten minutes, and then come out again. It is clear there are only two doors: the one to gain entrance to the office, and the other one leading to the stairs through the hall. After a while, the young man's turn comes. Two or three minutes go by; the door opens, but instead of the young man coming out, one of the employees appears who asks her to enter. She is taken by surprise, having been aware until then of only the one door everyone had left through. But when she enters the office – which is quite spacious, in fact, with many tables – she looks around and does not see the young man. In the meantime, the officials call her to a table where she has to fill out some lengthy forms, as is always the case in this type of office. But she continues to worry, nevertheless, for it all seems very strange to her. She thinks that perhaps there might be another door she did not notice, and that maybe they instructed him to leave through that alternate door. After all, she remembers at that moment, he was coming for a second time around, and she for the first time. The enigma remains unresolved until the end, as the story never explains what actually happened.

The effect of horror arises at two points (the disconcertment of the character being extremely intensified by the strong focalization): when it becomes clear to the girl that the young man has disappeared, and when she herself is invited for the second time.

Rhetorical devices: metaphors of nothing

At the beginning and at the end of the story, a subservient functionary of the mysterious office, who blindly performs partial tasks in the process of the dirty war (as the historically informed reader knows), speaks about the tasks delegated to him "from above" in mere hints. The allusive metaphors produce an exclusionary discourse: only the insiders can understand the indeterminate words. It just so happens that this discourse only refers to itself and does not even need to be understood by the organs performing it. For all intents and purposes, the illusory distinction between those who know and those who do not know is irrelevant, because such knowledge is futile. It is a knowledge of the void that ultimately transforms through Carlos' traceless disappearance into a frightening knowledge of annihilation. On the declarative level of this disappearance, all metaphors transform into their literal sense.[15] The mundane is discursively represented as an indeterminate, and the indeterminate refers to nothing, or to the nothing that the act of disappearing represents, without ever actually signifying.

Before turning to the dizzying aspect of the figures of speech and their silencing, I want to scrutinize how the anxiety of one's own disappearance is turned into the only referent of the narrative. The uncanny effect and the precondition of the fantastic are created by a

---

[15] A study on euphemism in national-socialist diction (for the notions of "völkisch" and "Endlösung") by Sneh and Cosaka provides the ideal framework of such an analysis. Sneh and Cosaka have shown that the transition to a pure, doubtless subjectivity by way of the annihilation of the other is executed, and that the figure of the bureaucrat and not the sadist best describes the executor of this operation: "No se registra la voluntad de lograr la angustia del partenaire sino la voluntad de un pasaje directo a un sujeto pleno, es decir por fuera de toda vacilación, del goce implicado an la angustia. Para ese pasaje no es necesarion la angustia del otro, sino lisa y llanamente, su eliminación" (Perla Sneh and Juan Carlos Cosaka, *La Shoah en el siglo: Del lenguaje del exterminio al exterminio del discurso*, Buenos Aires: Xavier Bóveda, 2000, 52).

setting that is equally an ordinary, orderly, and a familiar world: an office for something or another in a part of Buenos Aires where formalities are transacted on a daily basis. The act of filling out papers in the office is preceded by the familiar period of waiting in the waiting room filled by conversation about ordinary matters with the other people waiting. It is an official site in which, as a civil servant "on the other side of the desk", one has the leisure to drink coffee and all the time in the world to chit-chat about the weather and horse racing, but has no qualms about the purpose of the system (about the decrees and the execution of orders from the boss). Solely relevant is how ("nice and easy", "without worrying", "nice and clear"), not what ("things like that") is being performed. The superficially unperturbed and offensively flaunted banality of business ("the same thing every day") is, however, burst by the objects of this action being vehemently held in uncertainty. These opaque junctures, which appear nominalized on the discursive level as "something like that", "everything", or simply as "things", indicate what is at stake in these summons and the denomination of the agency.

On other levels as well, the referent is marked in the text as uncertain or illegible: on the writ of the summons, the signature is "illegible", the name plate of the office is "dirty and with a piece of paper pasted over". The unifying element between those waiting and the functionaries is the dense cigarette smoke that fills the waiting room as well as the offices and parked cars along the street (possibly occupied by informants), and thus represents a visual-olfactory density and opacity. This motif also occurs in Kafka's *Trial* with the same function. The functionaries themselves are faceless; they have nicknames ("negro López") or simple functions ("boss"). Whenever a face appears, then it is only in uncharacteristic form and never looking directly at another: "a clerk with a sickly face was looking at a form."

The discursive composition of the event is characterized by uncertainty at precisely such junctures where it is a matter of the identities of persons, and especially where the primary function of every bureaucratic office is performed, the entry of personal data. Precisely that moment when, while filling in the blank fields of the form ("It was the usual nonsense, first and last name, sex, address"), the protagonist María-Elena is distracted by the missing entry for Carlos, who had signed in before her, is the clearest sign of the text's movement toward erasure. "Usual nonsense" is here the most inscrutable of all metaphors of everyday life, as this "usual nonsense" of recording personal data becomes a denotation of the methodical act of making a person disappear.

Cortázar's short story is written in Argentine Spanish; it transfers the characteristic colloquial way of speaking in Buenos Aires into the written word. Whereas the passages that report the perspective of the functionaries retain the sociolect of a less educated stratum, the main part of the short story which focuses on María-Elena and represents her voice is more elevated, almost classical. The metaphors that find expression on the functionaries' side of the counter are taken from everyday parlance. I showed earlier how the way that things unfold takes on a much more significant function in the text than the things themselves. The highest aim – a frictionless course of events ("things like that had to happen without making waves") – is unflinchingly repeated in a number of metaphorical variations, and is the actual task ordered by the boss, "the boss's word". Frequent repetition reflects the repeated insistence of the boss's assignment: "he would repeat it every so often for just in case." The Spanish metaphor "sin escombros" is translated as "without making waves", which literally means "without rubbish" in the sense of without a remainder or without a trace. An essential feature of disappearance is thus already mentioned in this first passage in the form of a metaphor whose English translation remarkably denotes a further aspect of killing methods (although this was not yet officially known at the time of the translation[16]): drugged prisoners were thrown from airplanes into the ocean or Rio de la Plata. The frictionless, traceless course of ominous government business is also evoked in the metaphor "pueden proceder no más", which refers to the procedural, progression by procedure, but literally means "only proceeding forward" and leads directly into death when one orients oneself along the directed path.

---

[16] If starting in 1976 death flights ordered by the military took place every Wednesday, then presumably rumors circulated very quickly among the populace and must have been known to human rights organizations. The extent and degree of such practices first came to light in 1995 with the confession of Scilingo, who opened the door of military planes and threw out prisoners. See Horacio Verbitsky, *The Flight: Confessions of an Argentine Dirty Warrior*, trans. Esther Allen, New York: The New Press, 1996.

There are two passages in the short story: one leads through the door and into the government office, while the other leads out of the waiting room and into the street. The first passage through the door and into the government office is completed with the act of personal registration and ends with the passage through the exit door into an outer world perceived as freedom. The second passage, and this is also the title of the short story, leads, as it were, through the door of the "éxito", from the outside into the room of the government office and never out again. "Éxito" is death, and all who come through the door a second time, pass through the waiting room, and go into the office, like Carlos, but never come back again. In this way, the metaphor uttered by the bald-headed man among the people waiting, "Life is a waiting room", is reduced to a horrific literality that also contains its opposite, namely that death lurks on the other end of the waiting room.

The short story opens with the remarks of one of the civil servants who discloses in the first-person plural, "We just waited for them, each one had his date and his time". Day and hour are simple coordinates of time, they are "appointments" that, in a metaphorical constriction tagged with a possessive pronoun such as this one, denote those days and hours that are determined for a person, that is, his terminus or end.

A fatal disappearance is also a disappearance of meaning, nonsense, the void. "Pavadas" ("nonsense") is the narrator's word for the kernel of all government business, namely the "trámites" that are omnipresent in Spanish, which refer to both the act of completion of formalities as well as the documents themselves. It is the occasion at which the office becomes a scene of paranoia. The "trámites" to be completed by María-Elena consist of the usual personal data. They attest to her identity and consequently her life. She fulfills the required bureaucratic act with the glance around the room in which she expects to find Carlos, realizing there is no second door through which he could have left. The meaning of the "trámites" begins to lose its symbolic function at the moment when filling in the blank spaces gets associated with the disappearance of a human being. "Trámites" means at its root "path across/through" (from the Latin, *trames, transmeare*). Yet where there is no door, no path leads through, the passageway is a dead end, a *cul de sac*, a path into death. Significantly, the synonym for the "transition" is metaphor itself: *meta, pherein*. Thus, the "traslado" refers to the literal "trans-lation" and is, in the diction of the military dictatorship, the official designation for the murder of captives.

The obsession with "papers" ("trámites") in the logic of government bureaucracy that certify citizenship, gender, professional, and even human identity, points to their latent annihilating potential in the logic of death. Identity, human existence, is reduced to certification by paper; in the government office it becomes a death certificate.

The translation/transition and the metaphor of life into death, of presence into absence, occur temporally between the first and second time, in the repetition that gives the short story its name. In his study of the uncanny, Freud identified the "moment of the repetition of the similar" as the source of the uncanny, which can, though not with the same clarity as the motif of the *Doppelgänger*, nonetheless "subject to certain conditions and combined with certain circumstances, arouse an uncanny feeling".[17] Such circumstances of repetition recall distraught dream sequences in which it is impossible to elude the inescapable. In Cortázar's "Segunda vez", the second time, the second summons to the government office, becomes a nightmare. All of the desperate observations that María-Elena made during her first visit which were supposed to establish the normality of the passageway dissolve into nothing. Her premonitions that something just is not right here become dreadful reality (yet in a sense other than what she dared to think):

> Maria Elena got the feeling that something was bothering her, something that wasn't completely clear. Not on the form, where it was easy to go along filling in the blanks; something outside it, something that was missing or wasn't in its place. She stopped writing and took a look around, the other desks with the clerks working or talking among themselves, the dirty walls with posters and photographs, the two windows, the door she had come through, the only door in the office.[18]

Between the moment when it becomes clear to her that Carlos has disappeared and the moment it becomes clear to her that the same destiny awaits her during her second summons ("Thursday at eleven"),

---

17 Freud, "The Uncanny", 249.
18 Cortázar, "Second Time Around", 519.

another process of translation transpires: identification with Carlos. At first he was her predecessor, now he is her *Doppelgänger*, by whom she is guided into nothing. He is her harbinger of death, in the uncanny sense of the motif of the *Doppelgänger* in which Freud diagnosed a transformation of omens following the overcoming of a primitive phase of mental life: "From having been an assurance of immortality, it becomes the uncanny harbinger of death."[19]

"Second Time Around" operates structurally and linguistically with the overlapping semantic contexts of the sphere of bureaucracy and the sphere of death. Where at first glance government business is recognizable at the lowest level of its power, legible in the feather-brained, faceless paper pushers behind the counter, whose sole interests consist of drinking coffee, chit-chat, and horse races, in the next moment a space of death irrupts within the government office which transforms non-issues into voids.

Terror between bureaucratic fiction and the reality of death

The logics of both frames of reference – bureaucracy and death – are seemingly opposed and hence fulfill Todorov's criterion of the fantastic, which arises out of the collision between two irreconcilable explanatory frames. While it is not accurate to talk about a head-on collision in the short story, one may refer to a latency of the sphere of death that is manifest as a short-circuit of metaphors on the discursive level of the characters: if the void – annihilation – is the latent meaning of the government office and all its procedures, then every banal metaphor of a passage that becomes a passageway into nothing (of which the short story is full) – *trámite, traslado, sala de espera, éxito* – refers back to its literal meaning, or (in Freud's terms), its augur is reversed. The formalities at the government office do not serve the representation of living existence, but that of death, the transfer from one site to another becomes murder "sin escombros", killing time in the waiting room manifests its predetermined reality and the door leading out means the *exitus*.

Freud's uncanny is superior to Todorov's fantastic as an analytic model insofar as the moments of semantic transformation that are inherent to every metaphor can be understood as a superimposition of an ambivalence, whereas the fantastic strongly operates with figures

---

[19]   Freud, "The Uncanny", 237.

of opposition. It is the dramatic irony at the origin of the German concept of *das Unheimliche* (namely, that it is closely intertwined with its opposite) which constitutes the fantastic within this simultaneously realistic short story. With Freud it is even possible to encounter the problem of mimesis that every theory of the fantastic has to deal with sooner or later: what happens when the frame of this story itself remains unresolved within the story and has a correspondence in the extra-literary world? How do fictive *terreur* and real terror relate to one another? Does the story participate parasitically, does it bolster the effect of anxiety even more, or does it remain contained in its fictive world? Cortázar's short story operates with entirely classical techniques of fantastic literature. The problem that a person disappears in the middle of a banal world of bureaucratic regimentation – this is the fantastic effect – is first made plausible by a realistic, yet unspecific figuration of precisely this bureaucratic world. The story mimetically constructs out of necessity a fictive world that is subservient to the laws of necessity and probability, in order to then call them into question through an inexplicable event, which in this case can first be resolved for both the Argentine censor and readership of 1977 by recourse to the historical reality.

How does it get resolved, if one wants to stick with Todorov? For the purely uncanny, the experience of disappearance remains in reality inexplicable and in contradiction to the laws of nature, but was this indeed the real life experience of about 30,000 people? With Freud, the uncanny passageway between bureaucratic fiction and reality of death can be defined by a symbolic overlap where metaphor becomes the path to death. The official writs in the everyday world of bureaucracy go hand in hand with the fiction of government office in Cortázar's short story in the concept of the "trámites". It is significant that Cortázar did not separate his new style of fantastic telling of historical facts from his other, purely fictional texts. In "Segunda vez", Cortázar opened up new spaces for the intersection of reality and fiction in the fantastic and its function as a representation of real historical events while he lived in European exile. He had mentioned the new direction of his understanding of literature earlier, "while in times past literature represented somehow holidays that the reader allowed himself in his daily reality, today in Latin America it has become a direct way of exploring what happens to us and asking ourselves about

212 *Kirsten Mahlke*

the reasons why it happens to us".[20] Fear and terror can indeed be induced by the text, because it contains the ambivalence of the metaphor of death. This is, however, qualitatively different from the fear in reality, and hence fundamentally opposed to the agents of state terror, because it results in knowledge and exposes rather than conceals the abyss between sign and meaning. The real occurrence of the impossible is not the disappearance of human beings, but that one refers to disappearance when one means killing.

---

[20] Julio Cortázar, *Argentina: Años de alambradas culturales*, Barcelona: Muchnik, 1984, 114 (my translation).

MIDDLE HOURS: TERRORISM AND NARRATIVE EMPLOTMENT IN ANDRE DUBUS III'S *THE GARDEN OF LAST DAYS*

GEORGIANA BANITA

> I still believe the world is ending, but I concede that it seems to be ending more slowly than I once thought ... so I figured I'd make a book.[1]

It appears simple enough and perhaps a little obvious to suggest an analogy between the plots of terrorism and narrative plots. The term "plot" seems to overflow with meaning both in the study of political action and in the field of narrative. Surely no terrorist attack can succeed or even come into being without some measure of plotting, that is, scheming, conspiring, and thoughtful planning. Narrative similarly depends on a plot to buttress its other aspects, a structure that postmodern trends have rendered increasingly skeletal, yet which literature about one of the most devastating terrorist events in modern memory, the attacks of September 11, 2001, has hitherto seemed to favor over less focused narrative forms. Although there are exceptions to this tendency, most notably Ronald Sukenick's experimental novel *Last Fall* (published posthumously in 2005[2]), the preference for tightly plotted structures in narrating 9/11 comes as no surprise in light of the terrorist attack's own reliance on plotting and of the profoundly eventful nature of terrorism itself.

Yet even though it can safely be stated that most 9/11 fiction has adopted a straightforward approach to plot in the realist mode, the correspondence of terror plots and narrative plots in a post-9/11

---

[1] Art Spiegelman, *In the Shadow of No Towers*, New York: Pantheon Books, 2004.
[2] Ronald Sukenick, *Last Fall*, Normal, IL: FC2, 2005.

context poses questions that go beyond the mere reflection of a historical event in its narrative retelling. In this essay, I explore the practice of emplotting, or storytelling, as a space of mediation between the socio-political valences of terror and its narrative aesthetics. I argue that the emplotting of terrorism in post-9/11 cultural discourse may be better understood by studying its mutation into narrative forms that retain the original event's aura of violence and spectacle. Drawing on narratological, historiographic, and cultural approaches to storytelling and to the concept of plot – as formulated, among others, by Peter Brooks, Hayden White, and Hannah Arendt – I propose to investigate the formal structures and textual performance of Andre Dubus III's *The Garden of Last Days* (2008), a novel that is both symptomatic of a larger plot-oriented trend in 9/11 literature and critical of its hermeneutic scheme.

The son of Andre Dubus, a well-known American short fiction writer, Andre Dubus III does not feature frequently or, for that matter, prominently, in discussions of post-9/11 fiction, most of which have displayed a consistent interest in the plight of the American intelligentsia and of the privileged classes in the aftermath of the attacks. The protagonists of 9/11 novels are usually employees of companies located in the World Trade Center towers, or other individuals of comparably high social standing. While a teacher of creative writing at universities such as Tufts and Harvard, Dubus continued to work as a construction worker, and this is where the social canvas of his fiction differs from the by now familiar middle- and upper-class voices of 9/11 literature. Dubus' work, Lisa Abney notes, "delves into many troubling sides of contemporary society – urban violence, decaying relationships, loss of community and family, loss of identity, and unfulfilled dreams".[3]

The Garden of Last Days similarly emerges from the disturbing world of the American underclass. Its realistic view of America's underprivileged at the same time cannily elucidates the processes that allow terrorism to come into being. The stresses and strains of their hand-to-mouth lives compel the novel's American characters to become radicalized in various ways (tempers are lost and the law is broken on multiple occasions) that differ only in intensity and effect

---

[3] Lisa Abney, "Andre Dubus III", in *Twenty-First-Century American Novelists*, eds Lisa Abney and Suzanne Disheroon-Green, Detroit, MI: Thomson Gale, 2004, 75.

from the attacks of the Islamic fundamentalists. "Reconciliation", Ian Ward maintains, "depends not just on hearing the stories of those who suffered, but on hearing the stories of those who caused their suffering".[4] Dubus' narrative nurtures empathy precisely through the equal subjection of both ordinary poor Americans and Saudi Arabian terrorists to a set of social forces that alienate and impoverish both groups. This focus on terrorism's diverse demographics stages a complex set of relationships aptly mapped out by John Orr as a complicated diagram of power relations: "Terrorism ... is two things, both *event*, the things that happen, and *process*, that is to say, it consists of the relationships developing between protagonists, the dyadic relationship of terrorists and authorities, and the triadic relationship of state, terrorists and public."[5]

Its focus on class, poverty, and radicalization is not this novel's only original contribution to 9/11 discourse. Most fictions that focus on the terrorist attacks develop narratives that are triggered by the events and almost invariably are set in their aftermath, reflecting their broader cultural impact. Prior to the narrative incipit or, at the very latest, by the end of the first few pages, in novels by Don DeLillo, Jay McInerney, Jonathan Safran Foer, or Ken Kalfus, the attacks have already occurred, killing significant others, shattering marriages, and propelling lives into crises. *The Garden of Last Days* warns the reader on its first page that the setting of the novel is "Late Summer, '01",[6] thus exposing the narrative sword of Damocles waiting to collapse and sever the lives of the protagonists, most of whom remain blissfully unaware up until the novel's last pages. The reader's only complicit companion is Bassam al-Jizani, one of the 9/11 hijackers, for whom the plot (both terrorist and narrative) acquires the intensity and corporeal abandon of a last supper amidst a tangled knot of human relationships to which he is as indifferent as the others are oblivious to his own murderous plans.

---

[4]   Ian Ward, *Law, Text, Terror*, Cambridge: Cambridge University Press, 2009, 89.

[5]   John Orr, "Introduction", in *Terrorism and Modern Drama*, eds John Orr and Dragan Klaic, Edinburgh: Edinburgh University Press, 1990, 2.

[6]   Andre Dubus III, *The Garden of Last Days*, New York: W.W. Norton, 2008, 1. (unless specified otherwise, all subsequent references to this edition are indicated by page numbers in the text).

The merit of Dubus' novel lies in the interplay it stages between the unfolding of the plot and its predetermined resolution, as well as in its ability to encapsulate larger questions of narrative agency and morality within a spare, tightly-plotted story spilling over at precisely those moments that seem one-dimensional and self-contained. Before retracing these discretely self-conscious moments, however, it is worth elaborating on the complex theoretical imbrications of terrorism and narrative, which determine the use of plot in Dubus' novel and in 9/11 fiction more broadly. The issue of how terrorist plots are folded within narrative structures has remained largely unexamined, although the question has not been without importance, at least indirectly, in such studies as Margaret Scanlan's *Plotting Terror*. Scanlan, however, only nominally refers to the "affinities between … literary and terror-ist plots", detecting in terrorism-themed fictions primarily "an invita-tion to see in insurgent terrorism an occasion for exploring the roman-tic idea of the writer as rebel and for questioning romanticism's optimism about literature's social power".[7] My aim is to examine the way terrorist and narrative plots, especially through their endings, are caught up in a wider cultural field, as well as to look at the ways in which Dubus' novel not only engages with post-9/11 discourses of closure, but also presents its own performative critique.[8]

Terror, action, narrative

Any correlation between terrorist plots and their narrative counterparts must first of all be based on a clear understanding of the contentious role of narrative in the representation of reality. Historian Hayden White has famously dismissed emplotment as an inadequate tool of historiography, preferring instead plotless forms of historical represen-tation, such as annals and chronicles, which list events as they present

---

[7]   Margaret Scanlan, *Plotting Terror: Novelists and Terrorists in Contemporary Fiction*, Charlottesville and London: University Press of Virginia, 2001, 2, 10.

[8]   Closure-repellant narratives have already been the subject of valuable studies, the most perceptive of which, to my mind, is Russell Reising's *Loose Ends: Closure and Crisis in the American Social Text* (Durham and London: Duke University Press, 1996). The narrative endings discussed in this book "not only fail to resolve or con-clude important narrative issues, but exacerbate, problematize, and sometimes explode exactly the issues which generate the narratives and which, according to many theories of closure, are precisely those narrative energies that conclusions exist to domesticate" (*ibid.*, ix).

themselves to perception, that is, in unmediated form and often without causal linkages. Storytelling, White maintains, imposes on reality a set of structural and moral principles that it naturally resists: "Does the world really present itself to perception in the form of well-made stories, with central subjects, proper beginnings, middles, and ends, and a coherence that permits us to see the end in every beginning?" Certainly not, White suggests, and rejects endings in particular as ways of projecting values onto events, noting that "the demand for closure in the historical story is a demand ... for moral meaning, a demand that sequences of real events be assessed as to their significance in a moral drama".[9]

Writing about the "historical exceptionalism" that isolates 9/11 as a unique story in time and place, Amy Kaplan laments the view of American history as peaking in the 9/11 attacks, an event "so unique and unprecedented as to transcend time and defy comparison or historical analysis".[10] This idea of 9/11 as historical climax, a last extension to the "end of history" proclaimed since the end of the Cold War, is rooted in an understanding of narrative as a balm on history's wounds, a neat system into which destructive historical lapses can be encapsulated and defused. Leo Bersani and Ulysse Dutoit have usefully explained what happens when violence becomes embedded in plot: "it can be isolated, understood, perhaps mastered and eliminated. And, having been conditioned to think of violence within narrative frameworks, we expect this mastery to take place as a result of the pacifying power of such narrative conventions as beginnings, explanatory middles, and climactic endings."[11] Certainly the fantasy of mastery implied by narrativization accounts for the predilection of 9/11 fiction toward realist plotting. Yet even though it subscribes to these tendencies, Dubus' novel *The Garden of Last Days* also draws critical attention to the moral and ideological package that the 9/11 attacks as a moment of cultural closure deliver to us. He does so by exploring the micro-narrativity of events leading up to September 11 in the lives of

[9] Hayden White, *The Content of the Form: Narrative Discourse and Historical Representation*, Baltimore, MD: Johns Hopkins University Press, 1987, 24, 21.
[10] Amy Kaplan, "Homeland Insecurities: Reflections on Language and Space", *Radical History Review*, LCCCV (Winter 2003), 83.
[11] Leo Bersani and Ulysse Dutoit, *The Forms of Violence: Narrative in Assyrian Art and Modern Culture*, New York: Schocken Books, 1985, 51.

people whose trajectories intersect at once forcefully and randomly. The plot intensity of the novel, as well as its insistence on fortuity as an organizing structure, will in fact guide my analysis throughout.

According to Roland Barthes, narrative is in fact the very condition and foundation of thought; it is "international, transhistorical, transcultural: it is simply there, like life itself".[12] And if Fredric Jameson is right, narrativization can even be considered "the central function or *instance* of the human mind",[13] a form of human comprehension that is productive of meaning. Weaving individual actions into a single narrative is thus constitutive of their value and implications, as it enables the retrospective articulation of their importance both for the actors themselves and for the readers. Hayden White admits as much when he writes that "the kind of descriptive protocol used to constitute events as facts of a particular sort determines the kind of fact they are considered to be".[14] Yet *The Garden of Last Days* challenges this issue of signification, what Peter Brooks refers to as narrative's "stubborn insistence on making meaning in our world and in our lives";[15] it does so, paradoxically enough, by an acute reliance on plot construction. The novel's various blurbs, including one by Stephen King, accordingly describe the narrative as "compulsively readable", "riveting", and mesmerizing. The challenge I see at work here lies in the novel's dissolution of the doer-sufferer binary into which the 9/11 plot is routinely compressed by presenting the build-up toward the attacks as a series of contingent chain reactions.

In reading the novel from this perspective, I am drawing on Hannah Arendt's concept of action, the full meaning of which "can reveal itself only when it has ended ... frequently when all the participants are dead". The closure Arendt has in mind, of the kind that can codify historical processes most clearly, is radical to the point of complete extinction. Her words here unwittingly invoke the image of the suicide terrorist: "only a man who does not survive his one supreme act

---

[12]   Roland Barthes, "Introduction to the Structural Analysis of Narratives", in *Image-Music-Text*, ed. Stephen Heath, New York: Hill and Wang, 1977, 79.
[13]   Fredric Jameson, *The Political Unconscious: Narrative as a Socially Symbolic Act*, Ithaca, NY: Cornell University Press, 1981, 13.
[14]   Hayden White, "The Narrativization of Real Events", *Critical Inquiry*, VII/4 (Summer 1981), 795.
[15]   Peter Brooks, *Reading for the Plot: Design and Intention in Narrative*, Oxford: Clarendon Press, 1984, 323.

remains the indisputable master of his identity and possible greatness, because he withdraws into death from the possible consequences and continuation of what he began."[16] Conveying a sense of futility and uncertainty, Dubus' characters are still very much alive, and although one could argue that we, as readers, are privy to their future and to the attacks, constantly seeing their lives through the prism of this ending "beyond the frame", the sum of coincidences and accidents that drive the plot forward suggests that any ending is possible, and only a wily fate (or force of circumstance), a Nabokovian McFate, has selected 9/11 from among a range of options.

Inseparable from the question of how the narrativization of terrorism aggregates is a second problem about the ways in which such narratives are read. "I never feel like I have a story to tell. I write to find a story",[17] Dubus confessed to *Publishers Weekly* and this lack of authorial plotting, as disingenuous as it may sound, confirms the writer's investment in narrative as the medium of writing, of memory, and of terrorism itself, which, like any other kind of story, involves a hermeneutic relation and the same desire for elucidation that a literary text will spark, by dint of its sheer unpredictability. Dubus' method, a sort of narrative anamnesis, is founded on the nature of terrorist plots to rewrite the historical events that preceded them. Dubus applies this model narratologically by telling the story of four lonesome, rudderless characters whose trajectories are elucidated in two ways: first, as a result of the eruption of violence at the end of the novel; and second, through the reader's own awareness of what is to come, giving rise to a clandestine form of hermeneutic plotting. As in political acts of terror, the plot must remain secret, though for different reasons: the terrorist event requires discretion as part of its spectacular design; narrative plot must remain under wraps for the sake of readerly seduction and the creation of suspense.

Anthony Kubiak has argued that

> ... terror as a political weapon *depends* upon narrative ... that is coherent, logical, and transparent. Not only must the handbooks be clear

---

[16] Hannah Arendt, *The Human Condition*, Chicago: University of Chicago Press, 1958, 192, 193-94.
[17] Louisa Ermelino, "My Dinner with Andre", *Publishers Weekly*, 28 April 2008: 106.

and logical, the spectacle itself must be immediately readable and interpretable, no matter how 'insane' the act might seem to be.[18]

Perhaps the most important "readable and interpretable" plot thread of
both preparatory and spectacular terrorism lies in its jihad element,
that is, the narrative that convinces the perpetrators to sacrifice themselves in the first place, a narrative strict enough to preempt rebellion
yet sufficiently capacious and ambiguous to accommodate whoever
subscribes to its precepts. When Bassam's father learns that his son
has "taken up jihad", which to Bassam means that he is "prepared to
die for Allah" (255), the father explains that jihad is nothing but "a
struggle within yourself" (256) – in other words, not a suicidal meta-
physics whereby only the ending of a life bestows meaning on its
narrative, but an intradiegetic plot device guiding the self through a
series of transformations. Similarly, Dubus' novel never seems to
lapse into metafictional self-awareness, the relentless plot carefully
disguising the critique of narrative roiling underneath. This convergence of simplicity and ambiguity displays several features that can be
found individually in other plot-conscious 9/11 fictions.

Emplotting 9/11: reverberation, suspension, occlusion
Several writers of 9/11 fiction, particularly authors working within
classifiable genres, have relied heavily on plot as a narrative engine
that reinforces the deadliness and unavoidability of the terrorist event,
as in Jess Walter's *The Zero*[19] or William Gibson's *Pattern Recognition*.[20] The latter describes the attacks over a small number of pages
that provide the novel's narrative centerpiece, an island of stability
amidst its transnational crisscrossing. Ultimately the multiple plots
fold back onto this core section that significantly offers a two-scale
narrative of the attacks in Manhattan: as a massive blow to glass and
steel structures, but also as the simultaneous fall of a rose petal inside
a windowed box in an antique shop, under the puzzled and eerily
fascinated gaze of the protagonist, Cayce Pollard, whose father disappeared under the WTC rubble. The parallel between the towers collaps-

---

[18]   Anthony Kubiak, "Spelling It Out: Narrative Typologies of Terror", *Studies in the Novel*, XXXVI/3 (Fall 2004), 300.
[19]   Jess Walter, *The Zero*, New York: Regan, 2006.
[20]   William Gibson, *Pattern Recognition*, New York: Putnam, 2003.

ing and the petal falling in slow motion in its highly controlled aesthetic environment is an accurate rendition of how the larger 9/11 plot reverberates in the small-scale aesthetics of fiction. The challenge of representing the attacks in narrative is one of containment and aestheticization: storytelling condenses the broader narrative of terrorism into a simplified, clearly delineated textual space. The catastrophe may thereby appear decelerated or shrink into miniature, yet on both levels the general direction of the plot is unmistakably downward. As Don DeLillo writes in his intricately plotted novel *Libra*:

> ... there is a tendency of plots to move toward death .... A narrative plot is no less than the conspiracy of armed men. The tighter the plot of a story, the more likely it will end in death.[21]

The plot of DeLillo's own 9/11 novel *Falling Man* is, however, anything but tight.[22] The narrative meanders along interwoven plots – the story of a doomed couple alternates with a loose narrative on the terrorists' conspiratorial meetings – converging toward the attacks, which had already occurred shortly before the novel's opening gambit. Here the tendency of plot toward death materializes in the repeated descent of a man falling from the North Tower, the original and a performative copy calling himself Falling Man, toward an unmentionable ending. *Falling Man* on the whole shows little enthusiasm for the virtues of literary storytelling, exposing the use of plot in narrative as merely a strategy of conferring meaning upon dreadful and inexplicable events that would otherwise defy all sense of understanding. Plot, this novel suggests, prohibits a slower-paced and more engaged working-through of the events and of their attendant trauma. DeLillo's rejection of plot as an artificial means of serializing the eventness of 9/11, coupled with his paratactic approach to the imagery produced by the attacks, indicates that deferring and suspending the event may allow readers to inhabit it more intensively.

Taking this aesthetics of textual occlusion to the extreme, other post-9/11 narratives have attempted to divert attention from the attacks altogether and to emphasize the equally catastrophic nature of individual tragedies. The plot of Philip Beard's novel *Dear Zoe* hinges

---

[21]   Don DeLillo, *Libra*, New York: Viking, 1988, 221.
[22]   Don DeLillo, *Falling Man*, New York: Scribner, 2007.

on the accidental death of a young girl on September 11, 2001, while
Roland Merullo's *A Love Story* places the death of a 9/11 plane pas-
senger in the distant background of a medical thriller sustained by a
romantic plot.[23] In an instance of repression bordering on textual psy-
chosis, Richard Powers' novel *The Echo Maker* stages a sophisticated
plot of amnesia and identity loss partly in response to the alienation
felt by many Americans affected by the increasingly severe counterterrorism policies implemented by the Bush administration.[24] Plot,
then, can be both a vehicle of disaster and a narrative path of escape
from its consequences.

The Garden of Last Days contributes two original features to a
discussion of plot in 9/11 fiction: first, a seamless imbrication of narrative and terrorist plotting (Bassam and his plans are invoked
throughout, while DeLillo, for instance, devotes only the last section
of his novel to the 9/11 hijackers); and second, it instantiates, through
the deferral of its pending conclusion, what Peter Brooks called the
"altered situation of plot, which no longer wishes to be seen as end-
determined, moving toward full predication of the narrative sentence,
claiming a final plenitude of meaning".[25] In Brooks' words, rather
than triggering a "spectacular denouement," the 9/11 attacks in *The
Garden of Last Days* merely mark a "textual finis", the resolution of a
randomly entangled ensemble piece that could have taken a different
route at any one of its junctures.

The sense of an ending
Although it seemingly progresses teleologically toward an epiphanic
twist that reveals Bassam's involvement in the 9/11 hijackings, *The
Garden of Last Days* ping-pongs between monolithic and fragmentary

---

[23]   Philip Beard, *Dear Zoe*, New York: Viking, 2005; Roland Merullo, *A Little Love
Story*, New York: Shaye Areheart Books, 2005.
[24]   Richard Powers, *The Echo Maker*, New York: Farrar, Straus and Giroux, 2006.
[25]   Brooks, *Reading for the Plot*, 314. Brooks refers here to postmodern, poststructuralist plotting mechanisms, taking Allain Robbe-Grillet as his case study. It may be
argued that the 9/11 attacks explicitly demand a poststructuralist approach to storytelling, especially through the influence of information technology, surveillance, and
global mobility on the period immediately preceding the attacks and over the years
that have elapsed since then. For an earlier study of global power relations and
poststructuralism, see James Der Derian, *Antidiplomacy: Spies, Terror, Speed and
War*, Oxford: Blackwell, 1992.

narrative structures in an attempt to grapple with an event that itself revolved around a main plot trickling down along individual trajectories. This narrative oscillation gives rise to several paradoxes. The novel is plot-oriented, yet it does not move steadily along the rails of a single story. And even though it adheres to no overarching narrative structure, one can discern patterns in its organization. I must first briefly sketch the plot, reducing its richness to the narrative points that are at issue.

There are four main story lines, the first of which, focusing on a stripper, April (stage name Spring), who entertains one of the 9/11 hijackers, lays claim to a bedrock of historical fact. Some of the Saudi Arabian terrorists indeed spent their last days drinking in Floridian strip clubs in order to "deflect suspicion" (26). Bassam offers April thousands of dollars in return for a private performance in the club's exclusive Champagne Room, during which he expresses the wish to know why April has chosen this particular profession and to touch the genital scar caused by the birth of April's daughter, Franny (now three). A second narrative plot involves the kidnapping of Franny by A.J. (Alan James), a disgruntled club customer pained not only by his eviction from the club after manhandling one of the girls, but also by his battered wife's decision to keep him from seeing his son, Cole, by restraining order. A.J. accidentally discovers Franny, who has managed to escape the sloppy, adult supervision of the other strippers, and takes her for a ride, during which the girl is starved, sedated, and exploited as a stand-in for A.J.'s own son, Cole. The third subplot chronicles the thoughts of the elderly Jean – April's landlord and Franny's babysitter – hospitalized on the day the girl disappears and thus unable to look after the toddler; while the fourth narrative strand focuses on Lonnie, a young bouncer at the strip club who has his sights set on April (his sentiments are unrequited).[26] When she realizes, after the

---

[26]   The characters receive equal attention over the course of the novel – in alternating subchapters channeling each one's perspective – which contributes to the gradual distraction of the reader away from 9/11 as a final narrative punchline. Bersani and Dutoit have identified a narrative technique that accurately matches the democratic distribution of narrative space I am describing here: "the calculation, preparation, and control of climaxes result from the establishment of foregrounds (objects of desire) and backgrounds (insignificant, undesired reality). This is also a narrative strategy: the climactic significances of narrative are made possible by a rigidly hierarchical organi-

attacks of September 11, that a hijacker had been one of her clients, April seems keen to change her profession and to take her responsibilities as a mother more seriously. The kidnapping of her daughter, who is eventually recovered and allowed to join her mother, appears to have as much of an impact on April as the recognition of her intimacy with a mass murderer. Yet the novel's point of closure raises more questions than it resolves: it remains unclear whether April's resolutions can be sustained and to what extent the terrorist attacks have acted as a catalyst for her purported transformation.

As this summary makes clear, despite its critique of narrative form, *The Garden of Last Days* does have an ending, one that brutally interrupts the events and appears to recast their significance. In this, the novel confirms Frank Kermode's assessment in *The Sense of an Ending*[27] that narrative relies on retrospection in attaching relevance to events: *The Garden of Last Days* is clearly written and read with the outcome of 9/11 in mind. Yet the characters are constantly unsure of the effects of their actions and narrowly miss the importance of what takes place around them. In the end, it is not 9/11 that establishes connection and coherence among the narrative events, which remain as arbitrary and inscrutable as on the first page. In this, *The Garden of Last Days* works more subtly than other 9/11 fictions which use the attacks like a final trump card to impose some coherence within the great mass of the contingent.

Marie-Laure Ryan opens her study of plot deficiencies in narrative with a concise description of authorial versus textual plotting:

> In narrative, plot exists on two levels: the plotting of the author, who creates the storyline; and the plotting of the characters, who set goals, devise plans, schemes and conspiracies, and try to arrange events to their advantage. The plotting of both author and characters is meant to exercise control: for the author, control over the reader, who must undergo a certain experience; for the characters, control over other characters and over the randomness of life.[28]

zation of people and events into major and minor roles" (Bersani and Dutoit, *The Forms of Violence*, 41).

[27] Frank Kermode, *The Sense of an Ending: Studies in the Theory of Fiction*, Oxford: Oxford University Press, 1967.

[28] Marie-Laure Ryan, "Cheap Plot Tricks, Plot Holes, and Narrative Design", *Narrative*, XVII/1 (January 2009), 56.

Ryan argues that these divergent yet deeply imbricated plot levels are not always in sync, and occasionally the author's plotting is so heavy-handed as to completely unravel the causal chain of the characters' actions. In cases where the pivotal plot elements postulated by Aristotle (reversal of fortune and recognition) do not derive from probable circumstances as they are set up by the narrative, but are propelled by authorial intervention, Ryan diagnoses what she describes as "cheap plot tricks" or CPTs, some of which she dismisses as bad plotting, irrespective of narrative context. 9/11 as a narrative event could, I believe, in some cases be classified as a cheap plot trick – with a focus on "trick" rather than "cheap", since it is not my intention to valorize narrative strategies. The attacks are mentioned unexpectedly in the penultimate paragraph of Paul Auster's novel *The Brooklyn Follies*.[29] They conclude Julia Glass' *The Whole World Over* and Claire Messud's *The Emperor's Children*, intricately-structured novels that paint their characters into a corner and deploy the terrorist attacks as a classic *deus ex machina* device.[30]

Certainly any terrorist attack derives its effectiveness and *raison d'être* from shock and violence, so it could be argued that however gently a writer may wish to incorporate terrorism into a narrative, the result will inevitably be catastrophic. The story has no choice but to choke on the plot item it has been fed, especially when this occurs towards the end of a text and blocks further attempts at textual assimilation. As Ryan remarks, "a deus ex machina ending lingers in the reader's memory", while a preparatory one "at least holds the promise of future satisfaction".[31] However unsatisfactory such an abrupt interruption of the narrative in Dubus' novel may be – indeed, the multiplicity of subplots forecloses any comprehensive conclusion to the book – what lingers in the reader's memory is the interruption itself. "To disrupt narrativity", Anthony Kubiak writes, "is to disrupt body and mind, to induce a kind of madness – not merely to interrupt the story, or cause us to question its outcomes, or challenge our beliefs and suppositions".[32] To that extent the novel's invocation of Bassam's

[29]   Paul Auster, *The Brooklyn Follies*, New York: Henry Holt, 2006.
[30]   Julia Glass, *The Whole World Over*, New York: Pantheon Books, 2006; Claire Messud, *The Emperor's Children*, New York: Knopf, 2006.
[31]   Ryan, "Cheap Plot Tricks", 72.
[32]   Kubiak, "Spelling It Out", 295.

successful plot may be read as a terrorist-style action against the stability of narrative, an act of protest against the placidity displayed by
the four characters carrying the multiple plots. 9/11 and other incidents of terrorism are in fact so generic and unfocussed that they can
be used to terminate any plot, as they do not emerge from an evolving
narrative but are applied top-down, thwarting rather than tying the
loose ends of the story to which a narrative is attached.

Some narratives that ruminate on the evolution and psychological
makeup of suicide bombers, such as John Updike's *Terrorist* or Neil
Bissoondath's *The Unyielding Clamor of the Night*, also rush toward a
potentially violent denouement.[33] By drawing a dark, if threadbare,
curtain over the attacks themselves, Dubus spares the characters a
radical intervention from outside the text, and thus affords them some
degree of control over their own lives, a kind of control that the novel's irresolute figures initially lack. The randomness of their actions
contrasts with the purposefulness of narrative form, which leads them,
like lambs to the slaughter, toward a murderous ending that almost by
the by releases the tensions accumulated in the course of the characters' maudlin struggles.

Following a timeline starting Thursday, the week before the attacks, and ending on September 11, the narrative flows at a slow, almost real-time pace, petering out after 9/11 with a few glimpses of
how that fateful Tuesday impacted the characters' lives, either directly
through the attacks or as a result of events that merely happened to
occur on the same day. *The Garden of Last Days* begins with a picture
of innocence, "little Franny … strapped in her car seat in the back,
tired and happy with no idea how different tonight will be, how
strange it could be" (13). Franny, April, Jean, Lonnie, and Bassam
will remain "strapped" to the various contraptions of their lives (jobs,
medical conditions, religious beliefs, etc.), hurtling toward destruction
like the passengers strapped to their seats on the plane Bassam and
two other hijackers board at Boston's Logan Airport. The theme of
enforced seclusion resonates with Dubus' previous interests in the
claustrophobic lives of America's poor and socially isolated. As one
reviewer of Dubus' earlier work remarked, the writer "carries us deep
into the lives of his characters, from wardens to inmates to abused

---

[33] John Updike, *Terrorist*, New York: Knopf, 2006; Neil Bissoondath, *The Unyielding Clamor of the Night*, New York: Bloomsbury, 2006.

women, who live on society's edge in prisons of their own or of their state's construction".[34] "You do it because you think it is allowed" (178), Bassam tells April, guessing at the reasons why she dances and strips for a living. His is a world of restraint and restrictions, refracted in the novel's almost ritualistically plotted story line, which in turn recalls the ritualized practices of terrorism itself.[35]

For long stretches the reader also feels entrapped in this predetermined narrative that seems to leave little room for imaginative maneuver.[36] And yet, surprises abound: it is not the 9/11 attacks but the comparatively minor tragedies preceding them (the middle, not the ending) that form the core of the novel.[37] In this, *The Garden of Last Days* recalls Dubus' previous novel *House of Sand and Fog*,[38] which a reviewer described as "a throwback to a time when writing was more important than plot, and the characters mattered more than the cunning of the author who created them".[39] Issues of coincidence and accident provide the narrative axis around which the novel's subplots rotate.[40] The accidental connotations of 9/11, beyond the surprise caused by the terrorist attacks, have often been pointed out: 911 is the national US emergency number.

---

[34] Quoted in Abney, "Andre Dubus III", 78.

[35] On the ritualistic aspects of terrorism, see Joseba Zulaika and William Douglass, *Terror and Taboo: The Follies, Fables, and Faces of Terrorism*, New York and London: Routledge, 1996, 84. Also see Alex Houen, *Terrorism and Modern Literature, from Joseph Conrad to Ciaran Carson*, New York: Oxford University Press, 2001, 10: "In so far as terrorist events frequently appear to be choreographed by the perpetrators as media spectacles, and often involve attacks on 'symbolic' buildings, such ritualization is clearly evidenced." Bassam appears to be fascinated by the rituals of his religious faith and mission, and his interest in the strip club may have something to do with the strict choreography of the dance routines.

[36] Roland Barthes would argue that it lies in the nature of narrative to create systems of constraint: "it is impossible to combine (to produce) a narrative without reference to an implicit system of units and rules" (Barthes, "Introduction to the Structural Analysis of Narratives", 81). In the case of Dubus' novel, then, the tighter the plot, the firmer the novel's grip on whatever is left of the characters' agency and freedom.

[37] The beginning of the plot lies practically outside the narrative frame. It is "the roaring sound of the American jets taking off to bomb [Bassam's] Muslim brothers in Iraq and Kuwait" (91).

[38] Andre Dubus III, *House of Sand and Fog*, New York, W.W. Norton, 1999.

[39] Quoted in Abney, "Andre Dubus III", 79.

[40] Most ironically, Dubus himself was born on September 11, 1959.

The Garden of Last Days contains several such emergencies: Jean is taken to hospital after a heart attack scare; Franny goes missing; and a parallel is drawn between the Puma club's wrecked appearance after the police arrive to ransack the building, on the one hand, and the aftermath of the attacks at Ground Zero, on the other:

> ... the tables were covered with half-empty cocktail glasses and beer bottles and overflowing ashtrays, the chairs scattered all over. The red carpet – worn to a bloody gray in most places – was gritty and soiled with boot and shoe filth, spilled drinks, stray coins and streaks of ash. (224)

Both in the subtext, through such submerged correspondences, and on the surface, endings of all kinds and various degrees of finality are a recurring theme. Bassam is haunted by the sense of an ending and its flipside, the long desired entry into Jannah:

> This is not something he thinks but feels. An end approaching. And a beginning. Everyone here in a shadow world. (57)

In this provisional world his own life is a Moebius strip, as he hurries to experience sexuality with "the last woman who is the first woman" (115): his initiation into sex is at the same time his last sexual encounter. Even during the private performance at the Puma strip club, all Bassam can think about is the end of life and flesh, keenly asking one of the dancers: "What will happen for you after you die?" (152). The woman believes – and Bassam despises her for it – that human beings after death are nothing but worm food. In keeping with well-worn narrative rules, considerable narrative energies are also spent on foreshadowing: Bassam's eyes are "two dark holes" (71), regarding April with the same incomprehensible opacity as the dark holes torn into the Twin Towers.

Despite this obsession with endings, the narrative appears excruciatingly slow, unfolding in the reader's mind with a disorienting precision that recalls the reading deficiencies of the slightly dyslexic Lonnie: "Instead of seeing a graceful row of letters symbolic of specific sounds, he saw the broken arms and legs of insects, a pile of them that had to be put back together before their message could move and shine" (164). When they finally occur, the attacks fail to leave a clear imprint on the characters' lives, their effects intermingling with other incidental occurrences. After the initial shock of her daughter's disappearance, April loses her job but remains willing to dial the number of another strip club looking for similar employment. The realization that she danced for hours in front of a man who would conspire to murder thousands of Americans fails to trigger the expected resolution that a more conventional narrative would have used to round off the novel: April's life back on track, bolstered by a firm, newly regained sense of identity and self-respect. Instead, we are left wondering where the characters will end up next (those that are still alive). It is as if the novel refuses to settle on a center of gravity, such as the epiphany of a young mother or a shattering historical event.

Marie-Laure Ryan has persuasively argued that most narratives conform to a retrospective rather than prospective structure, which imagines a causal chain of events that lead to a predetermined climactic situation.[41] Here the objective may have been the 9/11 attacks (many of the book's reviews introduce it as a "9/11 novel"), or some of their immediate consequences, yet the story assumes a life of its own, escaping the purposeful plot it was meant to unfold. Terrorism itself is a kind of text that needs to be deciphered retrospectively. It is a narrative with inconspicuous beginnings, middles, and extremely forceful endings. It occasions a narrative unfolding of desire of a most dangerous kind, not sexual desire, which is what fuels April's profession, but religious fanaticism, a form of desire that has received little if any attention in the study of narrative plotting. Bassam's apocalyptic fantasies are partly motivated by his ideological convictions, which imagine life, in its everyday continuity, as a failure; in this view, the only aspect of life worth living is its ending, conceived as a pinnacle of great intensity worth striving and sacrificing for.

When on the night before the attacks Bassam is unexpectedly overwhelmed by a surge of fear, he identifies this emotion as "the fear of failing and remaining here in this life .... The fear of living" (495). It would certainly be worth considering narrativity and terrorist plotting from this religious perspective, although it should be said that narratives which seriously address the dogmatic underpinnings of the 9/11 attacks are still few and far between. Dubus, for his part, con-

---

[41]   See Ryan, "Cheap Plot Tricks", 67.

demns the doctrinaire pursuit of 9/11 as climax (in religious, cultural, and political terms) by inviting us to reconsider the middle of the narrative. It is an idea that finds confirmation in Peter Brooks' statement: "If at the end of a narrative", he writes, "we can suspend time in a moment when past and present hold together in a metaphor ... that moment does not abolish the movement, the slidings, the mistakes, and partial recognitions of the middle".[42]

In *The Garden of Last Days* – as the title suggests, a paradise of oppressive endings – the characters face the tyranny of plot, the pressure of circumstance on the ideas they embrace, and the tyranny of a conclusive ending. In the terms proposed by Bersani and Dutoit, who posit a "complicity between narrativity and violence", Dubus denounces the "sense-making orders of narrative" for their extreme linearity, single-mindedness, and intrinsic hierarchical bias that envelop the reader in a false sense of certainty stemming from the "security of being passively carried along an unfolding order".[43] *The Garden of Last Days* acknowledges the impact of the violent moment, but does not privilege its structural function as an explosive climax, continuing beyond the caesura that such violence should have imposed on the narrative. We do not linger on the catastrophe – although, as Kubiak and others have suggested, this is what usually happens in the aftermath of terrorism, when "the sense of time standing still is common to both victims and observers".[44] On the contrary, after spinning the central drama of the book over a few days, the timeline suddenly stretches out as the story moves from individual psychology to the larger historical context. Time does not stand still; if anything, it begins to run as if liberated from the stranglehold of dense narrative plotting. The novel, ending as it does very soon after the attacks are mentioned, does not permit a lengthy working-through of narrative trauma, but relies instead on the figure of anamnesis which implies the interminable performance of uncovering memory rather than its final result. In challenging the plot's impulse to totalization and completion, Dubus' novel criticizes those narrative tendencies that emphasize the violent act, in this case the terrorist attacks of 9/11, as the significant moment in a narrative, thus inviting a "pleasurable identification with its enact-

---

[42] Brooks, *Reading for the Plot*, 92.
[43] Bersani and Dutoit, *The Forms of Violence*, v, 89, 87.
[44] Kubiak, "Spelling It Out", 299.

ment".[45] In this sense, the novel deploys counter-narrative and anti-closural strategies of representation, gesturing towards forms of narrative emplotment that borrow something from the abrupt timelessness of terror itself.

Conclusion

Though complex and pointillistically described, the plot of this novel is contained within the space created by a few lines: several days in September 2001, Florida, in a few homes, on a few roads, and in the air. This is a very simple ordering frame for a bewildering event, a frame that purposefully reduces the 9/11 attacks to an afterthought. Dubus' novel is only deceptively centered on the destruction wrought by the hijackers in Manhattan and Washington (a clue to this is the setting of the action in unexciting Florida). Several details point to this apparently central space, yet the narrative subtly moves into different directions precisely at the moments we allow ourselves to be carried along by the progress of the narrative toward the climatic point. This strategy, I have proposed, deemphasizes 9/11 as a narrative subject, implicitly prohibiting a fascination with its message as an icon of cultural closure. Not unlike the work of the Assyrian sculptors discussed by Bersani and Dutoit, who "strategically saturated themselves in linear narrativity as a way of escaping from it, of disrupting its orders", in *The Garden of Last Days* "it is precisely in following a narrative movement toward centers and climaxes of violence that we move away from that movement (and those centers) to supplemental, non-narrative points of interest".[46]

Nor is Dubus alone in questioning the closural aspects of the 9/11 attacks, their fetishization as a space of radical conclusions. In his study *9/11: The Culture of Commemoration*, David Simpson cautions against presenting 9/11 "as an attack on culture itself, on any meaningful continuity with the past and with a projected future". According to this erroneous reading, Simpson writes, "9/11 was intended as a cataclysmic imposition of revelation and apocalypse, of eternally present time, on the complacent faith in merely historical and evolutionary temporality that characterizes our secular preference for pru-

---

[45]   Bersani and Dutoit, *The Forms of Violence*, 52.
[46]   *Ibid.*, 56.

dence, profit, and accumulation in the world of trade, a world of self-cultivation measured by the reassuring tick of a predictable plot."[47]

To counter both the predictability of capitalist temporality and the nihilist disruptions of terrorism, Simpson suggests that we take more time – for longer, more circuitous, and deeper reflection – before reaching a conclusion regarding the ways in which 9/11 may have ruptured our lives and enraptured our sensibilities. And even though George W. Bush's response to the attacks was far from impeccable, what comes to mind are his aptly chosen words on the "middle hour" of grief – the moment, soon after the attacks, in which his remarks were spoken. Cordoned off by individual narratives which, with the exception of Bassam, are all very much in development – April is building a new life in New Hampshire, Jean is returning to a solitary life, Lonnie enlists in the military and is killed in combat, A.J. goes to prison – 9/11 in this novel marks a stoppage rather than a conclusion, signaling the problems of demarcating between befores and afters both in historical, cultural, and narrative terms.

Certainly Dubus might have devoted more space to the attacks than the brief section in which their aftermath is described through the reactions of the characters we have come to know. Certainly the novel could have ended, climactically, with the terror in Manhattan, as other 9/11 narratives do. Dubus refuses this easy solution for historically specific reasons, revealing his novel's situation within a specific social context. That the novel should end with a scene conveying both stasis and perpetual movement is, therefore, no surprise. In Jean's garden, perhaps the garden of the title, the last days are not what they appear to be – final, conclusive, definitive – but days that last, caught in a heavy-footed inertia that provides a literally grassroots view of the attacks' continuing reverberations:

> A lizard flitted over the brickwork into the ferns. One of them trembled, then went still. The cat just stared after it as if she were through chasing things. Then another fern moved, and Jean's cat shot into them and she couldn't see her anymore, just heard her, her frantic search in the garden. (535)

---

[47]   David Simpson, *9/11: The Culture of Commemoration*, Chicago: University of Chicago Press, 2006, 6.

The Question of Genre:
Drama and Narrative Literature after 9/11

NARRATIVES OF TERROR:
A NEW PARADIGM FOR THE NOVEL?

MARIE-LUISE EGBERT

A recurrent object of study in analyses of 9/11 has been the role of the media in reporting on the events and their aftermath. The visual media in particular have been exposed for their apparently complicit role in the mechanisms of terror, offering, as they did, a forum for the global dissemination of the terrorists' "messages", and serving to spread the fear of terrorism on a similarly worldwide scale.

By reporting on terrorist acts, the media function as a platform for terrorists to instill in the public a fear of further attacks. Such attacks are aimed at civilians, suggesting that everyone may expect to become the target of a terrorist attack at any time and in any place. In the logic of terrorism,[1] the killing of innocent victims becomes significant and terrorism works its full force only through the stories told of such atrocious acts. By serving their informational function, which includes the telling and showing of terrorist deeds, the media can hardly avoid becoming instrumental in the mechanisms of terror.[2] While this seems

---

[1] In a general sense, terrorism can be understood as "a policy intended to strike with terror those against whom it is adopted; the employment of methods of intimidation" (*OED*, s.v. "terrorism," 2.). Consider also the following, sociologically oriented, definition by Rex Hudson: "Terrorist action is the calculated use of unexpected, shocking, und unlawful violence against noncombatants and other symbolic targets perpetrated by a clandestine member(s) of a subnational group or a clandestine agent(s) for the psychological purpose of publicizing a political or religious cause and/or intimidating or coercing a government(s) or civilian population into accepting demands on behalf of the cause." Hudson suggests this definition in a study prepared on behalf of the US government that gives the year 1999 on its title page but was apparently revised after 9/11. Rex A. Hudson, *The Sociology and Psychology of Terrorism: Who Becomes a Terrorist and Why?*, Washington, DC: Federal Research Division, Library of Congress, 1999: http://www.loc.gov/rr/frd/pdf-files/Soc_Psych_of_Terrorism.pdf (accessed 18 March 2010).

[2] In her introduction to a special issue of *Studies in the Novel* (Fall 2004) on literary representations of terrorism, Jacqueline Foertsch comments on the frequently voiced

to involve the representation of reality as experienced by the victims of terror, the question has been asked whether the attacks on the World Trade Center of September 2001 and their coverage by the media have not indeed affected the very relationship between reality and fiction.

In what follows, I will take a look at that relationship as conceptualized by Jean Baudrillard in *The Spirit of Terrorism*,[3] and will then go on to pursue the issue in two novels, Don DeLillo's *Falling Man*[4] and Patrick Neate's *City of Tiny Lights*.[5] The first deals with September 11, 2001 in New York, the second with post-9/11 terrorism in London. Against this backdrop, I will then pose the question of whether terrorism novels actually constitute a new paradigm within the genre of the novel.

"A fiction surpassing fiction": terrorism as the super-fictional
Writing in October 2001 as the world was trying to make sense of what had happened on September 11, Jean Baudrillard offered an analysis of the events that drew attention to the omnipresence of the visual and the virtual in Western culture:

> In the present case, we thought we had seen (perhaps with a certain relief) a resurgence of the real, and of the violence of the real, in an allegedly virtual universe. "There's an end to all your talk about the virtual – this is something real!" Similarly, it was possible to see this as a resurrection of history beyond its proclaimed end. But does reality actually outstrip fiction? If it seems to do so, this is because it has absorbed fiction's energy, and has itself become fiction. We might almost say that reality is jealous of fiction, that the real is jealous of the image .... It is a kind of duel between them, a contest to see which can be the most unimaginable.[6]

---

claim of a symbiotic relationship between journalists and terrorists, arguing that while the media transmit visual representations of terrorist events, it is beyond their power to actually explain terrorism. See Jacquline Foertsch, "Introduction: The Terror! The Terror!", *Studies in the Novel*, XXXVI/3 (Fall 2004), 287.

[3]   Jean Baudrillard, *The Spirit of Terrorism and Requiem for the Twin Towers* (2001), trans. Chris Turner, London and New York: Verso, 2002.

[4]   Don DeLillo, *Falling Man*, New York: Pocket Books, 2007.

[5]   Patrick Neate, *City of Tiny Lights* (2005), London: Penguin, 2006.

[6]   Baudrillard, *The Spirit of Terrorism*, 28.

This implies that the terrorist deeds of September 2001 appeared so strangely unreal to many observers because the collapse of the Twin Towers actualized catastrophic events as outlined in films like *Independence Day* (dir. Roland Emmerich, 1996) and in the numerous computer games that enacted similar scenarios.[7]

Baudrillard further pursues the notion of a competition between the real and the fictional by assigning the events of 9/11 the status of something that surpasses fiction, for which the term of super-fiction might be suggested:

> In this case, then, the real is superadded to the image like a bonus of terror, like an additional frisson: not only is it terrifying, but what is more, it is real. .... Something like an additional fiction, a fiction surpassing fiction.[8]

It is tempting to link this idea of the veneration of the real with Baudrillard's concept of the simulacrum.[9] According to this figure of thought, twentieth-century culture was informed by the replacement of the authentic or real by the simulacrum. Considered against this backdrop, his postulation that the events of 9/11 brought back the real

---

[7] On the perceived re-enactment of disaster movies in the attack on the World Trade Center, see also Slavoj Žižek, "Welcome to the Desert of the Real: 10/7/01 – Reflections on WTC", *The European Graduate School*: http://www.egs.edu/faculty/ slavoj-zizek/articles/welcome-to-the-desert-of-the-real/ (accessed 15 March 2010). Žižek similarly considers the issue of the contemporary predominance of virtual reality and states that if there is a symbolic significance to the collapse of the Twin Towers, it is not that of an attack on finance capitalism (located in Manhattan), but rather of the virtual, stock-market capitalism which dominates Western economy. Sabine Sielke explores the relationship between reality and representation in the events of 9/11 against the background of the foundational myth of the American nation. She draws an analogy to the Puritans' literalist belief in the Bible ("reality") and the reiterated confirmation of that belief through citation ("representation"): see Sabine Silke, "Das Ende der Ironie? Zum Verhältnis von Realem und Repräsentation zu Beginn des 21. Jahrhunderts", in *Der 11. September 2001: Fragen, Folgen, Hintergründe*, ed. Sabine Sielke, Frankfurt on Main: Lang, 2002, 262-63.

[8] Baudrillard, *The Spirit of Terrorism*, 29.

[9] See Jean Baudrillard, *L'échange symbolique et la mort*, Paris: Gallimard, 1976, and *Simulacres et simulation*, Paris: Galilée, 1981.

seems to hint at a new cultural era in which the simulacrum might be superseded.[10]

Terrorism fictionalized: two recent examples

The idea of a contamination of the real by the fictional is among the recurrent themes of Don DeLillo's novel *Falling Man* (2007). Keith Neuendecker, whose office was in one of the towers of the World Trade Center, very narrowly escaped from the burning building. Traumatized by the experience, he walks back into the life of Lianne, from whom he has been separated for some time. This also reunites him with Justin, his young son, and the family is thus formally reconstituted. Another narrative strand concerns Lianne's elderly mother and her lover Martin R., who turns out to have been a left-wing terrorist in 1960s' Germany. Finally, there is the story of Hammad, which chronologically precedes the rest of the plot. A young Muslim living in Hamburg, Hammad is drawn into the fundamentalist circle of Atta and will be one of the terrorists on board the plane that hits the first tower.

The overriding impression that emerges from the text is that of emotional detachment. Although they try to lead their ordinary former lives as best they can, the characters seem to live in limbo. This holds true for Keith in particular, who soon gives up his rediscovered family life and drifts into an existence of gambling, becoming a professional poker player. The characters are so detached that they seem ephemeral – they are "unreal" even by the standards of fictional lives.

Keith tries to reassure himself of the reality of his own existence. When revisiting his former apartment located close to his office in downtown Manhattan, which has meanwhile been declared a no-go area, his perception of the moment is inter-cut by filmic images:

> He said "I'm standing here", and then, louder, "I'm standing here."
> In the movie version, someone would be in the building, an emotionally damaged woman or a homeless old man, and there would be dialogue and close-ups.[11]

---

[10]   On the relationship between fiction and terrorism, see also Robert Appelbaum and Alexis Paknadel, "Terrorism and the Novel, 1970-2001", *Poetics Today*, XXIX/3 (Fall 2008), 401-402.
[11]   DeLillo, *Falling Man*, 27.

It is some time after the event, but the destruction caused by the planes has not yet gained reality for Keith. Standing in a place connected with his life before September 11, he feels alienated from it. He must tell himself that he is truly there, in a place covered by the debris from the towers. The place is so strangely unreal to him that he imagines it as part of a movie. Even later, when he has begun to play poker, Keith cannot easily tell apart reality and representation. In the lounge of a place where he will play poker, he

> ... stared into the waterfall, forty yards away. He realized he didn't know whether it was real or simulated. The flow of the water was un-ruffled and the sound of falling water might easily be a digital effect like the waterfall itself.[12]

DeLillo's novel also thematizes the part played by the media in giving proof that the terrorist attacks are real. Justin does not believe that the Twin Towers actually collapsed. They were hit by planes, yes, but they never collapsed. This is because he has seen images of the planes flying into the buildings, but none of those showing the Twin Towers coming down. His mother had deliberately withheld such pictures from him.

On the whole, then, *Falling Man* is much concerned with the relationship between reality and representation. While the feeling of alien-sation experienced by the protagonists is related to their traumatic experience, the contamination between reality and medial representation is specific to a period strongly informed by the visual media, which had in fact anticipated catastrophes of the kind that the characters have witnessed.

Patrick Neate's *City of Tiny Lights* is set in London. Published shortly before the bombings that hit London public transport on July 7, 2005, the novel looks at the implications of terrorism for the city's Muslim community whose integration into mainstream British society is called into question as these terrorist acts revitalize age-old stereotypes.

The son of an Indian-Ugandan immigrant, Tommy Akhtar is a private detective with a shabby office in Chiswick. He is commissioned by one "exoticmelody" (Melody Chase), a young prostitute, to find

---

[12] *Ibid.*, 203-204.

her colleague "sexyrussian", who disappeared after a date with British MP Bailey. Bailey is later found dead in a cheap hotel. The killing of that politician turns out to be part of a larger plot involving a Russian selling plastic explosive to a Briton of Arab extraction by the name of Azmat Al-Dubayan. The latter is wanted as a supposed religious fundamentalist. Al-Dubayan is the founder of the Post-Western Alliance (PWA) whose members feel excluded from the benefits of British capitalist society. They give vent to their extremist, anti-Western attitudes, but they do not have any religious or fundamentalist background at all. Al-Dubayan is in fact a mere opportunist who likes to bathe in the media interest that he attracts. It is only when the supposed Russian – who is really a CIA undercover agent – makes the explosive available to Al-Dubayan and the PWA that they launch the bombings in the course of which twelve people will die.

Concerning Tommy's role in these events, it is important to note that he has a background as a mujahideen combatant. His engagement with that group was caused by a guilt complex. When his mother had suffered a fit, he had failed to take her to hospital in good time and therefore considers himself responsible for her death. A Muslim, he channeled these feelings into religious fervor. Thus, in the 1980s, he joined Hekmatyar's mujahideen to fight on the Afghan side in the war against the Soviet Union and returned to England marked by the trauma of war. That war is recalled when he realizes what a long way the USA have come from actively supporting Hekmatyar to their present prosecution of terrorists in Afghanistan and elsewhere.

City of Tiny Lights is written in the mode of detective fiction and set among London's Indian and Pakistani immigrant communities. As is so typical of detective novels, the investigator figure is a misfit of sorts, who appeals to the reader through his very pronounced verbal humor and his generous offerings of worldly wisdom, to be collected in his *Little Book of Tommy*.[13]

As the true dimensions of what had first seemed to be just another lost-person case gradually dawn upon Tommy and he himself becomes the object of secret-service investigations, he feels as if he is acting out a film script. While he is generally critical of Hollywood

---

[13]   Neate, *City of Tiny Lights*, 153.

cinema for its lack of realism in some areas, his own encounter with two MI5 agents is portrayed just as in the movies:

> Little Book of Tommy, # 27: There are many things that the movies get wrong most of the time. I've already touched upon Hollywood fist fights and Hollywood sex and, off the top of my head, you could add nightclubs, gun battles, torture, police chiefs, Nazis, American presidents and annoying younger brothers to the list. There are also, however, certain movie archetypes that seem to reflect reality with surprising accuracy. I have never, for example, come across an intelligence agent of any nation who didn't look like he or she had walked straight off the set (even Stanton, whom I'd respected, played hard-bitten field agent to a T). And the "he" and "she" [Jones and Albright, two MI5 agents] who now confronted me outside Phoenecia, backed up by a pair of uniform, did nothing to contradict this assertion.[14]

Note, however, that it remains unclear here whether life imitates art or the reverse: the movies manage to "reflect reality with surprising accuracy" concerning intelligence agents, and every intelligence agent encountered in real life looks like its movie counterpart.

Tommy clarifies the direction of imitation as he remembers killing a Soviet soldier in Afghanistan. The soldier's death throes seemed to him similarly informed by the behavior portrayed in films:

> Either he was like a headless chicken and these were the last vestiges of instinct pulsing through him like an electric current. Or – and this is the interpretation I favour – he really did think he was Rambo and, at some subconscious level, he was reliving the bootleg he once saw in a blackmarket cinema in the heart of Moscow. It was a case of life – or in this instance death – imitating art.
>
> Jones and Albright were the same. It wasn't like Tinseltown had sent down their finest producers to model Agent X or Agent Y in Movie Z on a couple of MI5's jobbing pros. No. If anything it was the other way round.[15]

Thus, Tommy returns to the case of the two agents to point out that cinematic representation tends to contaminate his perception of real life. As he puts it, life imitates art. It is clear, though, that Tommy's

---

[14] *Ibid.*, 189.
[15] *Ibid.*, 191.

22 *Marie-Luise Egbert*

consideration of the past in these terms serves the function of creating
a distance between himself and the death for which he is responsible.
The notion that filmic realism replaces reality when things are getting
too serious for comfort is found yet again when Tommy accompanies
his teenage friend Avid Khan (who has been acting as an informant
for him in the Bailey case) on an underground train and Avid turns out
to be – unwittingly – carrying a bomb in his rucksack (having been
promised a meeting with the terrorist group's charismatic leader).
When the explosion of the bomb is imminent, Tommy feels that "It
was so real we could have been in a movie".[16] The underground
bombing is eventually prevented, but the extremity of the situation,
with the unimaginable being so close at hand, has triggered a feeling
of unreality, of facts that are so much out of the ordinary that it is difficult to credit them with being real.

The scene on the underground is a terrifying moment corresponding to the "fiction surpassing fiction" formulated by Baudrillard. It has
all the appearance of a fictional filmic catastrophe, except that it is
real.

Realism and the novel

From a historical perspective, the genre of the novel is linked closely
to the representational mode of realism, as opposed to the fantastic
mode of romance which antedates it in literary history. It is by virtue
of its realism, as well as its thematic openness, that the novel can deal
with every aspect of human experience, including the profoundly disturbing experience of terrorism. However, the very conventions of
novelistic realism were called into question in the twentieth century,
beginning with Modernist innovations concerning the representation
of the characters' consciousness, and yet more radically by means of
the metafictional elements so typical of postmodernist fiction. In the
latter kind of fiction, it is not uncommon to find metafictional observations on the constructedness of the reality presented in fiction and
on the status of the author as a creator of a fictional world.

Such considerations become relevant where they touch upon writers' affinity with terrorists concerning their power to change the
world, to re-create it through the violence they inflict, through the

---

[16] *Ibid.*, 288.

insecurity and fear that result from such acts, and through the political reactions they may elicit.[17]

As for the relationship between writers of fiction and terrorists, one may go so far as to claim that there is a kind of competition between them, that they both wish to gain control over people's imagination. Precisely this point is made by DeLillo in his earlier novel *Mao II*. The protagonist is Bill Gray, a novelist who observes in a conversation that he and his fellow-writers are becoming obsolete in an age in which terrorism (in this case the terrorist kidnappings connected with the conflict between Israel and Palestine) has begun to impact the public imagination:

> "For some time now I've had the feeling that novelists and terrorists are playing a zero-sum game." .... "What terrorists gain, novelists lose. The degree to which they influence mass consciousness is the extent of our decline as shapers of sensibility and thought. The danger they represent equals our own failure to be dangerous."[18]

Terrorists' plots can threaten to invalidate the work of the creator of imaginative literature. Indeed, the polysemous verb "plot", used both in connection with writing and terrorism, already hints at a similarity between these very different phenomena. Writers (and playwrights, film makers) plot the events of their narratives[19] while criminals and terrorists form a plan for a crime or conspiracy.[20]

The novelist and the terrorist, then, are united in so far as they are both agents in bringing about a change in the world.[21] Novelists achieve this by means of the fictional worlds they plot. These fictional worlds can have an impact on the readers' outlook on things or even on their behavior. Terrorists obviously change reality when they force

---

[17]   In the two novels studied here, there are no explicit metafictional comments, but DeLillo's *Mao II* (see next paragraph) is a good example of a novel on terrorism whose metafiction is overt.

[18]   Don DeLillo, *Mao II*, New York: Penguin, 1992, 151.

[19]   *OED*, s.v. "plot," 3.a. *trans.*

[20]   *OED*, s.v. "plot," 1.b. *intr.*

[21]   Margaret Scanlan also underscores the link between writers of fiction on the one hand, and "militants, journalists and politicians" on the other. What they share is the ability to construct reality, be it fictional or political: see Margaret Scanlan, *Plotting Terror: Novelists and Terrorists in Contemporary Fiction*, Charlottesville, VA: University Press of Virginia, 2001, 2.

politicians to act in a certain way, but also when they intimidate the public, thus asserting their power. In the case of the novelist, the agency is that of a creator, and this has caused him or her to be compared to a god. As concerns terrorists, the term "destroyers" might seem more appropriate, but the sheer impact of the terrorists' deeds on the public imagination seems to warrant the term of creators for them as well.

Do "terrorism novels" constitute a new genre?

That terrorist plots have in fact not invalidated the work of the novelist is forcefully demonstrated by the unabated flood of fiction that continues to be created. Especially in the post-9/11 era, it is fiction that offers a means of coping with the painful experience of terrorism. Yet terrorism was a topic for literature long before the events of 9/11. Ever since terrorism in the modern sense emerged in the late nineteenth- and early twentieth-century (Ireland, Russia), it has been dealt with in fiction.[22] In this sense the question as to whether narratives of terror might constitute a new genre of fiction must be answered in the negative.

It is clear, though, that the number of novels dealing with terrorism surged in the years after 2001. That great number surely expresses the need to tell of the trauma suffered by the victims of terrorism, a telling which can be undertaken in the imaginative mode of fictional writing. Even a cursory look at novels whose topic is terrorism reveals recurrent concerns, such as trying to grasp the particular nature of what has occurred, coping with the loss of a loved one killed in a terrorist attack, or trying to rid oneself of the images of mutilated bodies as seen in the streets of Manhattan. Another frequent topic is the family as a network that may or may not serve as support in periods of crisis – a topic central to the two novels studied above. Further examples of this are Ian McEwan's *Saturday*[23] – set in London on February 13, 2003, the day of the anti-war demonstration in protest against the United States' impending war against Iraq – and Jonathan Safran

---

[22] See Francis Blessington, "Politics and the Terrorist Novel", *Sewanee Review*, CXVI/1 (Winter 2007), 116, and Alex Houen, *Terrorism and Modern Literature: From Joseph Conrad to Ciaran Carson*, Oxford: Oxford University Press, 2002.
[23] Ian McEwan, *Saturday* [2005], London: Vintage, 2006.

Foer's *Extremely Loud and Incredibly Close*,[24] which concentrates on a child's perception of 9/11 and the loss of his father who died in one of the World Trade Center towers.

However, all of these are thematic concerns, and it would be difficult to pinpoint any formal or structural peculiarities of terrorism novels to allow one to talk of a separate genre of writing.[25] Where the emphasis is not on emotional responses but on the terrorist plot itself, the novels sometimes follow the mode of detective fiction, as in the case of *City of Tiny Lights*, or, to mention another instance, in John le Carré's *A Most Wanted Man*.[26] Le Carré adapts his spy-novel formula to anti-terrorist secret service activities in Germany in a period marked by suspicion against young Muslim students. But these are just two examples of novelistic genres in which terrorism is a topic, while virtually every subgenre of the novel would be eligible.[27]

Against this backdrop, one would be justified in positing the emergence of a new subgenre of the novel only insofar as that subgenre is defined on thematic grounds. The argument does not end there, since one may still think of terrorism novels as fiction that stands apart

---

[24] Jonathan Safran Foer, *Extremely Loud and Incredibly Close*, London: Hamish Hamilton, 2005.

[25] Appelbaum and Paknadel propose a typology of terrorism fiction for the period of 1970 to 2001. They detect a boom in the publication of such fiction in the 1970s (linked with left-wing terrorism in the West, the Irish Troubles and terrorism in the Middle East), and another one in the mid-1990s (to do with, for instance, right-wing, religiously motivated terrorism – e.g. the murder of Yitzhak Rabbin – and right-wing ultras in Northern Ireland): see Appelbaum and Paknadel, "Terrorism and the Novel", 395. The authors give a figure of 1,081 English-language novels concerned directly or indirectly with terrorism (*ibid.*, 399) and single out 25 for their typology. For each of these, the typology establishes genre, register (e.g. "comic suspense", "realist satire"), protagonist/focalizer, the specific climactic action and terrorist incidents, the identity of terrorists and targets, the terrorists' motives, methods and objectives as well as the location (country) concerned (*ibid.*, 410, 428-31). Not quite surprisingly, this does not yield a clear picture of typical features (*ibid.*, 406). A correlation which they can detect, however, is that "thrillers tend to follow the action and observe it from the point of view of *terrorists, counterterrorists*, and *victim-avengers* .... The mainstream novels tend to opt, instead, for the point of view of *victims, inadvertent collaborators*, and *victim-collaborators*" (*ibid.*, 411, emphases in the original).

[26] John Le Carré, *A Most Wanted Man*, London: Hodder and Stoughton, 2008.

[27] Appelbaum and Paknadel underscore the great range of novelistic subgenres with terrorism as a topic, "from the adventure story to the psychological drama", adding that the novels "adopt a wide variety of tones and express an equally wide variety of moods" (Appelbaum and Paknadel, "Terrorism and the Novel", 404).

when one considers the intricate relationship between terrorism and narrative that was adumbrated here. The notion of a relatedness between these two provides the basis for Anthony Kubiak's essay "Spelling It Out: Narrative Typologies of Terror", in which he attempts to classify narratives of terror.

Adopting a wide definition of narrative as a structuring principle in the human mind that even precedes language, he distinguishes between three types of "terrorist narratives".[28] Kubiak's first category includes propaganda speeches as well as written communications by terrorists themselves, in which they set out their motivations and call their followers to action ("terrorist literature"). The second category contains fiction about terrorism and literary criticism dealing with such fiction ("terrorism in literature"). As fictional examples, Kubiak mentions DeLillo's novel *Mao II* and Conrad's *The Secret Agent*. The third of his categories consists of novels and short stories that abandon conventional modes of storytelling concerning character, plot, and linearity ("literary terrorism"). Examples mentioned are experimental pieces of fiction, such as Donald Barthelme's "Game" and Robert Coover's "The Babysitter". Texts of the latter category, Kubiak argues, constitute cases of "narrative terrorism" inasmuch as they are "attempts to destabilize narrative itself".[29] This type of narrative is "terrorist" in a metaphorical sense and hence actually situated on a different plane than the other two.[30]

Kubiak himself is convinced that fairly conventional terrorist narratives of the second type may indeed be more likely than those of the third to cause terror on the part of the reader. They can do so by means of their imaginative power to create fearful scenarios, of mapping terrorist events in the possible worlds that they construct. While he mentions the specific case of Andrew MacDonald's *The Turner Diaries* as apparently becoming the blueprint for Timothy McVeigh's attack in Oklahoma City, his main point is not that novels about ter-

---

[28]   The term has apparently been adopted from Scanlan, *Plotting Terror*: see Anthony Kubiak, "Spelling It Out: Narrative Typologies of Terror", *Studies in the Novel*, XXXVI/3 (Fall 2004), 294-95.

[29]   *Ibid.*, 297.

[30]   Appelbaum and Paknadel criticize Kubiak's typology as "lack[ing] methodological rigor" (Appelbaum and Paknadel, "Terrorism and the Novel", 388, n.1 and 389, n.2).

rorism provide models for terrorists to act upon. Rather, he is convinced that both terrorism and fiction are putatively dangerous because of their ability to influence people's world view:

> The real interplay between fiction and terrorism is in the way that traditional narratives are able to construct belief in the world. The ability of narrative (fictional or not) to construct a world that is fearful, uncertain and dangerous is its link to terror.

According to Kubiak, this construction of belief can be achieved only through coherent narrative – narrative, that is, which precisely does not undermine the principles of narrative as the experimental writing of the kind that makes up his third category does.

One would certainly not wish to dispute fiction's potential to change the way we look at the world and, as a possible consequence thereof, to change the world itself. But as regards Kubiak's formulation of the "ability of narrative (fictional or not) to construct a world that is fearful, uncertain and dangerous", there seems to be an undue conflation here between these two different kinds of narrative. It is worth underscoring the ontological difference that exists between the worlds constructed in fictional narratives and those constructed through narratives of terrorist events outside of fiction. Fictional worlds are, after all, possible worlds and therefore crucially different from the real world in which there are victims of terror and where terror poses a psychic and physical threat. This does not, however, invalidate the observation that there is a felt contamination between fiction and reality as we have indicated, nor does it invalidate the great imaginative potential of literature.

In conclusion, it is undeniable that novels dealing with terrorism form a subset of fiction if one goes by topic, but they do not in themselves form quite a new paradigm. There is no doubting, though, that they have become a significant literary and cultural phenomenon, and this reflects the pressing need to approach terrorism and its consequences not just through political analyses. It is here that imaginative writing comes into its own by offering an alternative mode for reflection and analysis – a function acknowledged also by Kubiak.[31] Literature may help one to better understand and to oppose terrorism. Both

---

[31] Kubiak, "Spelling It Out", 298.

because of this ethical role that imaginative literature can have, which is so poignantly seen in some terrorism novels, and because of its capacity to draw attention to the role and power of the novelist as a creator, terrorism literature will continue to attract our critical interest.

THE IMPACT OF "SEPTEMBER 11": DRAMATIC AND NARRATIVE CREATIONS

HERBERT GRABES

The terrorist attacks on the World Trade Center and the Pentagon on September 11, 2001 have been featured in a great number of poems, stories, novels, and plays. It is especially the impact these events have had on individual lives that has been focused on in literary writing. Owing to the great number of victims and the material, psychological, and political damage done, this is no wonder. And as the catastrophe was deliberately brought about, the response was bound to be particularly intense and subjectively complex. The literature featuring 9/11 thus cannot escape being to a considerable extent *littérature engagée*, involved as it is in the real to a far greater extent than is usually the case. For the same reason, it has had – and will continue to have for some time – a heightened cultural and social importance that raises some questions. From one point of view, there seems to be the problem that, with literature being fictional and creative, if not to say always somewhat playful, it may be considered to be never factually truthful enough and ethically adequate. An example of this view can be found on the internet under the title "Does Literature Sell 9/11 Short?" in the *Guardian* books blog.[1] From the opposite perspective, the engagement with a catastrophic event with such a strong emotional impact can also be regarded as a severe hindrance to this literature's aesthetic reception – a kind of reception that cannot come about without out a certain amount of distance (or, in Wordsworth's words, "recollection in tranquility").

In this essay, I will therefore focus on the questions of how, and to what extent, this problem has been resolved in some of the literary

---

[1]   Anthony Cummins, "Does Literature Sell 9/11 Short?", *The Guardian* Books Blog, 23 February 2007: http://www.guardian.co.uk/books/booksblog/2007/feb/23/doesliteraturesell911short (accessed 28 September 2010).

works dealing with 9/11. As the novels have already received more critical attention than the plays, I will confine myself to discussing several plays and just one novel. Nonetheless, I hope that in dealing with different genres in this rudimentary form at least some of their strengths and weaknesses regarding the chosen focus will be revealed.

In order to show that we are indeed dealing with samples of "engaged" literature, I will first, with due brevity, demonstrate the way in which the works I selected feature 9/11. My first example, a series of dramatic monologues by Lavonne Mueller with the title *Voices from September 11th*, was published in 2002 and staged off-off-Broadway. The author's objective is to foster the impression of listening to authentic reports from average Americans on how they experienced the attacks. In order to make them appear representative, Mueller presents the "Voices" of seven women and four men from different walks of life and ranging in age between 17 and 67 years. As a final gag, she even includes Franklin D. Roosevelt's dog Fala, who – alluding to Pearl Harbor – encourages the audience by saying, "We came through those dark times. And you will come through, too." What all the "Voices" have in common is a strong patriotic tenor: at the very end, "the lights come up on the actors as they stand holding each other up (for moral support) so that they are looking like the famous Iwo Jima picture".[2]

The second play, Anne Nelson's *The Guys*, is a mixture of monologues and dialogues based on the playwright's personal experience. The piece was staged already on 4 December 2001, "twelve weeks to the day after the World Trade Center attack". Devoted "To the Captain, and to the guys. And to all the captains, and to all the guys",[3] the work is meant to be a memorial to the 343 firemen who lost their lives in the rescue operations at the Towers. The slight plot involves conversations between a fire captain and a journalist who gives him some help in writing the eulogies he has to deliver at the memorial services for the men from his company who were among the victims. The monologues of the journalist provide a biographical frame for this and commentaries on the immediate impact of the attack. But the really moving part is comprised of the captain's characterizations of his men and the eulogies based on them, because they show that, although

---

[2]   Lavonne Mueller, *Voices from September 11th*, New York: Applause, 2002, 86, 87.

[3]   Anne Nelson, *The Guys*, New York: Random House, 2002, xxv, xiii.

these fire fighters were neither well-known nor extraordinary people, they appear irreplaceable and invaluable in their individuality.

If *The Guys* can be considered as an expression of national mourning, this can hardly be said of Craig Wright's tragicomedy *Recent Tragic Events*, which premiered in August 2002. Written basically as a comedy that thrives on a series of bizarre coincidences and surprising turns, the play also proves to have a menacing aspect throughout and ends as a tragedy. The comedy part consists of a spontaneous party in the Minneapolis flat of a young woman on the evening of September 12, 2001. She has asked a bookish young man, who has come as her blind date, to stay home with her because she wants to keep trying to reach her twin sister in New York, from whom she has not heard since the attack on the Towers. Their talk and behavior become increasingly funny mainly through the uninvited visits by the young woman's somewhat crazy musician neighbor and his girlfriend, and later even turns absurd by the appearance of "Joyce Carol Oates", who is played by a sock puppet. When, after some forebodings in the last scene, it becomes clear that the protagonist's twin sister is indeed among the victims, the stage direction given by the Stage Manager, "Blackout",[4] has more than a literal meaning. What the play contributes to a rendering of the impact of 9/11 is therefore the awareness that not only those closer to the sites of the attack, but a great many Americans all over the country who had relatives and friends there, were first full of fear and then deeply shocked.

In contrast to the plays so far mentioned, Neil LaBute, in his 2002 play *The Mercy Seat*,[5] presents a New Yorker who had undeserved luck when he escaped certain death the day before because he was not at work in one of the Towers but was having sex with his boss in her apartment at the time of the attack. The protagonist also has the idea to make use of the fact that his wife and children must believe him to be dead so that he can start a new life somewhere else with the woman with whom he has had an affair for three years. This leads to a mostly heated discussion between the two that makes up most of the play. His plan does not work due to her strong ethical objections to his attitude and because she does not trust him enough to give up her privileged position. When she puts him to the test by almost forcing him to make

---

[4]   Craig Wright, *Recent Tragic Events*, New York: Dramatists Play Service, 2004, 60.

[5]   Neil LaBute, *The Mercy Seat*, New York and London: Faber and Faber, 2003.

a decisive phone call planned before the attack, in which he is supposed to tell his wife about them, it turns out that he had decided in
favor of his family, and the call is to his lover, informing her that he
wants to end their affair. So it was only the chance given to him by the
disaster to wipe out his former life and start anew that seemed attractive.

With Don DeLillo's *Falling Man* my last example is a very successful novel with a fairly wide scope. It centers on the lives of a New
York lawyer and his estranged wife and young son, to whom he
returns after having escaped with minor physical and considerable
psychological injuries from one of the Towers. Regarding 9/11, the
novel not only offers detailed renderings of the catastrophic situation
in and around one of the Towers after it was hit, but has additional
chapters allowing an insight into the mind of one of the terrorists during the planning phase in Hamburg, the flight training on the American Gulf Coast, and the flight into the Hudson Corridor and the first
Tower. Besides this, there is the brief affair the protagonist has with a
woman who also survived the attack and his increasing addiction to
the game of poker; his wife's storyline sessions with Alzheimer
patients and her visits with her mother, whose German friend was
once allied with the terrorists of the time after 1968 and claims to have
a better understanding of the jihadists; and finally her observations of
a performance artist who, due to his imitation of one of the victims of
the terrorist attack, fell or jumped from a tower to become the "Falling
Man" and thus unwittingly provides the title to the novel.

I will now look at the prospect these works have of surviving as
literature beyond their undisputed function as documentations of the
impact of 9/11. It can already be said that the plays I have chosen to
comment on differ considerably in this respect. The first one, *Voices
from September 11th*, is described in the blurb as "a moving collage of
voices from all around America", and what Lavonne Mueller intended
to create may have been precisely that. It can, however, neither really
claim to be a play, nor has it any tangible form when we read in the
"Production Notes": "Any six monologues may be performed as a
one-act."[6] What is even more aggravating is the fact that the "Voices"
that are meant to sound authentic often enough appear as mere dum-
mies for the author's own voice – a voice that by striving to be poetic
tends to be totally "out of character". To give just one example: "Ter-

---

[6]   Mueller, *Voices from September 11th*, iv.

ry's Father," a former army cook aged 67 who allegedly lost his daughter who worked at the Windows on the World Restaurant on the 107th floor, is given this poetic outburst: "I now imagine Terry flying out those windows on the world and melting like one of her ice-birds into the warm blanket of the sky."[7] Another feature that is hard to swallow is the frequent melodramatic exaggerations. Poor Terry, for instance, not only had no chance of escaping because she was so high up in the Tower but the fatal "Tuesday was supposed to be her day off, but somebody got sick and being the kind of person she is, Terry volunteered to go in".[8] So on top of being a victim of the terrorist attack she is also a victim of her own kindness.

Regarding Anne Nelson's *The Guys*, it has already been mentioned that the play is based on the author's true experience, and this may have helped to make it sound authentic. The decisive question is how the chosen combination of monologues, dialogues, and eulogies will survive as drama. The initial monologue of the author as journalist already shows that, as in Mueller's play, here the stage is mainly used as a forum for public storytelling as well. Her further monologues, which either frame or interrupt her dialogues with the fire captain, turn the play into a kind of epic drama as initiated by Thornton Wilder's *Our Town*[9] – with the difference that within the meta-dramatic frame we do not get any paradigmatic action but solely talk.

Among the features of *The Guys* that have been criticized is the fact that the journalist assumes a prominent position by rendering part of her own biography and by talking at length about her own reaction to the events of 9/11. It has to be seen, however, that she is meant to act as a mediator between someone like the fire captain, who has been directly involved in that event and has the official duty to read eulogies of the victims who belonged to his ladder company, and the wider American public, and that it is precisely her personal reaction that may serve as a model for most of the audience. What has also been criticized is the fact that the characters of the firemen whose eulogies are being written are drawn on the model of well-known stereotypes. Accordingly, the phrasing of the eulogies is said to be stereotypical.

[7] *Ibid.*, 9.
[8] *Ibid.*, 7.
[9] Thornton Wilder, *Our Town* (1938), in *Three Plays: Our Town, The Skin of Our Teeth, The Matchmaker*, London and New York: Longmans, Green and Co., 1958, 1-103.

What else should the playwright have done to make the few cases she could present in a short play look representative? The character sketches are detailed enough to create the impression of individual lives that appear most precious in retrospect, regardless of their being outstanding in one way or other or not. As the fire captain is made to say about Bill:

> There's just not much to say. This hero stuff, like they were some guys in a movie. But Bill – he wasn't like that. He was just an ordinary guy. A schmo. If Bill walked into a room, nobody would even notice.[10]

And as to the style of the eulogies for the firemen who lost their lives, how else can it be but stereotypical when the usual stock phrases to praise the deceased must be used to make them sound authentic?

What lies behind this kind of criticism is that the *The Guys* is a play which is thoroughly affirmative regarding Western bourgeois values. At least since the advent of Modernism, art and literature have, after all, been informed by an aesthetic of the strange, and being subversive or at least ironical regarding the rules and values of bourgeois society has since been one of the unspoken but basic preconditions for entering their domains. Here is neither the place nor the space to deal with that wider issue, but it may be mentioned that after more than a century under the sway of such a "negative" aesthetic it no longer seems original to continue in this vein. Moreover, the traditional bourgeois values have by now lost their dominant position to such an extent that their affirmation need not necessarily appear trite any more. *The Guys* is a brief, subdued play whose emotional appeal was certainly strongest in the months directly after 9/11. As an interesting specimen of the more recent narrative drama it may stand a chance of surviving, but its aesthetic appeal is slight, and it is hard to say how it will do on the stage in a decade or two.

Regarding Craig Wright's *Recent Tragic Events*, it has already been mentioned that it is an American version of the drawing-room comedy with quite serious overtones and a tragic ending. The quotation from Arthur Schopenhauer's *On Apparent Design in the Fate of*

---

[10] Nelson, *The Guys*, 12.

the Individual[11] that serves as its epigraph casts its shadow over the
ensuing trivial occurrences and strange coincidences that make up
most of the play, as well as over the constantly looming and finally
confirmed disaster that the protagonist's twin sister is among the victims of 9/11. It casts them as demonstrations of the questions of
whether life is ruled by chance or strict causality, and whether we
really possess free will or have to accept that all or at least much is
predetermined. To emphasize this, Wright employs a Stage Manager
who tells the audience at the beginning that there are two sets of
variables in the play and that the flip of a coin will decide which one
will be staged – with the characters in the play remaining ignorant of
the fact that there has been any choice. At the beginning of Act Two,
however, the Stage Manager admits that this was a hoax, since "everything that occurred on stage only happened because that was the only
way it ever could have happened", including his own speeches,
because everything was determined and written before by the author.
He also points out helpfully that "Joyce Carol Oates" is a mere character in the play and not the real Joyce Carol Oates and that this will be
made quite clear by "her part being played by a sock puppet operated
by the actress playing Nancy". And towards the end, the characters
begin a discussion about whether, as the puppet Joyce is going to say,
"we are free"[12] or whether we are puppets.

If Craig had spared us the Stage Manager – and it looks like a later
addition, because the dramatis personae for the first staging does not
feature one – the uncertainty about this alternative would still have
been clear enough. The experiment with the alleged alternative versions of parts of the play is most probably meant to signal that the
author is well acquainted with the fashionable trend in postmodern
times to let the real appear as a mere contingent instance of a multitude of possibilities. However, the playfulness resulting from that
strategy is strongly detrimental to the psychological realism and considerable emotional appeal the tragicomedy is otherwise meant to
unfold. Even more dysfunctional are meta-level commentaries like the
lecture about the characters in the play being trapped because of their
being already written by the author. The result is a contradiction
between such a foregrounding of the constructedness of what is being

---

[11] Arthur Schopenhauer, *Transcendent Speculations on Apparent Design in the Fate
of the Individual*, trans. David Irvine, London: Watts, 1913.
[12] Wright, *Recent Tragic Events*, 38-39, 50.

presented and the appeal to the compassion of the readers and viewers. What both the action and dialogue of the play bring out quite clearly, after all, is the disturbing impact of the uncertainty about the fate of someone dear on the psyche, and one does not want to be lectured about what one presently experiences.

For a convincing example of psychological drama one therefore has to turn to a play such as Neil LaBute's *The Mercy Seat*. As I said earlier the reaction to this play has been at least partly negative on ethical grounds. As LaBute has pointed out, the play is less about 9/11 in particular than more generally "about what a person would really do if they were afforded the chance to wipe the slate clean and start life over", although "the particulars of the plot mechanics could have been put into motion only by the catastrophic events of that notorious Tuesday". And *The Mercy Seat* is, indeed, above all else "a 'relation-ship' play, in the purest sense",[13] and a stark psychological drama with an ethical bent. Looked at retrospectively with the surprise ending in mind, it shows that the male protagonist Ben, when suddenly con-fronted with the situation that everybody except his girlfriend must think that he is dead, is suddenly so intrigued by the opportunity to start a new life with her without having to first fulfill the obligations in the old one, that he at least suspends the decision he had already made in favor of his family. He is quite aware of the fact that he is anyway prone to be directed in his decisions by current circumstances rather than by any principles:

> I always take the easy route, do it faster, simpler, you know, whatever it takes to be done, be liked, get by. That's me. Cheated in school, screwed over my friends, took whatever I could get from whomever I could take it from.[14]

His friend Abby, with whom he would like to elope, has serious prob-lems with exactly this kind of behavior because she strongly dislikes hiding the truth and urges him to at least let his family know that he is alive and put an end to "the *prayers* they are sending out for you right now".[15]Yet when the play ends, he still sits there with the cell phone in his hand and has not done anything. So LaBute is right when saying

---

[13]   La Bute, *The Mercy Seat*, iv, ix.
[14]   *Ibid.*, 32.
[15]   *Ibid.*, 50.

that *The Mercy Seat* deals with "a particular kind of terrorism: the painful, simplistic warfare we often wage on the hearts of those we profess to love". He adds: "I am trying to examine the 'ground Zero' of our lives, that gaping hole in ourselves that we try to cover up with clothes from The Gap, with cologne from Ralph Lauren, with handbags from Kate Spade."[16] Maybe for this very reason the play will be kept in cultural memory – along with 9/11 or without it.

Assuming that this will also be the case with Don DeLillo's novel *Falling Man*,[17] I finally have to deal with the question of how DeLillo found a solution to the paradoxical demand to do justice to such a decisive historical event as 9/11, an event leaving hardly anyone impartial and cool, and simultaneously provide the opportunity for a more distanced reading, a reading that would make an aesthetic reception possible. To give a preliminary answer to this question: he is largely successful, thanks to his widening of the narrative scope, the fact that he does not only write about the impact of the event but also about its causes and agents, about the preparations for the attack as well as the event itself. And regarding the aftermath, which tends to be the privileged subject of most writing on 9/11, DeLillo there distributes our attention among several quite different characters whose particular interests allow for considerable thematic expansion.

Published in 2007 and therefore at a greater distance from the attacks, *Falling Man* is a work in which the author makes extensive use of the advantage the novel genre has for detailed and extensive worldmaking, especially the presentation of the cognitive and emotional experience of individual characters. While in general staying within the domain of realistic fiction, or, to be more precise, of psychological realism, DeLillo has created a novel that is somewhat difficult to read. This is to some extent due to the employment of the narrative patterns of more than one subgenre, and above all to the constant, barely perceptible shifts of scene, agents, and perspective, which often enough leave readers temporarily at a loss before they realize where and with whom they actually are.

That *Falling Man* is nevertheless a novel centered on 9/11 is already signaled by its title, as the picture of a human figure falling or jumping from one of the burning towers was disseminated by the media worldwide. The motif of the falling man is taken up within the

---

[16] *Ibid.*, ix, x.
[17] Don DeLillo, *Falling Man*, New York and London: Scribner, 2007.

novel by the performances of an artist who – in business dress and with a safety harness barely visible – jumps from buildings, viaducts, or bridges in various parts of the city and then hangs head down until the police put an end to the spectacle. That there is more to these performances can be gathered from the fact that the name of the artist is chosen as a title for the third part of the novel. The "falling man" moreover takes on an uncanny shape when we recall that the initial report of the main character Keith's lucky escape from the disaster reads:

> There was something else then, outside all this, aloft. He watched it coming down. A shirt came down out of the high smoke, a shirt lifted and drifting in the scant light and then falling again, down toward the river.

And the final report of the earlier phase of his flight towards the end of the novel closes with the sentences:

> Then he saw a shirt come down out of the sky. He walked and saw it fall, arms waving like nothing in this life.[18]

While this may be seen as a symbol of the cruel fate of the victims of 9/11, the wider significance of the motif of the "falling man" is indicated by the comment of Keith's wife Lianne when she reads the performance artist's biography on the computer: "She thought it could be the name of a trump card in a tarot deck, Falling Man, named in Gothic type, the figure twisting down in a stormy night."[19] Readers acquainted with the "wicked pack of cards" of Madame Sosostris in T.S. Eliot's *The Waste Land*[20] will take this as an indication that the theme is fate, death, and the hope of a rebirth that remains quite uncertain. On closer observation, one will realize that death haunts the novel to such an extent that one could conclude that DeLillo wants to prove that the terrorist Hammad was right when he began to understand that "death is stronger than life".[21]

Not only is the death of several thousand people killed by the terrorist attacks on the Towers always in the background – Lianne is

---

[18] *Ibid.*, 4, 316.
[19] *Ibid.*, 281.
[20] T.S. Eliot, *Collected Poems 1909-1935*, London: Faber and Faber, 1958, 62.
[21] DeLillo, *Falling Man*, 218.

haunted by the image of her father shooting himself because "he did not want to submit to the long course of senile dementia", a process she is all too well acquainted with through her storyline sessions with "six or seven men and women in the early stages of Alzheimer disease", and her mother Nina's slow descent to death from first having to walk with a cane, then being in a wheelchair, then "the last hard months ..., ruptured blood vessels, loss of muscle control, the smeared speech and empty gaze" before the end of life.[22] In comparison, the performance artist's sudden death by heart failure after he had become chronically depressed because an injured back prevented further stunts seems more merciful – especially in view of the fact that, according to his brother, "Plans for a final fall ... did not include a safety harness".[23]

But death appears in a totally different light when turned from an unavoidable fate into a desired act of self-sacrifice by the terrorists that will "close the distance to God", as it did for the ten thousand Iranian Shia boys who wore plastic keys to paradise around their necks when they ran into the fire of the Iraqi machine guns on the battlefield in the Shatt al Arab. "We are willing to die, they are not. This is our strength, to love death, to feel the claim of armed martyrdom" – this is what the terrorist Hammad, whose thoughts are disclosed to us, was taught in the Afghan training camp where he was prepared for his mission. And this attitude towards death appears to be closely linked to the one towards life or, rather, one's fate. When Hammad skeptically keeps asking "does a man have to kill himself to accomplish something in the world?", Amir Atta, the leader of the group of terrorists, explains:

> The end of life is predetermined. We are carried toward that day from the minute we are born. There is no sacred law against what we are going to do. This is not suicide in any meaning of the word. It is only something long written. We are finding the way already chosen for us.[24]

In analogy, Florence Givens, the black woman who survived the attack on the Towers, not only tells Keith that she thinks that "dying is

---

[22]   *Ibid.*, 50, 25, 247.
[23]   *Ibid.*, 281.
[24]   *Ibid.*, 219, 226, 222, 223.

ordinary" but also asks: "Just, why don't we put it in God's hands?"
He admits that he does not "even know what it means, to believe in
God".[25] After 9/11 he seems to live mainly in the present, mostly as a
cool observer, as if he were always playing poker, watching seemingly
without emotion how the cards will fall, because even though he later
comes to master the game he remains aware of the high degree of
chance involved. This may be the reason why DeLillo has created in
Keith a character who becomes increasingly addicted to poker. In fact,
the description of this game and of Keith's thoughts and feelings
about it covers just as many pages as the account of the attack on the
Towers and of how the survivors experienced their escape. It is also
significant that Keith's wife Lianne wants to remain an "infidel in
current geopolitical parlance" and that her mother's friend Martin
Ridnour alias Ernst Hechinger was, as she remarks, perhaps "a terrorist but he was one of ours, she thought, and the thought chilled her,
shamed her – one of ours, which meant godless, Western, white".[26]

Yet these more general issues and themes do not allow us to forget
that *Falling Man* is foremost a novel about 9/11. How decisive the
impact of the attack on the World Trade Center is for the characters in
the novel shows in the remark: "These are the days after. Everything
now is measured by after."[27] At the same time, we are also dealing
with a family novel, a novel about a traumatic addiction, and a novel
about the more general theme of how to cope with death, a theme that
is linked with the question of how to find a meaning in life. In contrast
to political, social, philosophical or religious writings, literary works
rely much less on argument than on their being able to conjure up
concrete situations with individual characters and their thoughts and
feelings. Accordingly, DeLillo has not only succeeded in integrating
everything into the frame of "the days after" but also in letting the
wider issues appear as parts of the story. And that this can be done
quite well in a novel is, as can only be mentioned in passing, shown
also in Jonathan Safran Foer's *Extremely Loud and Incredibly Close*,[28]
where the trauma of a nine-year-old whose father died in the attack on

---

[25]   *Ibid.*, 112, 113.
[26]   *Ibid.*, 296, 249.
[27]   *Ibid.*, 173.
[28]   Jonathan Safran Foer, *Extremely Loud and Incredibly Close*, Chicago: Houghton
Mifflin, and London: Hamish Hamilton, 2005.

the World Trade Center is connected with that incurred on his grandparents by the bombing of Dresden in World War II.

To return to the question of genre-specific solutions to the problem of dealing in an engaged way with a recent historical event such as 9/11 while preserving a sufficient degree of aesthetic distance, the novel not only allows for a more comprehensive and detailed worldmaking but also leaves room for a broad unfolding of multiple plots and lengthy discussions of wider issues – all features of which DeLillo has made extensive use. At the same time, it seems difficult to preserve a high rate of intensity over several hundred pages, and there is also the danger of leveling issues of quite uneven importance by the rendering of a profusion of details – drawbacks of which *Falling Man* is not free. In contrast, dramatists have to be much more selective due to the restrictions of their genre, and their success depends more acutely on their ability to find telling incidents and render them in a way that makes for an intense theater experience. Being almost exclusively dependent on box office success, American theater, more so than European, tends to welcome plays on current issues that promise to draw a crowd, and the plays on 9/11 have to be seen within this pragmatic frame. This has generally not been detrimental to the quality of American drama, though that quality admittedly is quite uneven. Thus *Voices from September 11* may have been considered very moving by a patriotically-minded audience shortly after the event, yet relies far too much on melodramatic exaggerations and pious preaching of patriotic values to come even near the confines of dramatic art. *The Guys*, though also strongly patriotic and by no means free of melodramatic sentiment, in a rather quiet way, seems a much more convincing record of the general feeling of mourning immediately after the event. With its very modest format, it cannot make any great claim regarding dramatic art, yet it is a well-written specimen of the narrative type of play that has recently become trendy. *Recent Tragic Events*, basically a well-made play, which, through the events of 9/11, turns from a comedy into a tragedy, could have become a quite convincing psychological drama if there were less meta-level commentary that was obviously meant to sound sophisticated in a postmodern way but that is much too blunt and obtrusive to have the desired effect. When the issue of the contingency of human fate is being quite clearly demonstrated by example, its additional spelling out in philosophical commentary must seem rather insulting to an attentive audience. So it has to be said that the most "nasty" play of all, *The Mercy Seat*, is by far the best work in terms of the art of the drama, and, thanks to its chance to survive the phase of the actuality of its topic due to its dramatic qualities, it may also prove to be the most effective in keeping the events of September 11 alive in theater.

All in all it has to be said, though, that none of the dramatic treatments of 9/11 discussed here even comes near the intellectual scope and emotive power of novels like DeLillo's *Falling Man* or Jonathan Safran Foer's *Extremely Loud and Incredibly Close*. This does not mean, however, that the dramatic genre is principally not suited to deal with such real-life events of wider political and moral significance. One needs only to mention Arthur Miller's treatment of McCarthyism in *The Crucible*[29] to dispel such a general skepticism. Yet a play of that quality about 9/11 has still to be written.

---

[29]   Arthur Miller, *The Crucible* (1953), London: Heinemann, 1967.

NOTES ON CONTRIBUTORS

Georgiana Banita is Assistant Professor of American Literature and Media Studies at the Otto-Friedrich-University Bamberg. In 2010-11 she was a Postdoctoral Fellow at the United States Studies Centre, University of Sydney. Her articles have appeared in *Textual Practice, Literature Interpretation Theory, Biography, Critique,* and other journals and edited collections. She is the author of the forthcoming *Plotting Justice: Narrative Ethics and Literary Culture after 9/11* (Lincoln: Nebraska University Press, 2012) and is currently at work on a literary history of the American oil industry in its international contexts, as well as co-editing *The Look of Human Rights: Image, Narrative, Evidence.* Other research interests include graphic narrative, US cinema, and Canadian literature.

Hendrik Blumentrath teaches in the Department of German Literature at Humboldt University, Berlin. His main research interests include theory and history of media and signifying practices, modernist literature, and genre theory. He wrote his doctoral thesis on figurations of terrorism. His recent publications include a collaborative monograph on transcultural literature and film (*Transkulturalität: Türkischdeutsche Konstellationen in Literatur und Film,* Munster: Aschendorff, 2007) and a co-edited volume on Walter Benjamin, media theory, and the political (*Techniken der Übereinkunft: Zur Medialität des Politischen,* Berlin: Kulturverlag Kadmos, 2009).

Gudrun Braunsperger studied History and Slavic Literature in Vienna, Petersburg and Heidelberg. She received her PhD in 2001 for a study on Nechaev and Dostoevsky's *Devils* (published as *Sergej Nečaev und Dostoevskijs* Dämonen*: Die Geburt eines Romans aus dem Geist des Terrorismus,* Frankfurt on Main *et al.*: Peter Lang, 2002). She lives and works in Vienna as a translator of Russian and as an independent journalist for print and radio (ORF: Ö1).

Marie-Luise Egbert is Associate Professor (*Privatdozentin*) of Anglophone Literatures and Cultures at the University of Leipzig and is currently teaching as substitute professor at the University of Freiburg. She received her PhD for a dissertation on *Lexical Repetition in English-German Literary Translation* (Trier: Wissenschaftlicher Verlag, 1999). The author of a book on gardens and Englishness in British literature (*Garten und* Englishness *in der englischen Literatur*, Heidelberg: Carl Winter, 2006), completed as part of her *Habilitation*, she also co-edited the collection *Alternative Romanticisms* (Essen: Blaue Eule, 2003). Her other publications include articles on the eighteenth-century novel, postcolonial literatures and transcultural studies, literary translation, as well as media applications in teaching.

Michael C. Frank is Assistant Professor of British Literature at the University of Constance. The author of a book on the "anxiety of cultural influence" in nineteenth-century travel literature (*Kulturelle Einflussangst: Inszenierungen der Grenze in der Reiseliteratur des 19. Jahrhunderts*, Bielefeld: Transcript, 2006), he has co-edited volumes on forgotten texts and memory studies as well as three special issues of the *Zeitschrift für Kulturwissenschaften* (*Journal for Cultural Studies*), most recently, *Kultur und Terror* (*Culture and Terror*, 2010). His current research project is entitled "Narrating Terror: The Cultural Imaginary of Terrorism from Late-Victorian Fiction to Post-9/11 Film". In this context, he has published articles on the "alien terrorist" in post-9/11 discourse and film (in *Screens of Terror*, ed. Phil Hammond, Bury St. Edmunds: Arima Publishing, 2011), on Patrick Neate's *City of Tiny Lights* (in *Terrorism and Narrative Practice*, eds Thomas Austenfeld *et al.*, Munster: Lit, 2011), as well as on the discursive careers of the concepts of "terror" and "terrorism" (in *The Uncanny Familiar: Images of Terror*, ed. Felix Hoffmann, Cologne: Verlag der Buchhandlung Walther König, 2011).

Herbert Grabes held the chair of English and American Literature at the University of Giessen from 1970 to 2004 and is now Professor emeritus. He has been a visiting professor at the University of Wisconsin-Milwaukee, University of Wisconsin-Madison, and Simon Frazer University at Vancouver. He is co-editor of *REAL* (*The Yearbook of Research in English and American Literature*) and has published widely on English Renaissance literature and twentieth-century American literature and theory. His monographs include *Fictitious Biographies: Vladimir Nabokov's English Novels* (The Hague: Mouton, 1977), *The Mutable Glass: Mirror-Imagery in Titles and Texts of the Middle Ages and the English Renaissance* (Cambridge and New York: Cambridge University Press, 1982), *Das amerikanische Drama des 20. Jahrhunderts* (*The American Drama of the Twentieth Century*, Stuttgart: Klett, 1998), and *Making Strange: Beauty, Sublimity, and the (Post)Modern 'Third Aesthetic'* (Amsterdam and New York: Rodopi, 2008). The most recent of the many books he has edited or co-edited are *The Wider Scope of English* (Frankfurt on Main *et al.*: Lang, 2006), *Ethics in Culture* (Berlin and New York: Walter de Gruyter, 2008), *Literature and Values* (Trier: Wissenschaftlicher Verlag Trier, 2009), *Metaphors Shaping Culture and Theory* (Tubingen: Gunter Narr, 2009), and a volume on recent American drama, *Das neuere amerikanische Drama* (Trier: Wissenschaftlicher Verlag Trier, 2009).

Eva Gruber is Assistant Professor of American Literature at the University of Constance, where she has been teaching since 2004. Her research interests include Native North American literatures and film, conceptualizations of "race" in twentieth- and twenty-first-century American literature, and the field of literature and terrorism. Next to a monograph, *Humor in Native North American Literature: Reimagining Nativeness* (Rochester: Camden House, 2008), she has published articles and book chapters on Native writing and film in the United States and Canada, on the politics of translation, on space in Caribbean-Canadian writing, and on racial identities in contemporary American fiction. She is currently working on a project entitled *The Realities of Race: Black and White in the American Novel after 2000*, as well as editing a volume on Canada's best-known indigenous writer, Thomas King (*Thomas King: Works and Impact*, Rochester: Camden House, 2012).

Michael König is a doctoral candidate at the Graduate School *Practices of Literature* (University of Munster, Germany). He studied German Literature and Philosophy at the University of Tubingen. The title of his dissertation is *Poetik des Terrors: Darstellungen poli-*

tisch motivierter Gewalt in deutscher Gegenwartsliteratur (*Poetics of Terror: Representations of Politically Motivated Violence in Contemporary German Literature*). He has published several articles on reflections of September 11 in German literature. His other research interests focus on the connection between computer aesthetics and literature, and include the impact of surveillance techniques and data mining on recent German fiction.

Kirsten Mahlke is Professor of Romance Literatures and Cultural Theory at the University of Constance since 2011, where she researched and taught from 2002-2009. She obtained her PhD in Romance Literature from the Goethe University Frankfurt in 2002 and held a chair of Latin American and French Literature at the University of Heidelberg in 2009. She has published her doctoral thesis on early modern travel literature (*Offenbarung im Westen: Frühe Berichte aus der Neuen Welt*, Frankfurt on Main: Fischer, 2005) and several papers on sixteenth-century French literature as well as on science and fiction in twentieth-century Latin American Literature. She is presently working on the Argentinean Post-Dictatorship and the fantastic dimension of its representation in contemporaneous narratives.

Ulrich Meurer received his PhD in American and Film Studies from the University of Constance and has taught Comparative Literature at the Universities of Munich and Leipzig. Currently, he is Visiting Professor at the Department of Theater, Film, and Media Studies at the University of Vienna. His research focuses on media philosophy and history and intermedia word-image-relations. He has published a monograph on concepts of space in postmodern literature and film (*Topographien*, Munich: Fink, 2007), numerous articles on literary and visual culture, and has co-edited *Perseus' Schild: Griechische Frauenbilder im Film* (Neuried: Ars Una, 2008) and *FremdBilder: Auswanderung und Exil im internationalen Kino* (Bielefeld: Transcript, 2009). His future research project is entitled "Philokratia: Friendship in Early US-American Visual Culture".

Margaret Scanlan was formerly Chair and Professor of English at Indiana University South Bend, where she taught from 1976-2009. She received her PhD in 1972 from the University of Iowa, and is the author of *Traces of Another Time: History and Politics in Postwar British Politics* (Princeton: Princeton University Press, 1990), *Plotting Terror: Terrorists and Novelists in Contemporary Fiction* (Charlottesville and London: Virginia University Press, 2001), and the Ireland volume in Greenwood Press' "Customs and Cultures" series (2006). Recent articles include "Strange Times to be a Jew: Alternative History after 9/11" (*Modern Fiction Studies*, Fall 2011), "Domestic Terror: 1970s Radicalism in Philip Roth's *An American Pastoral* and Susan Choi's *An American Woman*" (*Journal of European Studies*, September 2010), and "Migrating from Terror: The Postcolonial Novel since 9/11" (*Journal of Postcolonial Writing*, July/September 2010).

Roy Scranton is currently working on a PhD in English at Princeton University. He received an MA in Liberal Studies at the New School for Social Research. His scholarly interests include twentieth-century American experimental literature, the literature of war, and questions of the phenomenology of the self and its literary construction. His articles and essays have appeared in *Theory & Event, CITY, The New York Times*, and elsewhere. His poetry and fiction have appeared in various journals including *The Massachusetts Review, New Letters, Denver Quarterly*, and *LIT*.

Martina Wolff received her PhD in Foreign Language Education in 2001 and has taught as lecturer, assistant professor and as visiting professor at the University of Cologne, the University of Applied Sciences in Cologne, and at Webster University in St. Louis, Missouri. Her main fields of teaching and research are intercultural awareness and differentiation in foreign language teaching, and American Cultural Studies in education, with a special focus on 9/11, new media and film. Recent publications include papers on the influence and representation of 9/11 in blogs, film (Spielberg, Inarritu, Nair) and literature (Mohsin Hamid, Shaila Abdullah, Ken Kalfus, Don DeLillo).

INDEX